THE GUARDIAN CODE

It's Not Your Fault
[And I Can Prove It!]

THE GUARDIAN CODE

It's Not Your Fault
[And I Can Prove It!]

SECRETS TO FINDING THE MAGNIFICENCE IN YOUR LIFE

STEVE SHENK

Copyright © 2013 by Steven Shenk.

All rights reserved.

Except as permitted under the U.S. Copyright Act of 1976, no part of this publication may be reproduced, distributed, or transmitted in any form or by any means or stored in a database or retrieval system, without the prior written permission of the publisher.

ISBN#: 978-1-60414-727-8

Originally Published by Grape Vine Blue, LLC, 2012.

Visit our Websites:

www.SteveShenk.com
www.TheGuardianCode.com

First Edition: January 2013.
Second Edition: October 2013

Cover Design by Fideli Publishing

COMPANION BOOKS:

My Book of Life

The Wisdom of the Guardian

PRINTED IN THE UNITED STATES OF AMERICA

Who am I?
Am I who I think I am?
Am I who you think I am?
Am I who I think you think I am?

*The Principles of
The Guardian Code
are all around us, hiding
in plain sight...*

Dedication

Why, in a universe of abundance, do so many have so little?
Why does everybody like a few of us, but the rest of us… not so much?
Why does sharing create prosperity as opposed to lack?
What makes some relationships last forever?

This compilation of wisdom from The Guardian is dedicated to you and me and every soul we know who has written questions in their life's book of experiences that deserve and require a teacher to appear and provide the answers.

Table of Contents

Dedication .... *vii*
Author's Note .... *xi*
Introduction .... *xiii*
Prologue .... *xv*
A Personal Note from The Guardian .... *xv*

CHAPTER 1
Michael Meets The Guardian 1
    The Teacher Appears 2
    Am I the Chosen One? 4

CHAPTER 2
People Think Life Has Handed Them a Lemon 7
    Folks Think Life is a Roll of the Dice 8
    That Lemon Is Really Lemonade! 9

CHAPTER 3
Your Life is Like a Perfect Building 12
    The Trash Removal System: "Be Ye Therefore Perfect..." 12
    You Start Out Perfect—How Would You Like to Stay Perfect? 13
    How People Think Things Work 15
    How Things Work 15
    Yeah! But Nobody's Perfect 16
    The Perfect Muscle 17

CHAPTER 4
The Magic of Faultlessness 19
    Just Solve the Problem 19
    How People *Think* Things Work 20
    How Things Really Work 21
    It's Not Your Fault Formula for Trash Removal 22

CHAPTER 5
Guilt: The "Un-Original" Sin 24
    The By-Products of Guilt 29
    Guilt Creates Victims 31
    The Upside of Guilt 33

CHAPTER 6
Victims Have Big "Buts" 35
- Victims Always Have a Long List of "BUTS" 36
- The Victim Mentality 38

CHAPTER 7
You Say You Love Me. Prove It! 44
- The Blackmail (Terrorist) Bind of Enablement 45

CHAPTER 8
The Past Does Not Exist 50
- Reality, Imagination, Illusion—and Really Goofy Human Nature 52

CHAPTER 9
The Law of Me 61
- Selfishly Unselfish: The Role of the Teacher in the Law of Me 64
- Bless the Beasts and the Children—They Live in the Law of Me 68

CHAPTER 10
Self-Image: The Great Mirror 70
- You Are What You Appear to Be 71

CHAPTER 11
Judgment 80
- The Dingo Concept 84
- No Negative Aspects 85

CHAPTER 12
Approval 87
- The Conditional Love That Destroys 87
- Whose Fault Is It, After All? 88
- No One Needs Anyone's Approval 91
- The Principle of Distraction by Action 94

CHAPTER 13
Unconditional Love 98
- The Cup That "Runneth Over" 98
- Helping and Helplessness…Sympathy and Grieving 100
- Wants and Needs—The Mentality of Lack 103
- The Law of the Ten-Fold Return 106

CHAPTER 14
Agency: The Freedom to Choose 108
- "If it's to be, it's up to Me." 108
- An Agent on Your Own Behalf 110
- The Hidden Contract 114

CHAPTER 15
The Wonder Hugger 117
    Distance is Disaster (So the Closer the Better) 117
    How People Think Things Work 118
    How Things Really Work 120

CHAPTER 16
The Big Push-Away! 124
    I Don't Like Me. Why Should You? 124

CHAPTER 17
Move Over Casanova and Don Juan, Here Comes Bob! 130
    How People Think Things Work 130
    How Things Really Work 131
    To Know Me Is to Love Me 131

CHAPTER 18
I Like Me Best When I'm With You 134
    Love: The Ultimate Validation 134
    How Things Work—To Know Me Is to Love Me 136
    How things Work—I Like Me Best When I'm With You 137

CHAPTER 19
The Four Confusions 140
    What People Think When They Don't Know How Things Work ... 140
    The First Confusion: The 'law of me' vs. The Law of Me! 142
    The Second Confusion: Sex vs. Love 144
    The Third Confusion: The Letter of the Law vs. the Spirit of the Law ... 148
    The Fourth Confusion: "Who Am I?" 151

CHAPTER 20
The Four Universal Laws 154
    What They Really Mean 154
        Law #1: The Law of Me 154
        Law #2: Agency 156
        Law #3: The Law of Justice 158
        Law #4: The Law of Creation 160

CHAPTER 21
A Return to Perfection 163
    You've always been perfect. (You just didn't know it.) 163

CHAPTER 22
Is The Pen Mightier Than the Sword? 169
    The Power of the 59¢ Pen! 169
    The Guardian's Six-Step Process…to Show the Past
        Does Not Exist 174

CHAPTER 23
Justice Versus … "Just Is" 179
    Debt, the death of liberty 185

CHAPTER 24
The Law of Creation 188
    You think it. You see it. You be it. You've GOT it! 188

CHAPTER 25
Goals and Objectives: The Power of Faith 199
    Visualization, Spiritual Creation and other Important Things 199

CHAPTER 26
Failure as the Pathway to Success 208
    The Hidden/Forbidden Zone 215

CHAPTER 27
Gratitude 217
    The Application of All the Universal Laws 217
    Gratitude… the Attitude to Live By 221

SPECIAL KEYS TO THE GUARDIAN CODE—THE ZONE

ZONE A
Baby, It's Not Your Fault 231
    Hands and Booties are for Shaking. Babies Are for Holding 234
        SHAKEN BABY SYNDROME (SBS) 237

ZONE B
The Abandoned Child 240

ZONE C
It's Not Your Fault for Dogs 243

ZONE D
Addiction 251

My Book of Life 258
    How It Works (…Is How Things Really Work!) 259

Acknowledgments 263

Index 265

THE GUARDIAN CODE ESSENTIALS 272

About Steve Shenk 273

Author's Note

You may not know it yet in your life, but you have the answers already. They are provided by something called *The Guardian Code*.

This Code, like a combination of numbers (or formula) that unlocks your universe of self-discovery and creation, is so simple that most folks don't even believe it exists. And yet it is so powerful that nothing has ever been built, achieved or even destroyed without it. Like every great truth, this Code has been used in every success ever accomplished by anyone—although most never even realize they are using it.

I'm Steve Shenk. I'm here to be your guide in understanding, finding and using The Guardian Code and its formula for removing what you don't want and creating the "charmed life" that you deserve. Still, if I'm to do my job properly, I have to adhere to the Guardian Code myself and observe the "Prime Directive" that the Guardians instill in us all. Not to interfere, but to observe, witness, and instruct—my job as your guide is to eliminate my job as your guide so you can move on without "training wheels" to the life of your choice.

It was originally Buddha who said: "When the student is ready, the teacher will appear." He knew—as all great teachers know—*that the Principles of the Guardian Code are all around us, hiding in plain sight.* And only the Elect who are ready for the teacher to appear will understand and be ready to embrace them.

As we apply *The Guardian Code*, we come to recognize that the problems and challenges that we fear are held in our mind. By beginning these lessons with us, and with the Guardians, you are already one of the Elect. By making the choices you have here—by learning and embracing *The Guardian Code*—you have become a co-creator in the most challenging and uplifting journey you will ever experience.

After you have completed your journey, it will be impossible for you *TO NOT LIVE BY THE CODE*. And once you understand *The Guardian Code*, you will realize it has been with you all along…in perfect proximity. It arrives in what at first appears to be a long string of lessons that are in reality all aspects of the same basic principles.

Once you realize how they tie together—how this Code ties them together—they will become so much a part of your true destiny that you'll use them every day of your life for the rest of your life. And the best day of your life will come when you recognize: It cannot be otherwise.

Welcome to *The Guardian Code*. Welcome Home!

— Steve Shenk

Introduction

THE GUARDIAN CODE: *It's Not Your Fault* is not your run of the mill metaphysical conversation.

It is more like practical magic. That's because it is about a number of meetings between a man we will call Michael and a very special mentor named The Guardian.

The Guardian is the personification of a great intelligence. Michael is the student representing all of us who want to know. I am the narrator. And we are keeping the message simple.

They say that, during a military campaign, Napoleon had an 'idiot' sit on a stool outside the flap of his battle tent. Whenever he prepared orders to be sent to his field marshals and generals, he would have an aide go out and read the orders to the idiot. If the idiot understood the orders and could repeat them back correctly, Napoleon would send them. If the idiot could not understand and repeat the orders, Napoleon would rewrite them.

Whatever may be said about Napoleon, the historians will have to agree on one thing: *He virtually never had confusion on the battlefield.* And his military campaigns have been the source for many a textbook on wartime strategy and tactics.

In my experience, the lousiest math teacher is the guy who is gifted in mathematics. The best math teacher is the one who struggles with the "On" switch to his calculator. Once he figured out the principles of mathematics so that *he* could understand them, he saw to it that anyone could follow his pathway to the answer. The subject would become what I call the 'any idiot program' for others.

I'm the first to admit that I was not cut out to be a salesman. I was too thin-skinned to take the proverbial "five No's" and keep on pushing. I hated the idea of any door being slammed in my face or someone on the other end of a telephone hanging up on me. I couldn't *make* people buy…anything. My failure helped me learn ways to *allow* people to order. I discovered, that if I could do it anyone could, and that became my 'any idiot program' for others.

I also have to say that I was a pretty lousy, domineering, judgmental, and controlling father. I demanded that my kids strive for approval but was stingy when it came to giving it. My experience of failure and discouragement may have led to an "any idiot" understanding that could be the path others could take in developing good relationships.

I'm slow-witted enough to acknowledge that once I come to understand a concept, I am able to develop a path that *anyone* can follow. That is probably the reason I was selected to narrate this work. The Guardian made his wisdom, understanding, and perceptions available to me. With that foundation, even I was able to grasp the "It's Not Your Fault" principle and pass it along to you. In the chapters to follow, I will narrate the ongoing discussion between The Guardian and Michael. This "any idiot" program has been written so that it might be a path easily followed by any student who is ready for his teacher to appear.

I extend my best wishes to each of you. As the Vulcans would say, "Live long and prosper." And to which I might add, "Let us all do it with liberty, grace, and dignity."

— *Steve Shenk*

Prologue
A Personal Note from The Guardian

Each morning when you wake up, you have a new life. It's not a matter of the situation your find yourself in—it's what you do about it that counts.

The only thing that can prevent each new morning from being the exciting "first day of the rest of your life" is if you choose to destroy it by beating it to death with remembered disappointments from the past.

What if I told you that the Past doesn't exist and that I could prove it?

As each new day dawns, there may be problems for you to deal with. And yet

I can promise that you'll have the power to handle them.

I can tell you that any feelings you have of guilt, pain, and helplessness are not your fault. If you are wrestling with indecision, self-condemnation, low self-esteem, victimization, or even addiction, *It's Not Your Fault!*

Taking guiltless—faultless—responsibility for your controllable interest in any situation will resolve all problems and fill your life with peace, joy, freedom, and happiness. Think about it.

— The Guardian

Scribes, authors, philosophers, religious leaders, psychotherapists, and great thinkers of every era and generation have been writing throughout the history of mankind to help people figure out How Things Work. People have been taught to 'take the blame,' then beat themselves up for a while and finally struggle hard to overcome 'their weaknesses.' A favorite approach used by so-called therapists with their clients for decades has been to work through the experience by reliving it over and over again.

That is not how it works. When you learn How Things Really Work, you'll find that placing blame or finding fault accomplishes nothing. Beating up the guilty party does nothing either. The concept that somehow weakness must be overcome by repeated mental recreation and visualization misses the point of how truly magnificent each human being is.

By taking responsibility, you hold the key. And that key is simply discovering and returning to who you really are. In doing so, you are fulfilling the measure of your creation. You're learning the hard lessons you have chosen to place inside what we often describe as *My Book of Life*. Sometimes, though, you need guidance. That's why I have come to you.

I am The Guardian.

It has been said, *When the student is ready, the teacher appears*. If you were not ready, you would not have discovered me now. You have chosen the time and conditions of our meeting.

All people are shackled by the bondage of limitation in their lives. That bondage of limitation in your life is caused by not knowing How Things Work. As you and I work together to help you become free from these limitations, you will learn lessons you never believed possible. You will remember your greatness, and you will know *who you really are*.

Believe me, it's going to be an exciting ride! Along the way, you will come to see fear, misery, anxiety, stress, depression, and pain for the trash they have always been and toss them out of your life for good. *The good stuff*—love, belonging, happiness, perfect peace, and all the success that comes with them—is already who you are, and I can show you how to get back to it. At the end of this adventure, when you finally slam shut the cover of this book, you'll feel like shouting out loud, "I love me best, because I'm me."

That's when we'll know we have accomplished our mission. So, sit down, hang on, shut up, and pay attention.

Your humble teacher,

The Guardian

CHAPTER 1

Michael Meets The Guardian

One Saturday morning Michael was watching TV. His sweetheart was at the grocery store, and he was less than excited about a couple of 'honey do' chores she had convinced him were necessary if he was going to have any peace of mind at all for the coming weekend. He had been dealing with problems at the office and relationships at home, all of which displayed considerable evidence of Murphy's Law. (You've heard of Murphy. He's the guy nobody has met but who is credited with the universal principle of disastrous results. Murphy's Law simply states: "If anything can go wrong, it will." And precisely at the worst possible time.) At this point, Michael was suspicious that one of Murphy's grandkids might be an undercover employee at his business.

Michael had channel-surfed to his favorite *Roadrunner* cartoon. He settled down into the comforting and secure clutches of his bucket-seated, four-on-the-floor, bored and stroked, zero-to-60-in-5-seconds, Lazy Boy recliner to savor the experience. He desperately needed the 'intellectual stimulation' of playing armchair quarterback to Wile E. Coyote in the eternal chase of that smart-aleck bird (The Roadrunner). As Michael tuned in, a dozen sticks of dynamite had just blown a huge red rock high into the air. The Coyote looked up, his ears wilting as the shadow of the falling boulder hovered over his head. The familiar whistle of impending doom squealed through the speakers as the coyote, disconcerted and with a deadpan face, looked directly into the camera with an "Oh, shoe polish! I'm about to become an accordion" expression. Michael had just decided that the coyote was a goner, when a loud sizzle and pop rattled the TV. The jolt was hard enough to dislodge a long-lost Beach Boys tape from the back of the entertainment center and send it clattering off of an air-conditioning vent.

The Teacher Appears

Suddenly all of the light in the TV screen was drawn into to a glowing dot in the center of the screen, condensing to a pinpoint just before it virtually exploded, shooting out of the screen in a blinding flash. No sooner had it done so than the room was entirely flooded with a hypnotizing yet comforting glow.

Michael blinked, instinctively using his hands to shield his eyes. Upon recovering from the shock, he realized that he was no longer in his living room but in a comfortable chair. This chair's armrest was aligned against that of a matching chair that faced in the opposite direction, forming a classic 'S' conversation chair that reminded him of the one that sat in the sitting room of his grandmother's house in Ohio.

Across from him in the adjacent chair sat a quite distinguished man with shocks of gray hair, tipping slightly toward white. The man smiled a warm, reassuring smile that somehow cooled Michael's overheated brain. The man's eyes revealed an intensity of wisdom and intelligence that Michael felt, rather than thought, carried a depth almost beyond comprehension.

As his nerves calmed from this disquieting experience, Michael realized that the setting for this conversation was outdoors. The Conversation chair sat on a lush, grassy terrace overlooking a wide, flat, flowing river crowned by a peaceful waterfall a short distance upstream.

No sooner had Michael's attention been drawn to the splash of the cascading water than the sound seemed to diminish and blend smoothly into a deep baritone masculine voice. The words became clearer as the voice boomed forth.

"This is The Guardian! He is the eternal witness. He is the Messenger. He's the sound of one hand clapping."

When the mysterious voice finally faded, Michael sat with his mouth open, not quite sure what to say. Somewhat stunned by the experience, he was still trying to get a grasp on this sudden encounter with a guy who had just been presented to him as some sort of a protector, observer, or guru. He also found himself trying to deal with a weird mental picture of one hand flapping around in midair, trying to find something to clap against.

The Guardian simply smiled and said, "Pretty impressive introduction, huh? This might be a good time to mention that I've never been able to figure out where that voice comes from. Oh well, as they used to say back in the 1970s, 'It's your dime.' So, how you spend it is up to you.'"

For a moment, Michael just stared at the older, distinguished-looking man. After all, he had just been bashed by a supernatural experience that was the equivalent of a two-by-four to the forehead. The shock of surprise had widened his eyes to the size of the headlights on his '68 Camaro. He knew he should have a gazillion questions, but at the moment he couldn't collect himself enough to ask a single one.

The Guardian was dressed in white, very much in the tradition of the old television commercial personalities "Mr. Clean," or "The Man from Glad," who enhanced their unblemished images by dressing completely in white. Michael was quite impressed with the fact that this man's pants were pure white Wrangler jeans (of "Wrangler butts drive me nuts" fame) and that he also sported a pair of the sharpest looking cowboy boots he had ever seen, notwithstanding the fact that they, too, were (you guessed it…) white.

The Guardian seemed to enjoy the cascade of emotions Michael was experiencing, letting them run their course until his newly chosen student had time to completely recover his faculties.

"So…" The Guardian savored the question. "How may I help you, Michael?"

In response, Michael unceremoniously blurted out, "Who are you? Where am I? And what am I doing here?"

At this point, The Guardian took command.

"Let me see if I can answer your questions. First of all, I am The Guardian. The title, Guardian, refers to a superior being of a *quasi-Angel* rank. I function as a kind of protector. Some see me as their *Guru*. Actually, I function as the Witness to people as they go through their life and deal with the situations that unfold. Most important: I am a

Messenger of Light and Wisdom to those who have prepared themselves to become true students.

"You see, Michael, the adage holds true: *When the student is ready, the teacher appears.* These are not just words. They are the truth."

Am I the Chosen One?

At that point, Michael was a little uncertain as to why he was The Chosen One, and said: "Does this mean that you think I'm ready to be some sort of a student?"

"That's not my decision," the Guardian answered. "It's really up to you. As far as your wanting to learn something is concerned, you tell me. Our records show that you spent several years in school—most of them because you had to, but some that were your choice. So…what were you looking for?

"You've studied the prophetic writings of the world's major religions. What did you want to know? You've checked into the teachings of a couple of dozen philosophers, scholars, psychics, and even a Native American Shaman. You must have been looking for something. You've read the biographies of great leaders. You've studied the histories of several ancient civilizations. You've read extensive works of Hermes and the Ancient Egyptians, Socrates, Winston Churchill, Benjamin Disraeli, the wisdom of the Aborigines, and the comparative beliefs and prophecies of the Native American tribes.

"You're the proud owner of a five and a half foot-high stack of dog-eared and underlined self-help books on subjects ranging from a dozen different philosophical disciplines through any number of approaches to getting rich and prosperous (preferably with the least amount of effort). And I'm sure there's probably a book in there somewhere entitled, *Wealth and Peace of Mind Through Ice Water Enemas.* (Just kidding.)

"You've driven thousands of miles, listening to hundreds of tapes telling you How to, When to, Why to, Where to, and What Not to do just about anything that the mind of man can conceive and believe. You even had a twelve-foot square pyramid in your backyard to see if it would sharpen razor blades and keep strawberries from rotting for two weeks in the middle of July.

"Is it possible that one could deduce from this excerpt of your life history that you may have been trying to figure something out, looking for something or searching for ultimate truths? Seems reasonable to me. One could also conclude, based on the evidence, that if you were accused in court of being a student of life that you would probably be convicted.

"To take the next step, you could use some help. So I'm here! I am The Guardian. This makes me an honest-to-goodness, certified, true-blue, one-of-a-kind guru-type quasi-angel, witness to truth and messenger of wisdom and life. In short, *a Teacher! So what do you want to know?*"

The way the question was asked triggered Michael to answer automatically: "I want to know *How Things Work!*"

With that, The Guardian slapped his knee and exclaimed: "Wonderful!" He continued, "Explaining How Things Work is what Guardians do best. Let's get started. My assignment is to work with you (and others among The Chosen) as you come to deal with real-life situations. So, if you truly want to know How Things Work, you are going to find out in ways you might never have dreamt of.

"We'll start by taking a good look at what people keep doing that hasn't been working, and why they keep doing it over and over again. Those recurrences, as you know by now, are one very good *definition of insanity*. When they do it, they make their lives incredibly hard. And that, to say the least, takes all the fun out of it.

"When you learn the simple principles of How Things Work, you'll not only wonder why so many people spend their lives doing the wrong things, you'll also want to share what you've learned with them.

"Michael, you're about to experience more joy and discovery in your life than you ever imagined possible. These simple principles are not new. They're proven successful, because they are the application of eternal universal laws. Great masters, prophets, teachers, and messengers have been sent to mankind at various intervals throughout the turbulent history of this tiny planet. Their job has been to share these universal laws with humankind and to their discovery to help guide them out of the darkness. (The problem has come in the translation.)

"The only reason that these principles will look so different to you is that they have been misquoted, misunderstood, and misinterpreted by so many, so often, and for so long. This has been going on since Adam and Eve first kicked the lid off Pandora's Box with that apple, causing what we now refer to as the mortality of the human race."

> ***Pandora's Box*** is the Box that Zeus, King of the Gods and ruler of Olympus, gave to Pandora to keep for humankind. He did so with strict instructions that the box never be opened. According to the legend, Pandora's curiosity got the best of her, and she opened it anyway. When she did, she released all the evils of the world and, with them, all the trouble, misery, afflictions and problems that would plague mankind. Note, there is conjecture throughout The Guardian forces that Pandora may, in fact, be Murphy's mother. And the subject is still a matter of investigation.

CHAPTER 2

People Think Life Has Handed Them a Lemon

(Understanding How Things Work Makes Lemonade)

"People who don't understand how things work tend to get discouraged easily," The Guardian said. "They reach a point where life looks so troublesome that it becomes virtually impossible for them to be happy."

Michael nodded his agreement. "A lot of the time," he said. "It seems like we spend most of our time being afraid, worried, depressed…even angry."

"The problem, Michael," The Guardian added, "is that the evidence around us seems to say, 'There are problems for which no one seems to know the solutions.' Just look at what you good folks have surrounding you 24-hours a day.

"Depression is the number one illness among American women and that group represents more than 10 percent of our total population. The emotional firestorm of stress contributes to the five most fatal diseases. Half of the marriages in the United States end in divorce, and millions of other couples stay together but live in the emotional despair of a loveless coexistence. Over 66 percent of working folks admit that they feel trapped inside of jobs that they don't like. Mental, emotional and spiritual suicide in the form of addiction is rampant in all generations. There is an epidemic fear of failure and (believe it or not) there's also a fear of success.

"People refuse to do anything about it because they're terrified of change. So, they choose instead to distract themselves with social placebos—entertainment, media, technology, drugs, and alcohol. And nothing provides quite as much of a deferral of pain as bad news, especially when it happens to someone else.

"Just look at how people are drawn to the problems of others as a distraction from their own troubles. In fact, bad news sells. The news media know this and have made a franchise out of it. Human beings are drawn to the perverse and sleazy. It has become a social ritual to stand around in the coffee bar and commiserate bad news about people other people know. The poor mistreated wife, the misunderstood husband, the abandoned children, the recent marital dispute, the 'broken marriage playhouse' of corporate America—all are played out in millions of conversations every day. People sit as judge, jury, and executioner in the courts of public opinion. They listen to half-truths and spin about entertainment personalities, politicians, or national figures and embrace them as facts, when in truth they are nothing of the sort. They all seem to have their little emotional narcotics of choice.

"These are prejudices and bigotries that are softened with words of PC—Political Correctness. They popularize TV programs that specialize in collecting material from all over the country and all over the world that focuses on negativity, social stupidity, and human cruelty.

"People take accusation as accuracy. They're quick to condemn and slow to forgive (if they forgive at all). They shun readily and embrace slowly. They hate fiercely and love only conditionally. They seem to take great delight in the losses of a once wealthy businessman. It makes them all feel better to hear of the boss's wayward son or the wealthy neighbor across the street who is losing his home. In fact, bad news travels best when it shows how 'the mighty have fallen.' It reinforces people's frightened belief that all of life is a gamble, and that if you risk too much you are doomed to fail."

Folks Think Life is a Roll of the Dice

"All this takes place because people are hurting," said The Guardian. "People hurt because they don't know how to make the fear and pain go away. That's because they don't know How Things Work! They think life is a gamble. They have a sense that they're out of control. They feel 'done onto' by the world around them. They think that other people and other situations have the power to make their lives good or bad, happy or sad. Success or failure, joy or despair are decided by a roll of the dice.

"For example, if Fred got a promotion, he was lucky. But if Fred's job was eliminated when the company downsized, he was 'down on his luck.' Or if Sally happened to marry well and got a gem of a guy, fortune had smiled upon her. By the same token, if Sally married someone she thought was a gem and ended up instead with a lump of coal (a guy that's kind of dirty and not worth much), she had caught a tough break. So, in seeing Life as a Great Game of Chance, people feel pretty helpless. Their days become as uncontrollable as the onslaught of an earthquake; they neither know how to predict it nor what to do with it once the earth starts moving beneath their feet.

"Their life becomes a desperate circus, and they start to perform very much like the juggler spinning plates at the end of a stick. (It is the plight of the circus juggler that he has to keep all his plates in perfect rhythm or all of them will crash.) John gets his 'job' plate spinning. Then his 'wife relationship plate' starts to wobble. He gives that a spin, when his 'teenage son plate' is about to topple. He hits that a lick. Then his 'physical fitness plate' needs an extra push. Just as he gets that going, his 5 year-old's 'daddy hug plate' almost takes a dive. So he has to give that a quick twirl, just before it does. He stands back to take a second look, and all of them are about to drop off and break. So he rushes in for the spin, and the whole insanity starts again."

Having heard this, Michael said, "It seems as if there's not much to be said for the human race. People seem to be unhappy most of the time. They're at such a loss about how to make things better that they are actually encouraged by the misfortunes of others. If that's really the case, then people are pretty goofy."

"Ah, but Michael!" The Guardian answered. "That's not the case at all! The fact is that, at the core of who they are, people are quite the opposite!"

That Lemon Is Really Lemonade!

"You hear about the guy over on the other side of town?" The Guardian asked. "He's been sitting around for three months collecting his unemployment while never once looking for a job. The other day, he cashed his unemployment check, got drunk, came home, beat up his wife, yelled at his kids and made an obscene gesture to the little old man across the street for calling the policeman who had just arrived to haul him off to the pokey. This guy is pretty much a stinker, and (because he is) you hear about him on the evening news. But let's talk about people you don't see in the news.

"What you don't hear about, or see, are people like our friend Tom. Tom goes to work, picks up his paycheck, comes home, kisses his wife, hugs his kids and sets about making his world a better place. He smiles through a sigh of exhaustion when his sweetheart asks him to fix the battery cable on the electric wheelchair for the old woman across the street and then comes home and applies some medication to the abscess on the family dog's left hind leg. All this needs to be handled before supper, and Tom does it without question or complaint. It's part of his social contract with the life he's chosen for himself.

"After eating dinner and helping to clear the table, Tom and his wife hurry down to the little league park to catch his young son playing baseball. And tonight's game will give him ample opportunity to lose his cool and scream at the plate umpire who is obviously both sight impaired and biased in favor of the other team. This person will call his nine-year-old son 'out' when he is obviously safe, a ridiculous call for which Tom is spared the onus of protesting too loudly, mainly because the rest of the crowd of parents is doing it for him. (Besides, Tom believes in leading by example. So, he already knows that nothing is more embarrassing than someone's dad who makes the game 'about him,' rather than the son he has come to support.)

"That's what I mean, Michael! You take all the men out there like Tom, those who have decided to make lemonade out of their lives, and they far outnumber the welfare cheating, wife-beating addict who manages to grab all the headlines.

"The human race is absolutely wonderful! We only hear about or see the exceptions, but if you compare them to the general population, there aren't very many. That means you and I get to focus on the rest.

"The Rest are nearly perfect, and I can prove it. It all depends upon how we choose to look at life: as lemons, or lemonade?

"In the Shakespeare play *Julius Caesar*, when Mark Anthony goes to make the funeral oration over his fallen friend Caesar, he immediately announces that 'The evil men do lives after them. The good is oft interred with their bones...' It's a point of common knowledge that everyone accepts, and yet it quickly turns out to be the most powerful oration ever given by one man for another, and for a very good reason.

"So isn't it time we celebrate the goodness for a change? That's the first step in making lemonade! And it starts by recognizing the perfection that exists—in everyone!"

What evil men do is what we see. The good is not newsworthy. Think about it.

— The Guardian

CHAPTER 3

Your Life is Like a Perfect Building

The Trash Removal System: "Be Ye Therefore Perfect..."

"Can't you really goof people up by telling them that they're perfect when they're not?" Michael asked, after he had thought about it for a while.

"How?" The Guardian asked. "If a person truly believes he can achieve something, nothing will stop him. A lot of the greatest achievements of mankind have been accomplished by people who didn't have a clue that what they were attempting to do was considered impossible. Besides, at some level, people already sense that they should be perfect. If they didn't, they wouldn't be disappointed in themselves for not meeting their own expectations. They already feel that they should be happy, should be successful, should be healthy, should be intelligent, and should be able to handle any situation that comes their way."

"That's quite a bundle of *shoulds*," Michael observed.

"Exactly!" The Guardian agreed. "And you'll notice that every one of the *shoulds* I just mentioned are subjects that people feel guilty about. Michael, I have one question for you: If you didn't think that success *should be* your natural state then why on earth would you feel guilty for not achieving it?

"If you didn't believe that health is your natural state, why would you get angry with yourself (Guilty) for getting sick? If you didn't think that you should be able to fix problems before they happen, why does it make you so upset (Guilty) to face them?"

You Start Out Perfect—How Would You Like to Stay Perfect?

"I think I understand what you're talking about," Michael replied. "But I'm still having a little bit of trouble with the idea that everybody is perfect—and I especially include myself. I don't think I'm perfect by any means."

To that, The Guardian smiled and said, "I understand *perfectly*. Look upon your life as a beautiful building, Michael. When the building is brand new (just born, so to speak) it's a marvel of modern design. It's perfectly clean and made for a specific function. In that form it is ready for furniture, technology, commerce, productive people, and all the good things that will help it fulfill its purpose.

"Through use, what almost always happens is that it gets filled with clutter, trash, and dirt. After that, it takes constant effort to keep it clean. And there is seldom a time during the remainder of its use as a building that anyone could say it's *perfectly clean*. The good news is that there is always the capability of *cleaning it to perfection*.

"There will be times, usually important events during the life experience of this magnificent center, when it really gets messed up. During these times, it takes a major effort and maybe even outside help to clean up all the dirt and toss out all the garbage.

"So you see, Michael, this beautiful building, as it fills the measure of its creation, never loses its potential to become perfectly clean. If those in charge truly come to understand *How Things Work*, they will simply throw out the trash and clean up the dirt after every event. That way, they will help the building regain its perfection.

"In fact, you would consider the building management to be both incompetent and ill-advised if, after the first major event, they declared this magnificent building hopelessly dirty, defaced, defamed, and corrupted. What if it was now only considered worthy to be used as an all-night dollar movie? That would be a terrible waste, wouldn't it Michael?

"Remember, I suggested that you look at your life as a beautiful building. When you were born you started out clean, innocent, and uncluttered—like a new building. As you set out upon the course of living, you gave yourself challenges and, in your innocence, thought that you had to do everything right the first time. So…did you?"

"No," Michael admitted, with a tinge of regret. "I made a lot of mistakes and did some things that were flat-out wrong!"

"What happened when you did the wrong stuff?" The Guardian asked. Michael answered. "Sometimes, I got into trouble."

"Naturally!" The Guardian observed. "And sometimes you didn't get caught—even when you thought you might. But the real question is: How did you feel?"

"Crummy!"

"Why?"

Michael thought about it for a minute. "I suppose it was because I knew better, and I felt bad for having done it anyway."

"Aha!" The Guardian shouted. "TRASH!" He paused for a moment to let the thought sink in. "So, what you have here is a perfectly clean life—like a sparkling clean building—that, in the process of everyday use, got some Trash dumped inside.

"There's a name for that Trash, Michael. It's called Guilt! You started out knowing in your heart of hearts that you are perfect. When you did things that didn't match your expectation of what a *perfect you* would do, you were startled, scared, and (to say the least) disappointed. You felt just like the ignorant, foolish building managers who —once they let the innocence, goodness, and potential get marred—felt they might be lost forever. I can also see that there are many times, thousands in fact, when you have wished you could take a huge eraser, go back and undo the disappointments in yourself—that if you did that, everything would be okay again. You could take back your perfection. Am I right?"

"Yes," Michael agreed. "I suppose you are."

"Well, Michael, I have some good news for you…"

> There is a *Guardian Trash Removal Team*. We call them the *Guilt Busters*.

When there is no justification for Guilt, does that mean that the individual is innocent? What is the adjective we most often use to describe a newborn baby? Innocent! What is a life that is Innocent? Is it Perfect? If there was a mechanism in a human life that was able to remove Guilt, could that life not remain perfect? Think about it.

— The Guardian

How People Think Things Work

"Most people think that when you let Trash *(Guilt!)* pile up in your life, you deal with it by finding fault—and obviously you start by believing it's your fault. And since you believe that it is your fault that the Trash got there, it becomes important to beat yourself up, so much so that you hurt yourself badly enough to match the size of your Guilt.

"A little sin, a little hurt, a huge mess up, and you might not be able to pack enough misery into one lifetime to pay for it all.

"People are convinced that the possibility of a big eraser for the 'Bad Stuff' in their lives is only a hope, a wish, and a dream. They become like the building management sitting atop the pile of trash after an event, beating on their chests while being miserably convinced that the building will never be perfect again—certain that it's their fault. (But take heart! That *Big Eraser in the Sky* does exist!)

"Folks deal with their own goodness as hopelessly as this unwise, ill-advised building management. Every time they experience major disappointments in their lives they become helpless, feeling all is lost through major disappointments in themselves. They have a strong tendency to wallow around in the Trash, being 're-disappointed' over and over again, never discovering how to throw the junk out and take back their own perfection."

How Things Work

"People have no idea that Trash Removal is How Things Work!" The Guardian made this statement in such a way that Michael would never forget it. "They never get to realize that *It's Not Their Fault.* So, Michael, every person is just like that building—magnificent and perfect at being who they are. When their lives get messy from being lived, all they need to do is shovel out the dirt, sweep out the trash, and restore the innocence of their perfection."

Listening intently, Michael asked, "Isn't it kind of conceited and even dangerous for us to start thinking that we're perfect?"

The comment caused The Guardian to chuckle to himself.

"What harm can it do? Besides, what if you believe me? It could be absolutely disastrous! You'd get rid of your Guilt! So, no one from that point on could pull on your emotional strings and get you to be arrogant, angry, and judgmental!

"Your wife would like herself best when she was with you. So, you'd have this beautiful woman feeling truly appreciated and dumping all that goodness back onto you *ten-fold!* (This works perfectly the other way around, by the way.)

"You would experience little or no anger, stress, worry, or fear on your road to tremendous success. You'd be a real mess. You'd be hopelessly happy!

"You'd once again become that perfect new building—that perfect, innocent child you started out to be."

"When you think about it, Michael, can you even imagine the possibility of a perfect God creating anything less than perfect children?"

There was a poster on the wall of an orphanage in New York. It was a picture of a scruffy, ragged little girl. The caption under the picture said, "I know I'm somebody because God don't make no trash." Think about it!

— The Guardian

Yeah! But Nobody's Perfect

By now, Michael was feeling a bit embarrassed for having challenged The Guardian about the goodness of people. Still, the message from all his life experience had become so imbedded in his mind that he found himself needing more convincing.

"I get your point," he said. "But what about the fact that we hear people all the time, saying, 'Well you know, nobody's perfect?'"

To Michael's surprise, The Guardian nodded his agreement. "Yep, you're right. You hear it all the time. You'll also notice that you usually hear it from somebody who just goofed up.

"You know, Michael, people say, 'Nobody's perfect,' but they really don't believe it. They prove it in every action they take and every word they speak. They try to do things right. But what is right? Perfection! And when they don't achieve it, they feel guilty. If they say something embarrassing, they get upset.

"Then again, what is embarrassment? It's Guilt for not having spoken (Guess what?) *perfectly!* If they didn't believe in and expect perfection, there'd be nothing to be upset, embarrassed, or guilty about.

"Michael, it should be obvious that there's a misconception regarding the magnificence of each person. People start in a State of Perfection. It would be hard for anyone to make the argument that a baby is not perfect. They're innocent—free of Guilt. Christians are counseled by Jesus the Christ to become, 'like unto little children.'

"Tell me then, at what point does a person cross the line and cease to be perfect? As he or she goes through the lessons of life's plan, that person develops both strength and wisdom.

"Compare spiritual, mental, and emotional growth to a physical developmental program. Some exercises take several tries and additional practice to accomplish. Worthwhile skills take effort and persistence to develop. Take an athlete in training for example. Does the athlete's need for practice and experience make him less perfect in his potential for greatness? No! The determination to run the race already proves his worth."

The Perfect Muscle

The Guardian turned toward Michael, holding up his arm as an example.

"Here's another way to look at it, Michael," he said, pointing to his arm. "You have a muscle in your arm. Does it start out as a perfect muscle?"

Michael seemed puzzled and answered. "I don't know. I'm so out of shape, I'm not sure if any of my muscles are very perfect."

The Guardian replied, "I'm not talking about its development to its potential, Michael. Let me ask it this way: How much more perfect can a muscle be than to be a muscle?"

"That's pretty much what a muscle is," Michael answered.

"So…" The Guardian continued, "Does a muscle start out perfect?"

"If you look at it that way," Michael said, "I suppose it does."

"Now," said The Guardian, "When that muscle, through exercise and the problems of burdens to lift, becomes more massive and strong, does it become more perfect? No. It remains perfect and simply develops to a higher level of its ultimate potential.

"One of the first concepts you'll need to learn more about is the ability to understand How Things Work. This is what I refer to as *The Magic of Faultlessness*. The principle that we're going to discuss further here is the simple little phrase, 'It's Not Your Fault!'"

With that exclamation, The Guardian raised his voice in a way that Michael found both terrifying and, at the same time, delightful. And suddenly he felt a sense of relief he had never quite known before.

People remain perfect all of their lives, while they train themselves for the potential they've chosen to obtain. Try though we have, over the centuries, no mortal has yet proven the optimum potential that a complex spiritual, emotional, intelligent physical human being can achieve. Think about it!

— The Guardian

CHAPTER 4

The Magic of Faultlessness
Just Solve the Problem.
(When everything is fixed, nobody cares whose fault it was.)

"So...there *is* Magic in faultlessness?" Michael asked.
"Absolutely!" The Guardian said. "Let me take you back a few weeks, Michael...You and your sweetheart had a little hassle, didn't you?"
"That we did," Michael agreed.

No one ever intentionally does anything stupid. Think about it.

— The Guardian

"I believe it was about a little problem with an overdraft in your checking account. When you found out about it, what happened?"
"We had a fight."
"Actually, you had a battle of accusations. You accused each other, back and forth, arguing about who had failed to record a couple of checks leading to the overdraft, didn't you? So...let me ask you: Would deciding who was at fault for the mistake make any difference in fixing the overdraft?"
"Well..." Michael reflected. "I had to defend myself, because I knew I was right. I hadn't made the mistake. She had."

"Isn't that a good thing to know... that you were right?"
"Yes! But she thought I was wrong."
"So you were angry about being wrongly accused—is that right?"
"I guess so."
"But didn't she think she was right?"
"Yes, but she wasn't."
"And yet if she was right then *she* would have been wrongly accused. Right? So once you figured out which one of you was right, that would have made the other one wrong. Right?"
"Well, of course."
To that response, The Guardian smiled. "All of this sounds pretty complicated to me, but knowing you were right was very important to you, wasn't it?"

If two people see the same information from the same perspective with the same objective, their decisions won't be defective. There'll be no illusion about their conclusion. Think about it.

— The Guardian

How People *Think* Things Work

"Most folks think that when a problem arises, it's important to know why it started and who started it. In short, whose fault it was that this mess came up in the first place. Isn't that the way people think, Michael?"

"Well yeah, I guess so. I mean it has to be someone's fault, doesn't it?"

"Aha!" The Guardian slapped his knee. "You say it has to be someone's fault, when the fault was already determined by the problem in your checking account. Let me ask you one thing: Did you still have *to fix* the overdraft?"

"Yes, we did," Michael acknowledged.

"Then finding fault did nothing but make everyone feel crummy. Didn't it?" "Yes, it did."

"Let me tell you how things really work," The Guardian said, letting his comment sink in.

> *Miracles will happen if every confrontation is begun with the statement, "It's Not Your Fault, and I can prove it." It's also not my fault, and I can prove that too. Finding Fault solves nothing. Taking responsibility solves everything. Think about it.*
>
> — The Guardian

How Things Really Work

"Michael, let me tell you How Things Really Work. Just one question before I do: Whose intent was it to forget to write those checks in the checkbook—the ones that caused the other checks to bounce?"

"Well, I don't know," Michael said. "I don't think anyone intended to…"

"And you see the problem with *finding Fault* is that it implies *intent*—to hurt, injure, discredit, and disrupt. The way most people think disagreements work is that the subject needs to become the issue of whose fault the problem, the argument (thus the failure) really is. It's a total waste of both time and energy.

If you can get the issue of Fault out of the way at the outset, it will allow you to address the true subject and resolve the problem that needs handling.

"You see, Michael, what you needed to do with your sweetheart was to say to her, 'I know *It's Not Your Fault*. And it's not my Fault either. What's more, I can prove it. Neither of us intended to mess up the checking account. So, once we decide what caused the problem and how it started let's just focus on solving it. Why should either of us care who created the problem?'

"There's nothing there for you to be mad about, Michael, and there was nothing there for your sweetheart to be mad about. There's nothing that either of you could do to change the past. (Because *The Past Does Not Exist!*)

"The key, Michael, is to ignore the Fault and solve the problem. That's the magic of faultlessness!"

"Sounds great!" Michael had to admit. "But what about all that Guilt?"

"We've already determined that Guilt is Trash, haven't we?" The Guardian said. "So what we need is an effective Trash Removal System—especially for garbage from the past."

It's Not Your Fault Formula for Trash Removal

It's Not Your Fault — and I Can Prove It!

Step 1: Go over the experience in your mind. Write the experience in the most detail possible. (Write it by hand with a pen or pencil. Do not use a mechanical or electronic device. Computers or word processors will not have the same effect.)

Step 2: Ask yourself this question: "What was my intent to become involved in this experience?" If the unacceptable result was not your intent, then you have proof of No Fault—It's Not Your Fault.

Write a clear explanation of your intent and honestly state your motives.

Write the results that you anticipated. (If no thought was given to results, it's okay. It was spontaneous. Write that down.)

Write any misgivings or reservations you had at the time (If only...I shoulda, woulda, coulda—from hindsight.)

Step 3: Ask yourself if there's anything you can do to fix the results of the experience (i.e. apologize, give it back, explain misunderstandings, negotiate settlements).

Write a detailed plan for the responsibility you choose to assume. (Note: Do not confuse fault with responsibility. Understanding this difference is essential to effectively removing the Trash [Guilt] from your life.)

As you go through the many experiences in your memory that give you a stab of embarrassment, concern, or hurt, you'll find very few where Guilt is appropriate. Most will only require assuming the responsibility for cleaning up an unintended mess

(This is Trash Removal that allows you to return your life to its innocent perfect state.)

If there is nothing that can be done or the repair is completed, the doing is over. All that can be done has been done: The Past No Longer Exists.

Step 4: Recognize that you have a choice. Ask yourself the question: "Do I want to allow the experience to be over and done with?" If you do, it's gone. The past no longer exists. The experience is over. All that can be done has been done. It can now dissolve into nothingness.

"That's it? That's all?" Michael asked.

"Pretty much," said The Guardian. "Most good solutions are simple. It's our need to complicate the plain logic of it that makes such a mess of things. And it's almost always because we choose to do so.

"And that's the caution here, Michael. Remember that you become the choices you make. You can, if you choose to, keep the Trash and allow it to foul up your natural state of perfection. If you recreate the sin, offense, or embarrassment again in your mind, it is because you choose to bring that Trash back into your life. When you do, you make it your fault all over again. And that's what Guilt is really good at—making you relive the past.

"That's the Magic of Faultlessness: It cuts all ties to the past. It cleans up that perfect building you started out with, and sets you free again."

CHAPTER 5

Guilt: The "Un-Original" Sin

"Is it possible, Michael, that Guilt is the basis of all problems between people?" The Guardian asked.

"My answer would have to be 'Yes!'" Michael replied. "Or else you probably wouldn't have asked the question in the first place."

"Good boy!" The Guardian said. "And Atonement is the solution. And it's the solution because the people we're offering it to may have only this single malady."

"Guilt!" Michael repeated. "But why Atonement? Doesn't that mean you need some kind of forgiveness?"

"The only people who need forgiveness are those who harbor bad feelings in the first place. (And they only need to forgive themselves for having the thought.)

"Break the word down, Michael. Atonement! At-one-ment. It means unification—with a Higher Source and with each other. It's the remedy offered in religions and all constructive belief systems. It is the means by which any individual may come back into grace (or harmony) and eliminate the greatest Guilt—*Judgmentalism.*

"Anytime you see Judgmentalism you are looking into the eyes of Guilt. Guilt creates the concept of Sin. There is a legitimate argument for the fact that in all civilizations throughout the history of mankind, every misdeed, most failure, every confrontation, every war—every sin of fraud, deception, murder, mayhem, lust, and hatred—are the result of Guilt or its evil stepchildren *anger, fear, jealousy,* and *rage.* In one way or another, all mental, psychological, and emotional pain is the result of the cancerous influence of Guilt."

> *Racism, prejudice, and bigotry are the result of judging others who look or believe differently than we do and pre-assuming on their behalf a challenge to our own beliefs. (I need everybody to be just like me, because if they aren't the question is raised in my own mind as to whether I am right.) Often adherents to a belief system will proselytize desperately to "save from hell and misery" the object of their attention when their true underlying need is to justify their own uncertain convictions. (This is a common application of the Horse Manure Principal, which states, in effect: "Eat horse manure. One hundred and fifty billion flies can't be wrong.") Think about it.*
>
> — The Guardian

The Guardian continued, "Often without even knowing it, we weave Guilt into everything in the past, all things going on in the present, and all things we project into the future. We feel Guilt in the presence of those before whom we are embarrassed, and we project our Guilt into the future by imagining what will happen when we fail to meet their expectations, or our own. (We even project our Guilt onto people we haven't even met, hating them and judging them without so much as a single personal encounter.)

"We judge our fellow human beings and ourselves with incredible harshness through the mechanism of Guilt. And then we crave redemption through that most terrifying of moments that we're taught to believe in— something called Judgment Day.

"So much of it is Biblical to be sure. But is that what's really in the Bible, Michael? Or did certain religious leaders choose to extract that message from it as a means of maintaining control over others? *Choice* is a key issue in this discussion. So let's take a good look at it.

Guilt is often the basis of many religions when that was anything but the teaching of their founders. In Christianity, the concept of Original Sin (having to do with carnal knowledge and the fall from Eden) took hold in the Fourth Century A.D., and seemed designed to condemn the innocent child—virtually out of the womb—to a life of imperfection, moral depravity, and Guilt. Some may call it Sin, but sin by any other name has the same root cause—Guilt.

Traditionally, priests, ministers, bishops, cardinals, and medicine men were all dispensers of Guilt. It came through Judgment and was often corrected through something called 'penance' and a forgiveness of sins. In the Middle Ages, that forgiveness could actually be purchased (in the same way you'd pay a traffic ticket), and those purchases actually had a name—Indulgences. Most of the time, indulgences were only available to those who could afford them. So people came to believe that there was literally a price to be paid for redemption. At the same time, they looked upon this concept as corrupt and the very notion of "forgiveness" to be flawed, especially since it seemed more available to those with enough money to actually pay for it. In a way, even in our modern Republic, people still believe that there are two kinds of justice—one for the rich and one for the rest of us.

So people are less and less inclined to think that we have a level playing field. And nothing is more of a seedbed for guilt and victimization than that. Think about it.

— The Guardian

"Wait a minute," Michael said. "Doesn't Guilt have an upside? Doesn't it make us use a tool called conscience? Isn't that a way to take responsibility?"

"It's true, Michael," The Guardian answered. "Put in perspective, Guilt can be a valuable tool we can use to help us keep on our life's path—if you understand How Things Work. And yet, in the wrong hands and applied with the wrong kind of leverage, it is the ultimate weapon many people use for controlling others. Even though they feel 'justified' in doing so, they're usually doing it to gain some kind of advantage. In other words, *it's a kind of power play.*

"First, you have to realize that there are two kinds of Guilt: *Organic Guilt* and *Synthetic Guilt*.

"Organic Guilt is everyone's personal police force. It's what comes over us when we feel like we're not living up to our own expectations. When we understand How Things Really Work, we quickly recognize this guilt for what it is and put it to work for us—as a means of helping us take responsibility for our lives and finding the solution that will get us back in touch with our purpose. Guilt like this can come in the form of self-policing, such as feeling bad about not paying your bills or getting that 'sinking feeling' when you're dieting and you see that delicious Snickers candy bar you've just got to have.

"The problem with most guilt is that it comes from outside you. So it quickly becomes Synthetic. By definition, *synthetic* is man-made. So it's artificial. (Synthetic Guilt is like an emotional hot potato. People can't get rid of it quickly enough.) So it's always transferred from one person to another...and that is done by finding-Fault.

That which I find in you that offends me, I have in me, for if I did not have it in me I could not see it in you. Students will note that the lack of Judgmentalism on the part of a Master, Sensei, or great teacher is the result of the attribute of guiltlessness. Think about it.

— The Guardian

"*Fault-finding* is what victims and victimizers do to dump the trash of their guilt onto others as a means of manipulating and controlling them. They do this to relieve their own guilt pressure."

"Guilt trips," Michael declared.

"*Guilt Trips!* Exactly!" The Guardian said. "People feel guilty out of a sense of fear of punishment ('the fires of Hell') for their acts. So they can't accept it for what it is: a prompting to grow or change. People have to do one of three things with their guilt. They either defend their guilt; they hide their guilt, or shift their guilt away from them to someone else. One thing is constant: They always get angry for being made to feel guilty. (So, much anger and rebelliousness comes out in people who are made to feel guilty.)

"Guilt almost always gets passed on to someone else, because most people need someone else to feel guilty about an issue, just so they can feel better. Still, it's impossible for a person to be insulted or embarrassed about something if they have no Guilt upon which to hang the alleged offense.

"Having said that, a most frustrating form of Guilt is the injustice of Synthetic Guilt created by a false or implied accusation. Here's an example: A police car pulls out and drives behind you in your same lane of traffic for a while. You experience stress as you mentally check your actions and condition of your vehicle. Then you feel a sense of anger at the possibility that you may be being watched (implied guilt). Later, you feel relieved yet resentful of the policeman as he pulls off onto an exit for having put you through your self-imposed inquisition.

"Michael, you've heard of the *Egyptian Book of the Dead* and the *Tibetan Book of Life*…Well, this is *The American Book of the Stupid*—the autobiography of the voyeuristic Victim. One of the most maddening things about Guilt (and something that sends us all ballistic faster than raw guilt) is being made by others to feel guilty. This especially applies to situations where the faultfinding comes as a bolt out of the blue—when you least expect it. It is an example of the worst possible infringement upon someone's agency. (The most classic example is the all-too-familiar speeding ticket. You're driving along enjoying your day, and you full of these emotional radar guns, and people known as Guilt-givers.)

"Some Guilt-givers are professionals. Traffic cops, meter maids, lawyers, TSA agents, the Internal Revenue Service, many fundamentalist religions, and some bosses in the workplace are masters of this. But some of these merely have a temporary impact in our lives and may be dismissed as passing influences.

"Unfortunately, most Guilt-givers (or *Fault-finders*) are often those with whom we spend most of our time—friends, family, parents, children, spouses, and significant others. Guilt-givers very often feel guilty themselves because they inwardly feel as if they don't deserve to be happy. And if they don't deserve to feel happy, neither should anyone else. So the guilt-giver continues to heap on Guilt in the form of statements and accusations, and yet all the while has no idea what they intend to accomplish. So guilt-giving and fault-finding becomes a nasty kind of social habit. People just dump their emotional Trash on someone else, often without reflecting on the consequences, and so they create a nasty cycle of unconscious abuse. They're dumping Trash without ever taking it out of the building.

"Think about it, Michael. Every action creates its equal and opposite reaction. So, the more extreme the behavior the more extreme the Trash dumping that probably caused it.

"The worst expression of guilt transfer comes in the form of physical and emotional abuse. This is particularly true in the cases of small children and animals who are both helpless and totally dependent upon those responsible for them to form their Self Images in the early stages of their lives.

"People who are the most abused, abandoned, controlled, or constricted have the strongest sense of guilt. Abused women and children usually have an overwhelming sense of culpability and a constant feeling that 'it's all their fault.' Abandoned children own a tremendous sense of guilt. They often feel that it's their fault for being abandoned, as if it was something they did that caused them to be left behind."

The By-Products of Guilt

The Guardian continued: "*Abuse* is the flashpoint of emotional response. Cases of abuse often result from the frustration of wanting (and needing) to get someone else to behave in the way the abuser needs them to. The abuser believes the victim should act or think in a certain way and punishes them verbally, psychologically or physically when they fail to do so. *This always comes from not knowing* How Things Work. Both parties experience Guilt over how things should work and feel guilty when they can't make it happen that way. So this flashes quickly through the filter of infringement, judgment, and battered self-image. The victim feels helpless. The abuser temporarily feels righteous, and the flash of emotion and reaction sends them into the next series of abusive events; so much so that it falls into a *cycle of addiction*.

"The abused (Victims) become addicted through feelings of helplessness. And the abuser momentarily experiences a false sense of power over the abused, one that almost daily requires new forms of abuse to maintain the illusion of 'rightness.' In the family, abuse through fault-finding takes place in the form of parent-to-child abuse, spousal abuse, physical abuse, verbal abuse, and self-image abuse.

"Oddly enough, Michael, the easiest examples to follow don't occur in family relationships as much as they do in the workplace—especially in the field of sales.

"*Con and manipulation* are often applied, using the threat of abuse as leverage. This is often put into play to force compliance on the part of 'the guilty.' It usually happens when a third party is brought up as the source of enforcement. That can include everything from a mother threatening a child with "Wait until your father gets home," to police or armed forces that act as instruments of repression for many world governments. In the case of certain nations, enough abuse and repression will often bring about revolutions by the repressed. And in the family dynamic, equal and opposite reactions on the part of the 'guilty' child will end in rebellion and even delinquency. (When you think about it, there are very few juvenile delinquents, gang-bangers, or hard-core criminals who didn't come from a home where guilt and abuse were heaped upon them as daily fare.) When fear takes hold, it virtually paralyzes 'the guilty' until they're afraid to take any action whatsoever for fear of being at fault. So they actually come to be more at fault for doing nothing at all. Let's take the salesman who goes out and has a bad week. He's so afraid of rejection that he just doesn't work at all. He sleeps late to avoid hard sales calls because he's terrified of rejection.

"*Rejection* is an aspect of judgment, disapproval, and abuse. And more often than not it's self-inflicted. (In sales, it's seldom personal. And yet it becomes a way of telling ourselves that if people like us 'they will buy.' So, for victims, the very act of someone's not buying means they don't like them, they don't trust them, and they don't believe in what they represent. That's because *the victim never understands* How Things Really Work.

"Sales and sales companies represent the highest-paying profession in the world for a very good reason. If it were easy anybody could do it. Salesmen have to live with rejection every day of their lives. And the only difference between the quitter and the sales superstar is the simple understanding of How Things Work. Not until a salesman understands his own value and learns to have faith in what he represents will he ever come to grips with his own personal genius. But once he does, no amount of rejection can diminish what he's doing, and the true value he brings to his customers. And the truly great salesperson is the person who realizes that no one can make you feel guilty over rejection or anything else unless you choose to let them.

"Once again, we finally have the opportunity to become what we choose to be. And we start by recognizing that Guilt is a highly communicable disease that is viral in nature. So it's invariably passed on from one victim to another. Like any disease, it can be crippling and (in extreme cases) even fatal. And, just like any other disease, it can best be dealt with by proper evaluation, diagnosis, and prevention—starting with the recognition that *Guilt creates victims.*"

Guilt Creates Victims

"Individuals in dependent positions," The Guardian continued, "are always the ones most easily victimized. Particularly if the individual is a child, an animal, or someone vulnerable, abused or low in self-esteem, the *Victim* is much more inclined to take on the Guilt of others in the form of 'vicarious victimization.' And everything can become *a judgment against them.*

"All judgment of someone implies condemnation and also invades their sense of Agency. Someone's Agency represents 'who they are,' and who they are defines their freedom to choose. This creates even more anger and denial.

"Victims always have big boxes that they get themselves into. They try and give the Guilt away or pass it along to someone else. If you refuse to take it on, it really upsets them, because that means they have to confront it, and that is the last thing they're willing to do. The Guilty often rationalize wrong or dishonest behavior to relieve themselves of 'guilt pressure.' *(A classic example:* Not paying a debt because the one to whom the debt is owed 'has plenty of money anyway').

"Anything that causes people pain will almost always carry *some level of Guilt* with it. And sometimes it will come for reasons no one can explain…at least not consciously," said The Guardian as he watched Michael's reaction.

"Survivors of disasters often feel guilty for having survived. People who get through a serious car accident tend to feel guilty because they weren't hurt, while others were. Soldiers in wars and battles—those who lived—

often feel guilty for having survived while their comrades-in-arms died in action. Some have emotional scars they carry with them all their lives. (Much of Post-Traumatic Stress Disorder [PTSD], is caused by this. And recent estimates indicate that more than 120,000 veterans of the wars in Iraq and Afghanistan are currently coping with varying levels of PTSD.)

"'What did I do to deserve this?' is often the question that gets asked. This is a dangerous question, because it's usually accompanied by a sense of denial that follows, and the underlying 'guilt trip' never gets tagged for what it is.

"This almost always occurs because people think they know How Things Work. Or else they think they have to know How Things Work when they really don't. A lot of the time guilt trips get laid on people by a kind of 'friendly fire.' This is an addictive form of hidden Guilt that appears to be 'the decent thing to do,' when it's really not.

"Doing the right thing very often turns out to be someone else's version of what is right and wrong. And the saddest kind of victim is the one who relies on someone else's moral compass to determine how they should live their lives. By doing that, they have surrendered their entire identity and, in doing so, lose any chance they have of taking charge of their future.

"It makes somewhat perverse sense that the penance and the misery of the 'sinner' should match the magnitude of the offense. We have accounts from medieval times of people making pilgrimages to the Holy Land and traversing the last significant distance of their journey on their knees just so they can prove their repentance to God and anyone else watching. In the outward display, there is nothing to relieve someone's personal anxiety. So this behavior is really only misdirection—like the child who knows he is in trouble with daddy and spanks himself in hopes that will satisfy the punishment requirement. (He's not thinking of his own misbehavior. He is only dealing with the Guilt from external judgment. Would the same boy be feeling guilty if daddy didn't find out what he did? Of course not.) Most Guilt comes from our perceptions of the judgments that others place upon us. That is the basis of Synthetic Guilt.

"Does most Guilt really come from outside us? We know about the impact of traffic tickets or IRS audits. What about this statement: 'What happens in Vegas stays in Vegas.' The implication here is that this is a Guilt-Free Zone where virtually no one will pass judgment upon you. (And that little statement has caused it to be one of the most memorable and successful ad campaigns in the last 20 years.)"

The Upside of Guilt

"Virtually all Guilt occurs because people think they need it to determine who's at fault when in fact they don't. They need to be told, *'It's not your fault.'* To tell someone that 'It's not your fault' is the emotional Wonder Hug. That statement, together with the Hug, are virtual magic bullets that go to core issues—to soothe, heal, and repair without the need to explain things. By not finding fault, we release the need for Guilt to be placed *anywhere*! That allows anyone involved to realize that, 'I do not hold any Guilt,' in the experience."

We have already revealed the universal law that states: "No one ever does anything intentionally stupid." This doesn't necessarily mean that what was done was either correct or appropriate. That is why understanding the Guilt Trash Removal System is so valuable. Think about it.

— The Guardian

"As soon as we are truly able to free ourselves from any Guilt or Fault," said The Guardian, "we're usually elated and are soon able to love and forgive anyone else involved. And so their sense of guilt, pain, or shame doesn't really bother us at all. Although it may seem cold, it is actually the act of the great soul to be untouched by events around them, but also to convey to others that, 'It's Not Your Fault, either.'

"One of the best ways to get rid of Guilt is to use the nifty Six-Step Method for Trash Removal I told you about earlier. Take whatever it is that's making you feel guilty. Write it down. Go through the six-step process of getting rid of it, and then put it out of your mind forever. (And be sure you don't pass it on to someone else.)"

More and more people are actually beginning to acknowledge the validity of the 'It's Not Your Fault,' concept. A recent cartoon in The New Yorker showed a family of four lost deep in the African jungle. In it, the father is addressing his wife and children with this ironic caption: 'Okay, I acknowledge that we're lost. The important thing is to stay focused on whose fault it is.' Funny stuff, when you think about it.

— The Guardian

"So ultimately, the best way to deal with Guilt is to recognize it early on and get rid of it forever," Michael said. "That way, if people have no Guilt on which to hang any of the language of the victim, it becomes impossible for them be insulted or embarrassed."

"That's it!" The Guardian emphasized. "Where there is no Guilt, there can be no offense, no fear, no anger—and no victim!"

"So, what do you have then?"

"You would have the gospel of love."

The things about you that offend me are qualities I actually have myself, for if I did not have them in me I could not recognize them in you. One of the greatest things that can be said about any human being is that they are 'guileless.' Look at the spelling of the word, 'guile,' and the word 'guilt' and tell me the linguistic root of these words. Is it reasonable to assume that the truly guileless person is devoid of personal guilt and thus sees nothing objectionable in others? Think about it.

— The Guardian

CHAPTER 6

Victims Have Big "Buts"

"We have two ends with a common link.
With one you sit. With one you think.
Success depends on which you use.
Heads, you win! Tails, you lose."

Michael said, "I'm a little confused about one thing you told me. You emphasized the fact that Guilt creates Victims. At what point does someone become a Victim? Why do they stay that way? And how do we recognize that in ourselves… if that's what's going on?"

"Good questions!" The Guardian noted. "And since giving examples seems to be the best way of making a point, let me take one from your own life…

"I note from your life records, Michael, that you have a friend named Jim."

"Yeah, Jim! Jim's a great guy!"

"And a wonderful friend in many ways," The Guardian acknowledged, "but with a propensity for stopping himself from reaching the greater heights of his true potential…because Jim is a Victim."

"You may be right," Michael agreed.

"As you'll recall, Jim was a member of the high school band, playing drums at football games and in the school's jazz ensemble. He claimed that he had the ability and the drive to take his music to the next level—to play professionally. Talent-wise, he was probably right. Still, Jim always seemed to have an excuse for not being able to take that talent further. Can you recall? Do you remember the afternoon he returned from a talent tryout in Los Angeles?"

"I do, as a matter of fact. There were professional agents looking for raw talent. I wasn't at the tryout that day, but I recall Jim telling me all about it.

"'We were kept in this crowded room for hours,' Jim told me. 'They told us we'd only be there for a few minutes while they were setting up, *but* it was about two hours before I even got called to go into the auditorium. The drum set they provided was nice, *but* we didn't have a chance to warm up or tune the skins. They had some musical accompaniment for us, *but* I'd never heard the songs before. So it was really hard to match things up. I mean it was a good experience and all, *but* I'm not sure I'd want to work with those guys anyway.' At least that's what he told me."

"Jim didn't get the gig, did he?" The Guardian asked. "We might have guessed as much. In fact, there have been a lot of other opportunities since that time, including full-time jobs, part-time musical performances, even marriage. Jim lives alone today; he's in his late 40s and still wondering what went wrong. He could have been a star, BUT things didn't go his way—it wasn't his fault."

Michael said, "So are the excuses Jim's fault? You keep saying that, 'No one ever intentionally does anything stupid.' And yet when people experience Guilt and bad things you say to them, 'It's Not Your Fault.'"

"Good point!" The Guardian answered. "But what would you say is the difference between the statement, 'It's Not Your Fault,' and the whining cry of the victim who says 'BUT It's Not My Fault'?"

Michael said, "It seems like the 'buts' that victims use to excuse their failures allow them to use the 'no-fault disclaimer' to blame other people and outside influences for all their problems."

"The keyword that you just used, Michael, is Blame. Every time the victim explains his or her failure it will always be followed by a statement of Blame. Someone else will always be responsible. And, whatever the excuse, it will always have a big BUT in front of it."

Victims Always Have a Long List of "BUTS"

"Jim isn't the only victim we know, *but* they all have one thing in common: They all have big BUTS. (And you see them all over the place.)

"I could have made it as a pro, BUT the coach didn't like me—it's not my fault.

"I could have finished school, BUT I got pregnant.

"I could have had a great career, BUT I got married instead.

"I was not drinking at the party, BUT they put vodka in the punch.

"I didn't put those wine coolers in the trunk, BUT they did it when they borrowed my car.

"I should have gotten the promotion, BUT I was a threat to the boss.

"I would have been there on time, BUT the highway construction—what a mess!

"Retirement should mean traveling and seeing the world, not working part time at a 7-Eleven, BUT I thought they planned Social Security better than that.

"I *wanna, coulda, shoulda, woulda*, BUT (fill in the blank). Michael, there are two types of people in this world. There are Victims—the 'Done-untos' who have no control over their destiny or their circumstances.

"They're tossed and turned on the winds of fate. They gravitate towards psychics, fortune-tellers, and soothsayers, hoping to get good news about the frightening unknowns of the future. These poor unfortunate souls are absolutely convinced that what happens to them indiscriminately rains down with pure envy, worry, concern and depression. The motto and battle cry of their meaningless existence is, 'But It's Not My Fault' (BINMF).

"The second group is those who, oddly enough, are faced with exactly the same circumstances and conditions as those of the previous group—the same concerns related to work, relationships and the tasks of daily life. They have kids who get goofy. They sometimes forget about work, relationships, and certain elements of routine. But there's a major difference between this group and the first. They understand that no matter what happens in their lives, they have total control over how they allow people and circumstances to affect them.

"They also realize that understanding this concept enables them to see the glass half-full as opposed to half-empty. They ascribe to an oft-quoted cliché that states: 'If it is to be, it's up to me.' And whatever the circumstance may be, whether they like it or not, they realize that, within their own personal universe, everything is their responsibility.

"It's their responsibility and they determine how they allow it to affect them. No, they didn't make their teenage son get drunk at the party and wreck the family car. That was in his universe, and they have no control over that. Did it affect them? Yes! He wrecked the family car, and they feel some parental disappointment at what their son did. And yet they do have a choice as to how they allow it to impact them in their own little universe.

"They can avoid the depressing situation where people run around commiserating about the fact that they failed as a parent. Do they want to spend hours lamenting the loss of the most perfect vehicle that ever entered a highway? Do they want to go back into the past and relive, over and over again, the call from the police department—the shock, the anguish, the financial loss, and the anger at the news about the son and his accident? Do they enjoy revisiting the agony in their lives by renewing that experience dozens of times a day for weeks and months? Or do they sit down, talk to their son, and realize that his choices aren't theirs; that they need to get another car, and get on with life? Yes, they were jolted by this emotionally charged event that came without warning. But now it's history. It no longer exists, and the fact is that they're not in misery and can truly enjoy an unconditional love for their son.

"There are no further thoughts about transportation needs because, for all intents and purposes, their lives are delightful, joyous, and full of love—and it is their fault.

"After understanding these principles, is it possible to have patience with the thought process of the Victims? I would suggest that it's very difficult because the Victim's thought process can be categorized in three areas: those with mental menopause, mental masturbation, or mental flagellation.

The Victim Mentality

"The question you have to ask is what's it like to have a *Victim mentality?* How would you like to sit in the corner curled up in the fetal position in a state of total depression because you allowed yourself to be a Victim? It's your choice. You are the one who has control. So, you're only a Victim when you choose to be.

"It's true that victims are the 'done-untos' of this world. A Victim cannot have good self-esteem for the simple reason that they have given their power away to someone or some outside source as a means of justifying their evaluation of themselves. They are the employees *done-unto* by their miserable boss, the misunderstood good Samaritans put upon by their manipulative friends, and the unemployed mid-level executive whose house is being foreclosed upon by greedy bankers. Their numbers are legion. And they all feel that their walk in life is 'externally controlled.'

"History is replete with people who were raised in ghettos who went on to achieve great things. Many of those in poverty or poor economic conditions turn out to be jerks, 'bangers,' or unproductive members of society, but there are also many exceptions.

"In the psychological circus this often triggers the big debate between *nature versus nurture,* or *heredity versus environment.* If heredity were the true determinant, any number of us would be predestined to be losers. If that were so, there could be no Judgment in heaven, because what we did in life would not be under our control.

"That would mean that the day a baby is born, that baby is already on its way to Hell (or in the rare instance, Heaven)! That human being is already foreordained to succeed or fail.

"The truth is that, because we have control over one thing, we have control over all things. Otherwise, there could be neither Judgment nor Justice. Those who hate 'lazy minorities' would be right; because the day those babies are born in the ghetto they are already condemned to be lazy, useless 'problems to society.' Following that perverse path of logic, the same day that first set of babies is born, condemned to the ghettos, it's also predetermined that a select few will be power brokers and presidents of major corporations.

"Heredity? Environment? Both are flawed and need a different perspective. In a free society (or not), we are all able to choose. An individual's self-image is totally determined by how that man or woman allows outside influences to affect them. Would there be any bad self-images if everyone took responsibility for who they are? The answer is a loud, resounding No!

"That's because you can't blame anyone else. As long as you can blame somebody else, you won't take responsibility. As soon as you realize you have control, you don't have time to thump your chest and whine.

"It's also important to remember that the Past (history) does not exist, except to the extent that we allow it to do so in our minds. If something is past, it only has power over the present if we choose to recreate it. This is something, Michael, that you should remember quite well."

"I do," Michael was quick to admit.

"Would you care to share it?" The Guardian asked. "It's been sitting there for years—something your father told you that happened to him that has stuck with you ever since."

The Guardian's comment encouraged Michael.

"My father's father was a strict old man, raised in the German tradition. My father told me how Grandpa once planted a small tree on his farm in Iowa. As soon as Grandpa stuck the tree in the earth and firmed up the ground around it, he hauled off and belted my dad, knocking him to the ground.

"'That's so you'll remember the planting of this tree,' he told him. "Well, you know what my father chose to remember—that the SOB hit him after he planted the tree. You see, he lived to be 96, and he recreated that moment over and over again. My father was 75 when he told me about it for the first time. His dad was long gone, and the tree had long since been chopped down. Did that experience exist any more? No, but it was still recreated in my father's mind. And he was still being victimized by constantly reliving the negative impact of it."

Hearing this The Guardian said, "There's a by-product of victimization that may be its biggest tragedy. Some people are afraid of success because they will no longer be able to hide behind the *But It's Not My Fault* (BINMF) shield. They can no longer point a finger someplace else to lay off the blame for messing up. If they are successful, they have to burst the bubble of denial. It scares the dickens out of them because they don't understand what makes someone successful, and they might not be able to duplicate it again. So it's safer not to be successful in the first place, because you might have to prove you can do it again. You could be a Victim.

"If you walked up to the average Joe Lunch-Bucket and said, 'Why do you want to continue being a Victim?' He would say. 'Oh, I'm not a Victim. I make things happen!'

"'Okay,' you'd have to say, and ask. 'But what do you make happen? You make yourself into a victim so that you always have a scapegoat—somebody else to point at.'

"The reason a once-successful businessman (who is now floundering) will not release himself from his denial that he has victimized himself lies in the fact that he'd have to admit that he messed up. Instead he says, 'There must be some reason this happened (because I did everything right). So, it must be the fault of my subordinates—or the circumstances, the market, the stupid people out there who did this to me. It's got to be something, other than my fault. I've got to be a Victim, so that I can release myself from any responsibility.' (This would have worked BUT…)

"Why do you think, Michael, that so many people are that way—wanting to hang on to the misery? This is the Victim mentality of society. And you know that it's a lot more work to be a Victim than to live in the *light of the knowledge* that you have total control of who you are?

"The plans for slavery and liberty lost along with the bondage of *Dependency* have always gone something like this: 'Just do what you're told and be *done-onto.*' Even though you think they'd know better, so many people let themselves be controlled. Why? Because it gives them the structured framework they feel they lack. So they're willing to give their freedom to that image that says, 'Do what I say. Behave yourself. And I will take care of you. Accept this, because it's part of your lot in life. Since you have no self-esteem and even less sense that you have any control over what happens to you, just put up with whatever I give you.' Victims need this vicious myth because, like the residents of a boneless chicken ranch, they have forfeited their freedom of choice.

"It's truly a dependent relationship in the worst sense. The *Victim* needs the support of the skeleton—the framework. And the *Controller* or *victimizer* needs his skeleton filled out by having a Victim to control. It's called *codependency!*

"People who are not *self-actualizing* risk turning themselves into total Victims. So, at some point, someone has to ask the question: What would happen if one of them suddenly came up with a great idea—that they control everything in terms of the effect it has on them? ('I can choose to allow myself to be affected by this or not.') What happens then? It blows the lid off the downward spiral of codependency.

"One thing you can be sure of, Michael: Victims have their own language and their own code. It all starts with dependency, and it makes them pretty easy to spot."

There are four easy ways to spot a Victim. And once you get the hang of it, Victims are easy to spot: 1) Victims always spend their last dime before they make arrangements to get the next one. People who are in control of their lives don't spend their last dime until they have their fist around their next one. 2) Victims lose things all the time—more often than not, they're 'stolen.' Positive people are well organized, seldom lose things, and always seem to be in the right place at the right time. 3) Victims always seem to be equally creative at being in the wrong place at precisely the right time, and are always convinced that Murphy's Law applies to them more than anyone else. They lose their money. Their purse was stolen. The car they bought is a lemon. Their appearance is sloppy. Their grammar is poor. And they're always rationalizing the reasons that everything happens to them. 4) Victims are never in control of their lives. People in control of their lives are always the ones you admire. They seem to have their act together. And other people want to be around them. They're always the ones victims see as 'lucky.' They're the ones who get all the breaks, while the victims never have any. Think about it.

— The Guardian

"Keep one thing in mind, Michael. *Dependency is the only source of fear.* The extent to which we are dependent is the extent to which we have given power over ourselves to those people, substances, or circumstances upon which we depend. Every single fear we experience is the result of a dependency being threatened. The fear of losing employment, one's home, a relationship, health, youth, food, and life itself are the result of the dependency on each of these. In fact, you will be unable to find a single fear that is not connected to a dependency no matter how great or small. Independence—or simply taking control over all dependencies—is the only path to purely fearless *Liberty*.

"And the terrifying thing about Liberty, Michael, is that it depends on taking responsibility for your actions. Why do so many feel they need to be victims? Because as long as people can continue to be victims, they can 'cop out.' And they can use codependency as a means of maintaining a hold over others—as a kind of power play."

"Are you saying that victims use their 'victimization' as a kind of manipulation?" Michael asked.

"Virtually 100 percent of the time," The Guardian answered. "Because as surely as night follows day, Victims will find a way to become victimizers. And codependency is the weapon that they use."

CHAPTER 7

You Say You Love Me. Prove It!

Joe Gillis: *You tried to kill yourself. What a silly, ridiculous thing to do.* Norma Desmond: *I'll do it again! I'll do it again!*

— Sunset Boulevard

"One thing that we need to be clear about," The Guardian emphasized. "Victims don't actually have relationships. They take prisoners and demand ransoms. It's a tyranny called *Codependency*, and it usually amounts to one victim, *the Enablee*, attracting another victim, *the Enabler*, to participate with them in a game called *Emotional Blackmail (a.k.a. Emotional Terrorism)*."

"Wait a minute," said Michael. "Why do victims find other victims to save? Don't they have problems enough of their own?" he asked. "Seems to me that they'd be doubling their workload."

"Good question!" The Guardian noted. "First, remember what I told you earlier. *Self-actualized people*, those who are in control of their own personal universe, cannot be influenced by others unless they choose to be. And they are the very people who have learned to spot and avoid victims and victimization in all its forms."

"So it gets to be a vicious cycle," Michael realized. "Victims victimize other victims."

"That's about what it amounts to. Victims rush in to save other victims in the hope that being needed will somehow make them important. They

> **Enablee** is a term coined by The Guardian, mainly because he found the term 'co-dependent,' which describes the enablee, to be confusing. In the old school of thought, you'd have to have a 'co-depender' (which is equally confusing). So he opted for a word that actually works.

truly believe that if they can save someone, if they can do something to fix someone else's problem or help them achieve something, then they can relieve their own sense of exasperation at not knowing what to do or How Things Work.

"In truth, at a subconscious level, we realize that no one can help us; no one can do anything for us. In reality, this realization becomes a life-changing experience, because it reinforces the law of Agency.

"As we mentioned in the earlier in Law of Agency... The Law of Agency, the Second Universal Law, makes up our *Freedom to Choose*. (So, if you mess with my Agency, you mess with who I am.)

"Victims will always mess with someone's freedom to choose. That's how they rope in more victims—through the *blackmail (terrorist) bind of enablement*."

> *The behaviors exhibited by Enablees to control and manipulate their Enablers are the same as those used by terrorists against their victims. (Enablees are, however, often less covert.) Think about it.*
>
> — The Guardian

The Blackmail (Terrorist) Bind of Enablement

"Keep in mind that we have two kinds of victims here: the *Enablee* and the *Enabler*," The Guardian said. "The Enablee forces the Enabler to make what the Enabler sees as life and death decisions. The Enablee figuratively climbs to the top of the cliff and says, 'I'm going to jump off. Catch me!'

"The Enabler says, 'No, no, no! Don't jump off!' 'Catch me,' the Enablee insists. (And here's where the blackmail comes in.)

"The Enablee says, 'If you don't catch me I'll splatter.'

"The Enabler says, 'I'm not going to. You're on your own.'

"The Enablee says, 'Okay!' and jumps. That's when the Enabler scurries back to the appropriate position on the ground, arms outstretched just in the nick of time, and saves the Enablee from certain destruction. And the Enablee snuggles—safe, warm, and secure—into the rescuer's arms, reassured yet again that they'll never have to truly take responsibility for anything because they can, at will, *make the Enabler prove that he or she loves them.*

"So the Enabler pays the endless ransom for the 'sin of caring.' And the Enablee has a wonderfully twisted manipulation going for them, one that seems to work every single time.

"We hear periodically about some rather ingenious plots of kidnappers deciding on a 'mark.' First, they make sure (in most cases) that their mark is a wealthy person. Then they do their research. They study the habits and patterns of the mark's loved ones. And then, when the time is right, they snatch their *victim*. They depend upon the love and the protective nature of the mark to save the victim by 'caring enough' to pay the ransom and do exactly what they're told. Doesn't it become interesting then that, when consulted, the experts always seem to say: 'Don't pay the ransom!'

"Their reasoning is quite solid when you think about it. When kidnappers have no more reason to place value on the victim, *the mark will probably lose the loved one.*

"We see this very same scenario with terrorists who take hostages and hope that the hostages are significant enough to the threatened government, airline, agency, or corporation to make them respond. The question always comes down to this common denominator: *Do they care enough to yield to the terrorists' ransom demands?* And yet, without exception, the experts will recommend not paying which, in essence, takes away terrorists' power.

"I have a question," The Guardian said. "What do the alcoholic, the unemployed husband, the lazy, uneducated, unemployed 23 year-old son living at home, a not-really-an-addict ('I can quit anytime') cocaine junkie, a jobless friend who just got fired from another job, a high school kid who just really doesn't feel like getting his homework assignments in so he can graduate, and a daughter who just got pregnant because she couldn't bother to use birth control, all have in common?"

"They're victims," Michael recognized immediately.

Look at the track record of Israeli terrorist response teams. The Israelis have an absolute carved-in-granite policy never to negotiate with terrorists. They completely ignore the 'care enough' blackmail model to do what the terrorists insist is the 'right course of action.' The Israeli response to this is: 'Do what you've got to do. But we refuse to recognize any hold you think you may have over us.' The result is that terrorists, who have been known to hold out for days, either abandon their position or surrender within minutes of being notified that an Israeli anti-terrorist team is on the scene. Think about it.

— The Guardian

"Accurate. But they're more than that," The Guardian said. "The thing that all these and thousands of other *Enablee archetypes* have in common is that every one of them is nothing but a kidnapper and a terrorist with an ironic twist: they kidnap and hold themselves for ransom to whichever *mark* happens to be *their Enabler of choice.*

"They coerce the Enabler with the same tool that terrorists use. They declare themselves the victims and say, 'If you care enough, you will pay the ransom. You will comply with my demands (in all their many forms): You will enable me to be an unemployed, drunken husband. You will buy my food and feel sorry for me because I'm your 23-year-old offspring who can't find employment. (So you'll continue to need a little hit to get me by and I will look for a job tomorrow. So, let me sleep here tonight.) And if you really care whether I graduate, you'll write my term paper for me. (If you value me as a son you won't make me do it myself, because I'm just not up to it.)'

"So…we have kidnappers and terrorists who hold themselves hostage and force parents, loved ones, and friends to do their bidding because *somewhere along the way, these Enablers have been conditioned to care enough to 'do the right thing.'*"

"It's easier said than done," Michael said. "Because friends, loved ones—and especially family members—have so many ways of pushing your buttons."

"I didn't say it would always be easy," The Guardian acknowledged. "But it is essential. This is something people in charge of their destiny come to realize, and they take the steps that are necessary to correct it.

"Remember, Michael…What's the first thing that the experts on terrorism and kidnapping recommend?"

"Not to pay the ransom," Michael answered. "And not to negotiate."

"Exactly!" The Guardian said. "There's also something else they've learned when dealing with terrorists: It's always best to bring in a terrorist response team that is in no way tied to the mark. That way they have someone with no emotional ties to the hostage. Someone who doesn't have trouble maintaining the policy of not negotiating.

"In the Israeli model, for example, if one of the men in the terrorist response team had a wife who was a captive they would immediately remove him from the team. That way they could take the very tough (but necessary) stance of saying, 'Shoot her. We don't care. We're not negotiating.'

"*Emotional involvement, caring, family ties*—these are the hooks that the terrorist (a.k.a. Enablee) uses to reel us in. They do that because very few Enablers are capable of withdrawing from the terrorist response team and turning over the negotiations to a third party. (But this needs to happen, either virtually or in fact.)

"It's not easy to step back from the emotional ties you have to the (terrorist) Enablee and say, 'Tell them to starve if they must. Tell them to file for bankruptcy if they must. Tell them to become an addict if they must. Tell them to jump if they must. There will be no negotiations. We will not obey the demands of the terrorists. *We will not be blackmailed or pay the ransom.*

"Unless the Enablers can understand these concepts, what they fear most will happen. Literally every time. They always will lose the victim… one way or the other.

"*In the real world,* once the ransom is paid, the victim has no more value to the terrorist. So, the terrorist has no incentive to give back the victim.

"*In the blackmail bind of personal relationships,* the mark (Enabler) will be rewarded by having to ransom the Enablee terrorist time and time again in a downward spiral—all the way to the bottom. And even though this is the direct opposite of what the Enabler wants, he is almost certain to get this as a result until he refuses to negotiate with the emotional terrorists in his life."

"Then there are no simple answers to this complex issue," Michael said. "Oh, but there are," The Guardian corrected. "Most complex problems have simple solutions. When you're dealing with emotional blackmail, the answer is an old-fashioned concept called *Tough Love*. Another way of expressing it is a War on Drugs campaign started by First Lady Nancy Reagan in 1985. The message was simple, yet effective. And everyone remembers it to this day: 'Just Say No.'"

"That's all there is to it?" Michael asked.

"That's all there is to it!" The Guardian repeated as he got up from his chair, stretched, and strolled away.

> **"Just Say No!"**
> Evidence suggests drug use and abuse significantly declined during the Reagan Presidency. According to research conducted by the University of Michigan, *more young people in the 1980s were saying no to drugs.* High school seniors using marijuana dropped from 50.1% in 1978 to 36 percent in 1987 to 12 % in 1991, and the percentage of students using other drugs decreased similarly.

CHAPTER 8

The Past Does Not Exist

"I've shut the door on yesterday and thrown the key away. Tomorrow holds no fears for me since I have found today."

— Vivian Laramore

The Guardian offered a definitive thought: "If you remember nothing else, remember this one thing: *The Past Does Not Exist.*"

"I'm sorry, I just don't get it," Michael answered. "Everything we're taught from day one, is that virtually 98 percent of all our behavior in the present is dictated by something that happened to us in the past,"

"Let's say that another way," The Guardian suggested. "The past does not exist. But remembrance of the past does. And with it comes something called *selective memory*. Some people believe selective memory is a good thing. They're the ones who see a human fault or a bad situation as a chance to correct the unpleasant memories of it; that usually involves cases of trauma or abuse that can have complications later.

"The rest of us treat the past in a different way. Boy, how we love to dwell on it—and in it! We relive our mistakes, repenting of sins both known and unknown (just to make sure we're covered), rethinking poor decisions, beating ourselves up over missed opportunities, and a whole list of things 'we didn't do.'

"Still most people dwell on it, because it's all they have. Or, at least, it's all they *think* they have.

"Every time I think of the past, there's a little ditty that I love to recite: *The past is gone. The future hasn't arrived. So it is now, and now is a gift. That's why they call it the present.*

"If you have a hard time with this concept that the past doesn't exist, prove to me that it does. Can you do it? You can find the evidence that it happened. You can see the skid marks on the pavement. But is the car still there with the dented fender? No. Does that even exist? No. It's history. So the only place the past exist is in our minds. You are re-entering that chamber of illusion of what happened in your memory.

"Try wrapping your mind around this one: *Our illusions are illusions that we create as an illusion of past illusions we created.*"

"That's a mouthful," Michael agreed.

"It's also a mind full," The Guardian added. "And that's the whole issue. Just ask yourself this with regard to the past: How are you reacting to it? And how are you letting it affect you? Are you making it happen to you all over again? Maybe you're even embellishing the embarrassment, pain, guilt, anger, and fear…on and on, *ad nauseum*.

"If you are, it's your choice. If you want the past to exist, then fine! It will! If you want to recreate that crime or sin you committed over and over again, do it.

"Perhaps you remember the time in your junior high science class when the teacher used litmus paper to test for the acidity of a liquid. He would dip this small reddish strip of paper in a beaker, and if the paper turned blue it proved that this liquid had an acidic content. The term, *litmus test*, has been used ever since when making a practical application to prove a theory. So, let me offer you a litmus test about living in past experiences.

"First, can you prove it (whatever it was) happened?

"Second, can you still do something about it? If so, do it. If not, forget it and move on. If you still find yourself hanging onto something in your past that you can do nothing about, then you're clinging to something that no longer exists. You've failed the litmus test to prove the existence of the past. (Because it doesn't.)"

"What about mistakes we made in the past?" Michael asked. "Perhaps that's the strongest bond that keeps so many of us trapped there."

"That's because you're not calling it what it is, Michael. In fact most people don't," The Guardian replied. "And because they don't, they automatically place themselves in Guilt mode.

"Part of our ability to take out the Trash from the past means identifying it for what it is. A lot of people refer to stupidity and errors of judgment as 'mistakes' as a means of softening their actions so they can sweep them under the rug. And sweeping Trash under the rug is no way to get rid of it; it's just a refusal on their part to deal with the truth.

"One example is the term *abortion*. It's not called *murder*, yet woman after woman knows in her heart that the *abortion* murdered her baby and stopped its life. So these mothers invariably carry the Guilt over it for the rest of their lives by going back into the past and reliving it.

"They may have tried unsuccessfully to soften that Guilt by calling it 'freedom of choice' and continuing to rationalize their decisions. Still, the Guilt often continues to build and compound itself until it eventually destroys them. Anytime you soften what you think of as a sin by calling it a 'mistake' you magnify the Guilt and perpetuate the Judgment you've placed on yourself. (There are seldom any real 'guilt-ridden' mistakes.)

"Think about it, Michael. Does anyone really sit down and say: 'Okay, I think I'll do something. I think I'll call this one a mistake.'

"It wasn't a mistake. It was a decision. It could be an erroneous decision; one that didn't turn out the way you thought it might. You may have made an error in judgment. But at the time, you made the decision to proceed with the action. You made the decision to act. And if you call an intentional decision a 'mistake,' down the road you're going to be dealing with the Guilt you're feeling for labeling it as something it is not."

Reality, Imagination, Illusion—and Really Goofy Human Nature

"I have a question about all that," Michael said. "Don't some people tell themselves so many lies that they begin to think it's the truth? They call it creating their own realities."

"They do, Michael. But an illusion by any other name is still an illusion.

"They say that if someone sees an event on television or in the movies three times, it has the same psychological effect on them and their nervous system as if they had actually lived the experience itself. That's how many so-called experts explain the fact that someone can walk into an office building or public place and blow people away over a silly little disagreement—because they've experienced that act so many times on video games or at the movies that they've become numb to it. When young people see an actor murdered in one show, but then see him turn up on another show days, weeks, or months later, they lose touch with reality. It doesn't compute that what they see on the screen isn't real life. (This is proving to be even more of an issue with video games where a character is killed then restored to life by the acquisition of an additional bunch of bananas [or something]. The modern term for this phenomenon is *desensitization.)*

"I know what you mean," Michael said. "We are such a media-conscious society, many people can't separate Hollywood from real life."

"I remember a story I heard and you might recall it as well, Michael," The Guardian added. "Many years ago, a popular soap opera character, a doctor, was written out of a daytime TV 'soap' with his character (supposedly) transferred to Carson City Memorial Hospital in Nevada. There is no such hospital in Carson City, but there is one called the Carson-Tahoe Regional Medical Center. Apparently, during the week after this TV doctor supposedly moved, a hospital administrator said the medical center received over 200 calls wanting to know if this fictional doctor was now on staff. More than 200 television viewers (and quite probably hundreds more who didn't call) didn't grasp the fact that this was all make-believe."

"Scary, when you think about it," Michael replied.

"A definition of an Illusion," The Guardian said, "is 'holding onto something that doesn't exist, and in fact never existed.' The same applies to the past.

"People hang onto the past because it's all they have. The mistake that almost everyone makes is that they try to keep the whole thing, when the only past you should hang onto is the part you can learn from. The only value in experience is to take out the salient, learnable, useful parts and let the rest of it go."

"What about betrayal or crimes against relationships?" Michael asked. "Do they exist?"

"Only to the extent that we recreate them," The Guardian answered. "And if we're stupid enough to recreate things about which we think we should feel guilty, we simply punish ourselves needlessly. (Remember: If we can't do anything about it, then there's absolutely no reason we should keep recreating it.)

"We talk about people being damned by their sins—and it is a dam, like a river being dammed by dirt, debris, and concrete. So people are dammed or stopped by their perceived 'sins.' They stop creating and concentrate all of their feelings on self-recrimination, and that is a double-edged sword.

"When folks are in a state of denial, they feel like victims. ('They did this to me; the state did this to me; my boss did this to me.') But when we beat ourselves up over past transgressions, we literally deny our power and victimize our own existence. And it becomes an impossible cycle, an impossible rut, out of which to extract ourselves. The people who don't deny responsibility (not knowing How Things Work) may turn and blame themselves. And, unlike blaming someone else (someone they can yell at…) they can't release their frustrations. That's why most religions provide people with an exit path from this cycle.

"For example most Christians believe that Jesus Christ has provided something called *The Atonement* so they could dump this Guilt (Trash) and get rid of it. There is the concept of *Repentance*—a step-by-step procedure that acts like a Guilt release valve, so we have a place to channel and release it. *(Every belief system has to give people a way out for their Guilt.)*

"Among Christians, the concept of repentance goes even further. If one is truly repentant, God not only forgives, He forgets what happened. If the past doesn't exist for God, then what is left for us to remember?

"Remember that I originally mentioned the concept of seeing an event three times—and the fact that repetition had the same impact as actually going through that life experience. What do you think it does, then, to repeatedly relive those things that are a source of guilt and despair? Do you think it takes three repetitions, or just one?

If you have truly repented (and that means you are not recreating the event in your mind over and over and over again), the past is gone. At the point where you have asked for forgiveness, at the point where you've made restitution and at the point where you've decided you don't ever want it to happen again, it's done—unless, of course, you go back and relive it over and over again, which might be looked upon as committing the sin again. Think about it.

— The Guardian

"If your relationship with God is a concern for you, ask yourself this question: As you've gone through what you need to go through to settle your mind, did it affect Him? No, because we can't have any effect on Him, only on ourselves. No unclean thing ever becomes a part of His presence. So, it can't affect Him, no matter what happens.

"If we take care of ourselves and forgive ourselves and don't recreate it again, it doesn't exist. If you take bitterness, guilt, resentment, worry, fear, and anger out of your life, what are left but love, joy, gratitude, and happiness? Therefore, where do you think those dark aberrations reside? Only in the past.

"No thought or word is as profound at the time it's uttered as it can become later—after the event itself. Abraham Lincoln had no idea of the significance of his address at Gettysburg at the time he gave it. He had scrawled it on the back of an envelope. And after he gave the address, the crowd there barely responded with polite applause. And yet, look at how history has played it, how revered it is now. (This is an example of recreation through remembering the past. This event was enhanced through re-creative remembrance. So also rests the danger of exacerbating the negative through re-creative remembrance.) As Lincoln said in his closing remarks:

> *...We here highly resolve that these dead shall not have died in vain—that this nation, under God, shall have a new birth of freedom—and that government of the people, by the people, for the people, shall not perish from the earth.*

"The Past, or any relationship with it, should be about the positive things—inspiration, ideals, tradition, and resolutions to greatness—not the emotional junk, the Guilt and the Trash.

"That's why it's both ironic and tragic in a way that Lincoln's immortal words, believed by pundits to be the most quoted speech ever given, was virtually ignored at the time he delivered it. And yet this example perfectly illustrates how selective we are about the past.

"When most people hear the concept that *The Past Doesn't Exist*, they resist it with an almost violent kind of passion. After all, we have libraries full of books that talk about history. We have scriptures that chronicle events from the past. We have cemeteries. We look in the mirror and see the two black eyes from the guy who punched us in the nose, and we change the bandages on the puncture wound where the neighbor's dog bit us. We continue to pay attorney's fees to recover Uncle Rich's gold-plated enema bag that, in all fairness, should never have been included when our good-for-nothing cousin contested the will. We sit at the kitchen table with our spouse, asking ourselves what we did wrong after getting a call from the local police department about our seventeen-year-old son who received enforced relocation from the party he told us he wasn't going to.

"Think about the fender-bender you may have had. You called the police and spent a good hour and a half answering questions while the officers filled out reports and reports and reports of events in the past. If the past did still exist, why would that policeman have to stay overtime and miss a perfectly good supper while he tries to get someone to give a clear recollection of what happened? All he'd have to do is drive up, watch the accident occur and then write a report. If a judge needed to look at the case, all he'd have to do is walk out to where the event was still happening and watch it. There wouldn't be a discussion or trial. In fact, the entire legal profession and a great deal of litigation would be eliminated because these activities in our society deal almost exclusively with what happened.

"In fact, a very interesting sci-fi novel could be written explaining the fact that we would never be able to get a thing done or put anything behind us as we would probably still be freeze-framed at the beginning of the Revolutionary War, trying to see through the fog of musket smoke from 'The Shot Heard Round the World.' In other words, if the past continues to exist we would never be able to progress to the present, and there would be absolutely no possibility of the future.

"When you get down to it, we get amused and sometimes aggravated with people who seem to be living in the past, especially when their recollections are almost totally selective.

"We all know an Uncle Harry who, from his position as third-string tight end on the high school football team, saw exactly three minutes of game time for his whole career—all in the fourth quarter of the last game of the season because everyone else even remotely capable of filling his position was either injured, wounded, or dying. At the same time, his quarterback, looking for anyone else to throw the ball to on a pass play, was hit just as he threw the ball to someone else. The errant pigskin wobbled like a 'ruptured duck' into flight toward Uncle Harry (who was running the wrong route) and it smacked him right in the wedge between the face guard and the temple of his prison surplus 1950s helmet, sticking there and bloodying his nose in the process. Out of reflex and self-preservation, Uncle Harry pulls the ball down just as he's stumbling over the goal line into the end zone and watches with some surprise as the referee throws his hands up in the air, signaling 'Touchdown!'

"Uncle Harry, now a legend in his own mind, has relived the incident a thousand times until he actually believes he was the hero of a game he was never supposed to play by catching the ball not really thrown to him by a quarterback who didn't want anything to do with him. Still, the memorabilia and headlines say just the opposite. And that is the event Uncle Harry recreates at every given opportunity—not the moment, just the memories, impressions, and perceptions of the moment."

"Seems like Uncle Harry is having a pretty good time remembering or misinterpreting that event," Michael observed.

"But is he?" The Guardian challenged. "Let me ask you? Is there anything sadder than someone who is living in the past—especially when that memory is so selective…even defective?

"Napoleon once observed: 'What is history but a lie agreed upon?' His point was well taken. No one truly knows what happened except for the people who were actually a part of that particular (historic) event. And they are long since gone.

"Take a walk through a cemetery, Michael. The names and dates on the grave markers identify a life that was, but is no more and people who were, but are no more. So, in fact the past does not exist except to remind us that everything must change—and does. There is only Now.

"Remember what I said about the things we should take from the past—the lessons?

"Take a hot iron, for example. For those of you who remember what it was like to iron your own clothes, the hot iron represented both a danger and an opportunity. As long as you remember that you don't touch the iron with your finger to see if it's hot, you have learned from the past.

"Does that mean you're living in the past? Of course not! You remember getting burned by testing the iron with your finger and that it hurt. (You may even have the tiny burn scar to remind you.) But if you start to dwell on the scar on your thumb and feel flawed and disfigured because of it, you are living in a past that doesn't exist. And you're turning yourself into a Victim.

"Let's kick that up another notch or two. How do you control the effect of having your house destroyed by fire, by an earthquake, or by some other disaster? You can't. But you can choose to control the impact on your family and your immediate environment.

"When Thomas Edison, the famous inventor, saw his entire laboratory and factory burn to the ground, his response was simple and profound. 'I am 67 years old. I can't get back what I've lost. But I can begin tomorrow by rebuilding again…' And he did. He had his employees report to work the next day to help clear the wreckage and rebuild all that they had created together. (Every one of them showed up the day after the fire, and within eighteen months they were back in full operation, as if the fire had never taken place.)

When the fire was destroying his buildings, rather than commiserating over the disaster, he is said to have called for others to come and enjoy the spectacular event with him. Thomas Edison lived to be 85 years old, continuing to invent and build until the week he died. Thomas Edison—the holder of more than 1,500 patents and the inventor of everything from control of electric current to the motion picture camera—never dwelled in the past and never concerned himself with the future. By his own self-description, he flourished in The Now, and understood better than anyone that this moment is all that matters. Think about it.

— The Guardian

"What Thomas Edison had that made him so successful was an element called Attitude. And a Positive Mental Attitude (PMA) is really the key to understanding that you are the center of your universe. Your Attitude, they say, determines the degree of your Altitude—how far you'll rise toward your potential.

"The biggest trap about living in the past lies in the fact that we always spend our time in the wrong part of it. We can have 90% of our lives in good working order, and yet the other 10% (all the bad stuff) is what we concentrate on and stew over. What did Jesus say about someone losing a silver coin out of the many they had? They literally dropped everything and went in search of that single coin, leaving all their abundance behind in pursuit of their loss. That is exactly what people do when they let the past rule their lives.

"Because the future hasn't occurred yet, the only things we have are memories, and we naturally project them toward future events that we're 'afraid' might happen again in our lives. We worry about the future, obsess about the past, and often fail to acknowledge the present. So, most people spend most of their lives living where life no longer exists—in all the days gone by! Isn't that amazing, since we now know that *The Past Doesn't Exist?*

"Keep in mind: *Now* is a very short period of time. And the *Now* from a minute ago is gone. Take what I said from that minute, and let the rest go. It no longer exists.

"The present is like glory. It's fleeting. In the Academy Award-winning film, *Patton*, the General reminisces over battles and winning and the experience of some of his grander missions in life. He points out that in ancient Rome, when the conquering general would return in 'a Triumph' at the head of his legions, they would always post a lowly slave to stand behind him in his chariot, holding a laurel above his head and constantly repeating the words: 'Remember…All Glory is Fleeting.' So *the Present*, like glory, is fleeting, fading quickly into the past, which (repeat after me…) *does not exist.*

No thing, no one, and no experience can have an impact on your life unless you allow it to. Those who live in the past, those who obsess over it, those who allow any experience from the past to affect them other than their choice to learn from history, are fools, and they only victimize themselves. No ifs, ands, or BUTS about it. Think about it.

— The Guardian

CHAPTER 9

The Law of Me

*"We talk about your skin and the dimples on your chin
The polish on your toes and the run in your hose And God knows we're gonna talk about your clothes! You know that talking about you makes me smile. But every once in a while,
I want to talk about me."*

— "I Wanna Talk About Me!" by Toby Keith

"It's very simple, Michael…as most things are," The Guardian said, beginning the lesson. "People wrap a lot of little coats of thought and emotion around everything that they do. They think that most of what they do is relative to how someone else thinks about, talks about, or acts about—them! It's called *The Law of Me*. It's the First of the Four Universal Laws. And The Law of Me states one idea with complete clarity: *Everything that you do is measured against how it makes me feel about you.*

"That's because most people function strictly from the rules that govern this Law. If you're being nice to that individual, it's because you want to see yourself in the light of being nice to that individual, and the way you're nice to that individual is always in accord with how you want to feel about *you* when you're with *them*.

"The people we like best are those to whom we would like to say, '*I like me best when I'm with you.*' People have these coats of emotion they wrap up around themselves whenever things go wrong. So, when you're angry with someone or when you feel like striking out at them, it's almost always because of how their actions and attitudes have affected the message you've chosen to receive from them.

"Keep in mind that the *Law of Me* states that: *Everything that happens to or around me—everything that's said and attitudes expressed—are always interpreted as a message about me.* Let me give you a couple of examples.

'Let's say a driver on the freeway cuts too close in front of you, just so he can make a turn. What's your first reaction? You feel 'done-onto.' You get upset about it. And you let him hear about it.

"And what's the other driver thinking about you? He's probably thinking, 'What's wrong with *that* guy? First, he ignores my turn signal, so I have to cut in quickly to make my turn. Now he's scowling and growling at me because I did what I had to do. (That guy must be a real jerk.)' So everything about either one of you is about *you*; it's *never* about the other guy.

"Here's another example: A marriage is in trouble. Two people are thinking of divorcing. She sees everything that he does as an intention to hurt her feelings, make her angry, or make her feel unimportant in his life. He feels that she is critical of everything he does. She has become extremely independent and no longer includes him in her life. They both feel guilty and unlovable because the other one doesn't like them. What they don't realize is that he isn't doing anything to her. His feelings and attitudes are never about her; they're only about him.

A most important law that we all must remember is that when someone acts or speaks in a negative way toward us it is never about us, it is always about them. Believe it. It is always about them. Think about it.

— The Guardian

"Not surprisingly, not a lot had changed since the early days of their relationship...when they were still 'in love.' In the beginning, he buys her flowers that are really about his own Self-Image—feeling good about his being affectionate and considerate. She takes the flowers and the meaning behind them to signify that she is worthy of someone's kindness and consideration. So she likes herself better because he gives her flowers. As the relationship starts to go a bit sideways, he gets her flowers because it makes him feel good about himself for showing affection, although he now starts to feel a bit 'done-unto' because she is critical of him."

In a romantic relationship or a marriage, the difference between making love and having sex lies in the physical expression of it. Making love is the physical expression of no-fault, no-judgment unconditional acceptance of one person by another. Having sex is the seeking of counterfeit approval and never finding it. One is spiritual and clear; the other is both polluted and superficial. Tell me, Michael, would you rather be with a woman who judges, evaluates and rewards you with her 'approval' based on the orgasmic output you elicit in her? Or would you rather be with a woman who savors a touch or a hug from you as readily as she enjoys complete physical intimacy? A truly loved woman can release the troubles of the world as easily by holding hands on a quiet walk as she can from the ecstasy of a nude embrace. So the choice is yours. Which would you rather have: unconditional (it's not your fault) appreciation and acceptance? Or the judgmental hoops and traps of reward and punishment, endlessly searching yet never finding the peace of being able to say, 'I like me best when I'm with you?' Think about it.

— The Guardian

"I understand, but I don't understand," Michael admitted. "Why would she start to be critical of him?"

"Any number of reasons, some of which may be valid but all of which will be about her," The Guardian answered. "She takes the flowers and feels good about them, but then starts to wonder what the real message is—whether they might be an apology for the fact that he no longer really likes her all that well. He can say, 'I love you.' But now she is starting to question whether she should really feel good about herself because he might not mean it like he used to. So it reaches that point of no return because everything she thinks and does is really about her, and everything he thinks is really about him. And neither of them can get back to 'liking themselves best when they're with one another,' because in the end (as in the beginning) it's *all about me*. He feels it's all about him. And she feels it's all about her.

"Remember, Michael, that we live in a fault-finding society and a fault-finding world. Once something—anything—goes a little bit out of balance, the first thing we have to do is find out whose fault it is. And as soon as anyone senses that they might be involved, they immediately start making adjustments to make sure that they're not found at fault. This prompts a lot of good people to waste a tremendous amount of energy and creativity to keep from being blamed for things they never did in the first place. This happens tens of thousands of times a day every day, and whether it's business or personal, finding-fault always destroys relationships."

On an individual scale, fault finding as it applies to the Law of Me is both sad and self-destructive. On a global scale, it can be dangerous and occasionally even disastrous. There are records upon records to show that many international calamities such as airplane crashes, the Titanic, even Pearl Harbor, all quite probably took place because people concealed, delayed, or ignored critical information for fear of being found at fault. In other words, they were afraid to take responsibility for their actions. Think about it.

— The Guardian

"If finding fault destroys relationships…and most people apply the Law of Me to finding fault, then what's the upside?"

"That's the whole point. People don't apply the Law of Me consciously, because they lost that ability as little children. Now as adults, they try to avoid 'being blamed for things' because they no longer understand How Things Work. They don't realize that *it's really not their fault.*"

Selfishly Unselfish: The Role of the Teacher in the Law of Me

"Keep one thing in mind, Michael," The Guardian said. "We can only see from our own perspective. In The Law of Me, it's the only thing that matters."

"So, what you're saying is that I see things only as they make me feel about Me." Michael realized. "Seems awfully selfish and self-centered pretty much across the board when you put it that way. Does that mean no one cares about anybody else?"

"Of course not," The Guardian corrected. "After all, I'm here helping and counseling you, am I not?"

"Yeah!" Michael agreed. "But I have to note that, according to you, you're doing it all 'because of you.'"

"Well, it is true. It makes me feel great to share wisdom, knowledge, and understanding with you (or anyone). Since I already understand these principles, I definitely get an additional sense of fulfillment by seeing you grasp and apply them. As I facilitate your growth and learning, it gives me great joy to be able to share your exhilaration when I see your eyes open to these truths for the first time. It's the same type of fulfillment that an adult experiences when he's helping a child learn to walk. The adult can't walk for the child, but he or she becomes the facilitator, and that is a special kind of 'high' all its own.

"Have you ever noticed that when someone becomes an expert at something, they actually love to share what they've learned—and to teach others? The reason is simple. Anytime someone achieves a level of skill or expertise that is beyond the ordinary, it has usually taken a struggle to get there. They've had to exercise to gain the strength or develop the skill. They've had to struggle, meditate, and break through barriers to learn the truth. When they finally break the barrier to reach a goal, they experience such a rush of exhilaration that it virtually becomes contagious.

"The way that human nature works is that everyone needs a goal or an objective for which to strive. The verse from Proverbs 29:18 clearly emphasizes this: 'Without a Vision, the people perish…' Without dreams, life is no longer life; it is mere existence.

"The question then is bound to come up: 'What happens when the vision materializes?' What happens when the dream comes true—when the goal is achieved?

"Everyone has heard the quotation: 'Life is a journey, not a destination.' What happens when that destination is reached? Very simply, the journey—life—ends. This happens tens of thousands of times in everyday life.

"A salesman sets his yearly goals and builds tremendous intensity around them. As a result, he becomes totally focused and single-minded. Finally, in the last hours of December 31st he completes his objective—the one previously thought to be impossible. After the beginning of the New Year, he goes into a sales slump. The journey was over. And the Glory 'was fleeting.'

"An athlete sets his mark, perhaps a new record, and struggles for months or years before he finally achieves his objective. After that, he 'plateaus out.' Maybe he even leaves his sport and tries something else for a while. When you have an athlete who is highly motivated to break a record or be better at his sport than ever before, there's not much fulfillment in doing it again and again just for the sake of doing it. (There has to be something else… something more.)

"Why do great salesmen train, great athletes coach, and great masters teach? Because by facilitating the journey of those who would emulate them, they renew their achievement vicariously, as well as the virtual rush that goes with it."

"So," Michael had to ask, "Does the Law of Me apply to everyone, including the great trainers, coaches, and masters?"

"Of course," The Guardian answered. "Parents experience a renewal of all their achievements in life as they support the striving of their child in learning to walk, riding a bicycle, walking away from a fight, or achieving financial success. But this all requires understanding. The danger comes (and it can become severe) if the parent, coach, trainer, or master doesn't understand How Things Work."

"I guess that's when a lot of Trash can get dumped in," Michael said, thinking about it.

If you have ever been to a Little League baseball game you will often see fathers, who were never good ballplayers themselves, pushing hard for the achievements of their children in order to vicariously experience the success they were never able to achieve themselves. Think about it.

— The Guardian

"Exactly!" The Guardian confirmed. "If a master receives his reward by seeing a student he is facilitating actually achieve his goal, he is *correctly putting the Law of Me into play*. He experiences fulfillment by sharing the struggle and seeing his student reach his destination. He rejoices with him as they pause halfway through the journey and enjoy the progress they have made. But this also comes with a caution.

"Those who do not understand the Law of Me mistake the destination for the process of the struggles that come with the journey. This is the teacher who enables mediocrity by giving the answer. This is the parent who pampers the son or daughter by giving them a new car instead of allowing them to take steps to earn it. This is the coach who encourages cheating as means to an end rather than developing the championship skills that are necessary to win. This is also the application of the Law of Me *without* an understanding of How Things Work.

"In fact, the Law of Me is very strict and absolute. And it says: *No one can do anything to or for anyone else.*

"You can only affect me, Michael, to the extent that I allow it. Others can only affect you to the extent that you allow it.

"When Jesus (in Matthew 6:1) emphasized giving alms in secret rather than making a spectacle of it, he was alluding to keeping the Law of Me in perspective. People are innately sensitive to being good as opposed to looking good. They want to feel good about themselves. So they make a great public display of being good by trying to look good. And yet this is something that is almost always temporary and superficial. When you look good only for the sake of appearances, it's so very unrewarding that, beneath it all, you feel at fault. So 'doing your alms (giving to the poor) in secret' and not for the praise of others keeps the truth of the Law of Me in perspective. The true reward of the master lies in the fact that *the student is discovering the answers for himself.*

How does the inflated ego of the alms giver affect the self-image of the recipient of their alms? Think about it.

— The Guardian

"A perfect example of the two applications of the Law of Me lies in the parable of the fish. The Chinese philosopher Lao Tzu once observed: 'Give a man a fish and you feed him for a day. Teach a man how to fish and you feed him for a lifetime.' A true master would add the following statement to this concept: 'Teach a man to teach a man how to fish and you will feed generations.'

"The man who receives the fish has his moment trivialized because he learns nothing from the experience. The master who teaches the student to fish revels in the fact that he has quite probably created an entire generation of fishermen—and, in doing so, created a legacy.

"In the Law of Me, the Enabler is just like the teacher, trainer, or coach who tries to find shortcuts to the answer or the 'win.' They are acting as Enablers in the teaching process. The Enabler, by assuming the *Enablee's* burden, is not allowing that person to learn from the experience and grow from it, because he doesn't understand How Things Work. And because he doesn't understand How Things Work, he's enabling that person to remain a Victim."

"Once again, we get back to the issue of Guilt (Trash) and Victimization," Michael observed. "So, how do we find our way back to that 'perfect building'?"

"By recognizing, Michael, that we never left it," The Guardian answered. "By becoming again as a little child."

Bless the Beasts and the Children—They Live in the Law of Me

"Children and animals function in complete accord with the Law of Me," The Guardian said. "They know that everything in life is measured against how they feel about themselves. They are honest in that emotion.

"A dog will nuzzle his head under his human's hand to get a pet or a hug. He loves his human companion unconditionally, so he expects the same thing in return and never evaluates whether or how much. The reason that dog can love so unconditionally is because he knows that love is all about him feeling good about himself. So he wastes no worry over the message of 'his worth.' He feels no need to interpret that message from the hand that pats his head. (It's not about the human; it's about him, the dog.)

"In the same way, love from a child is the comfort of love expected and received unconditionally. A child will throw her arms around her mother or father and blatantly expect a hug in return. Most children will even ask out loud for a hug. They're honest in their desires and their needs to express themselves. After all, it's all about them, and they know it!

"Sadly, most adults interpret this as selfishness. That's because, along the way to growing up they've been taught to mask their thoughts and actions by pretending that what they think and do is about others. So the adult will often play the game of striking a bargain. They give their significant other a hug then wait for the return message: *Will he or she hug me back? How sincere will it be, and what does it really mean? Will it be what I want? If not, what is there about me that isn't as lovable as I'd hoped?* (So, it's all about them, but they'll be the last to admit it.)

"Unfortunately, that same adult (in this case, the parent) will start playing that game of reward and punishment by giving or withholding affection as a means of bargaining with the small child. And that's where so much of the Trash (in the form of very conditional love) starts to get dumped inside.

"Keep in mind, infants are perfect learning machines. They see, hear, taste, and feel everything and everyone in their realm of experience—their personal universe. So, the evaluation or comparison that they make comes as a very simple question: *How does this experience make me feel about me?* This is the Law of Me. The little child gets that from the beginning, before the games begin—before the filters and masks get layered on top.

"That's how something called Self-Image gets created."

"That doesn't sound so good," Michael declared.

"Well, Michael, it's all good," The Guardian answered. *"It just depends upon whether or not you understand* How Things Really Work.*"*

CHAPTER 10

Self-Image: The Great Mirror

*"I could tell my parents hated me.
My bath toys were a toaster and a radio."*

— Rodney Dangerfield

"Our self-image is the blueprint for the world we create for ourselves," The Guardian continued. "We literally project it onto the screen of life for all the world to see."

"Then the Law of Me only works in your favor if you have a good opinion of yourself," Michael concluded.

"So, guess what, Michael? Self-image is either your biggest problem or your most important asset. It all depends upon what you see when you look in the mirror.

"Understand this, Michael: We carry on a running mental conversation with ourselves. (It's called 'self-talk' in psychological circles.) We are constantly having self-conversations about our relationship with the world around us. We're constantly evaluating our relationships, positioning ourselves against objects and around objects, in our travel and movement. Once in a great while we actually take the time to look and see what is happening around us, but most of the time we're deep in some conversation with ourselves.

"In accordance with the Law of Me, that conversation primarily involves two areas: 1) the image that we have of ourselves, and 2) the image of ourselves that we project to others.

"Who am I? Am I who I think I am or am I who you think I am or am I who I think you think I am? This is a conversation everyone has with himself, whether he (or she) does so consciously, or not. Think about it.

— The Guardian

"Most of us, when we project outward, create an image of ourselves on our own behalf. Almost without fail, we evaluate everyone and everything around us from our own center. So that's where the subject comes in: 'I'm not what you think I am. But I am what I think you think I am.'"

"So, it's all about *me*," Michael said. "It all reverts to that Law of Me."

"Interesting, how it all ties together, isn't it?" The Guardian mused. "Yes, it's true. All relationships, wants, and needs are about *me*. But it's more than that. It's also what your 'me' chooses to project to others. If you want to be good at something—anything—you have to be able to step outside yourself and examine what kind of first impression you make upon others.

"A great way to do this is to have a picture taken of yourself, and also make a recording of yourself talking about the things that you'd normally discuss with a friend. Then sit down and honestly look at the photo and listen to the tape. By stepping outside yourself this way, you'll gain some smattering of objectivity. You will soon find that you'll almost always be treated by other people based upon the impression you are creating with that photo and that tape. (It sounds superficial, but it's just human nature.)

You Are What You Appear to Be

"You're also going to find that you'll be most acceptable in the circle of people who look, sound, behave, and dress like you do. You'll also find that you're most comfortable there.

"Those who dress above you, speak above you, energy above you, and 'personality' above you will treat you as an inferior. (After all, they're not totally comfortable with you.) Those who dress below you, speak below you, energy below you, and 'personality' below you will treat you as a superior.

> *The 'mirror technique' of telling yourself who you will become and what you will achieve is a valuable application of the personal Law of Creation. This technique is extremely effective. It has been used successfully by many entertainers and public personalities. As an example, it has been said that Barbra Streisand adopted this very method to train herself to sing so beautifully. Think about it.*
>
> — The Guardian

"Inside this social process of natural selection, the victim will scream: 'You must accept me as I am. I demand that you dig down past the poor hygiene, poor grooming, sloppy dress, vulgar language, slop and slime of me, and ignore the stereotypes that this kind of social misfit is sure to represent.'

"In the first place, this kind of behavior offends other people, often without their being consciously aware of it, because it invades their sense of Agency.

"Let's take an example: A woman—otherwise sloppy, overweight, and unkempt—gets a tattoo. Unless she has gotten it for some intimate personal reason or to cover up a blemish (unlikely), she will more than likely have it exposed in a place that will boldly express her rebellious nature. As individuals, we can go through all the rationales we like to justify that person's decision, and yet we will still experience a bit of a mental hiccup whenever we see that woman and that tattoo. (It may not be fair. It may be biased, and a classic example of stereotyping someone else. It may not be right. *It just is*.)

"Above all else, you have to be true to yourself, Michael. Have you ever considered that you can be your own person by putting your 'best foot for ward' to others? In a way, you're playing their impressions of you like an instrument. And yet it's not manipulation. You have simply chosen to become wiser, more intelligent, and more impressive. In that way, you're very much like the computer whiz who creates his or her own system for surfing the Internet. The other systems may be fine, but you have found a way that works best for you, and in that way you command your own destiny. You find a way to outsmart everyone else and master every situation.

Minorities in any situation, rather than kick against the pricks of resistance and demand to be accepted, would be very wise to find the things that appeal to the other races and play them like a fiddle. Out-dress them, outsmart them, out-talk them—not in a malicious way, but because that's just how things are. Think about it.

— The Guardian

"It has become a cliché, Michael, but it's invariably true that *perception becomes reality*. You see, we not only have self-images, but also a whole library of images dictated by the images other people have of us. And as we act in ways that our self-images dictate, we are treated in ways that those images have predetermined for us. It just can't happen any other way. It is the Law. We can project the concept that you should act outside the image you've created for yourself, but it becomes an oxymoron—a contradiction in terms.

"When you accept the fact that we play the people we're dealing with like instruments, it's the equivalent of playing life like an instrument. And it's amazing how most people feel that they have erred in their 'first impressions' of other people, when in fact they are almost always unerring.

"Most people are not wise enough in the ways of this Law to do anything but project onto the *Screen of Life* the opinions that others hold of them. Their self-esteem is totally reliant upon the impressions others have of them either as winners or as victims. So, the old concept holds true: 'What you are speaks so loudly that I cannot hear what you say.' That's why dogs bite some people and not others. That's why some people are prosperous and successful while others get nothing on their plate except further applications of Murphy's Law.

"So the rule applies: 'The picture that I paint of who I am to myself is the image I will project to the rest of the world.' Very simply, *truth is truth*, whether it is for a Christian, a Muslim, a Buddhist, or an atheist. And it says, 'The picture that I paint of who I am will be based directly upon how much or how little I like myself.'

"This, of course, is called *Self-esteem*. (High levels of self-esteem are sometimes mistaken for arrogance when, much of the time, nothing could be farther from the truth.)

"The trap comes when the individual starts to confuse *self-esteem* with *self-gratification*. And even though we're dealing with two kinds of 'feel-goods' here, we know at our core which of the two makes us feel better. What really motivates us is what ultimately gains our own self-approval. *Self-gratification* is very often shallow and temporary. *Self-esteem* is that which is earned—things that we say and do that justify liking ourselves better.

"People with high self-esteem will invariably say, 'I like me best when I'm with you. I like me best when I'm in a job. I like me best when I paint the picture that we see of me as right and good and selfless.' The ultimate compliment we can give ourselves is to say, 'I like me best when I'm with…me!'

If you want to be good at a sport, separate yourself and get rid of the negative feedback that tears down your self-image. That way your image of yourself is what you will do with what you project onto the Screen of Life. By being by yourself, you don't have to be thinking, "Who is watching and what do they think?" with every move you make. That way—when preparing, when practicing, when in the middle of a game— you can perform only the 'good stuff.' And that becomes your Self-image. Think about it.

— The Guardian

"Every principle is a two-edged sword. If applied directly, it brings success and a *strong self-image*. *High self-esteem* eliminates ego. It eliminates Judgment. It gets rid of Guilt. People with high self-esteem act in accord with their own positive Self-Image. They stay on purpose. As the Greek Oracle of Delphi encouraged every man to 'know thyself,' people with high levels of self-esteem are able to do that. Shakespeare, in *Hamlet*, encourages us to remember: 'This above all else, to thine own self be true.'

"Ultimately, we project onto the movie Screen of Life, exactly what our self-image tells us that we deserve. People with strong self-images realize at some level that the past doesn't exist; it's an illusion. They focus only on the present.

"People with *low self-esteem* invariably recreate a self-image that comes from the past. They measure their self-worth by how they perceive themselves being treated by a family member, supervisor, bully, schoolmate, or any of the purveyors of judgment and opinion in whose presence they find themselves. They accept the Guilt for the nuisance level they believe they created and develop a victim mentality along the way. They feel deprived and will turn even the most positive encounter into a reason for justifying their feelings of unworthiness—that they don't deserve to have the good things of life.

"When we are dependent upon others for the picture we project on that Screen of Life, we have a problem. We are denying our responsibility and thus form a dependency on others to help with that projection.

"This is particularly true of a teen or young adult (with crummy self-esteem to begin with) who looks to mom or dad for approval. When they don't get it, they assume that it's somehow their fault. That is what's called *a negative assumption of responsibility*.

"So then what's the self-esteem of someone on welfare? What's the self-esteem of any loser (or those we define as 'loser')? Why is it that people go and find someone socially and morally lower than themselves? Again, it reverts to the fact that they need to feel better about themselves because they don't believe the 'good' of who they are and what they can accomplish. They are victims, or else they're in search of other victims even worse off than themselves that they go rescue, as a means of validating themselves.

People with low self-esteem very often try to use financial leverage to create images of themselves that will broadcast their worth to everyone else. They may not be personally attractive, but they can adjust the image they project to others by the house they own, the car they drive, the clubs they belong to, the trophy wife, and the other 'cool possessions' that they have. In doing so, they are creating status-symbol billboards about who they are in hopes of convincing everyone else that they are who they seem to be. Ultimately, they only attract others who are projecting the same illusions of status. Think about it.

— The Guardian

"Self-Image becomes the sum total of the way that we have allowed the experiences of the past to affect us. And since we now understand the fact that *the past does not exist*, why would we give away the ability to determine our own self-esteem? How could we do that if we weren't in possession of that Agency (that freedom of choice) and, through that, capable of determining this image ourselves? We can only be affected to the extent that we give away our freedom to choose, and (by giving away that Agency) turn ourselves into victims.

"A poor Self-Image and low self-esteem can lead to a myriad of social problems. They are the reasons why the woman who has been beaten by her mate and leaves him will go find another 'wife-beater' to justify the image that she has created for herself as someone who deserves to be beaten. Just like the dog acting as if he expects to be kicked and the kid on the playground who looks like he needs to be hit, the abused woman will gravitate toward the wife-beater with the low self-esteem who needs to have power over another human being, even if it means expressing it in the most despicable of ways, by degrading her.

"The cycle of low self-esteem creates a kind of *social conundrum* (a seemingly unsolvable riddle), because even if you tell someone with low self-esteem they are 'better than that,' they can't accept the compliment because it's coming from you and it's something that's being 'done-onto' them. So society has virtually millions of people running around working to gain approval from others. And yet that very approval creates victims because these people have become totally dependent upon others for what they think of themselves. *'I expect you to tell me who I am. But when you do, I am the Victim of who you think I am. Very simply, I am not who I think I am. I am not who you think I am. I am who I think you think I am."*

> *This concept is not as complicated as it seems. And it might be better expressed in a popular anecdote about world famous actor/comedian Groucho Marx. Groucho (who had very few problems with self-esteem) tried for years to get into the Los Angeles Country Club, a notoriously snooty golf club that had restrictions against admitting both Jews and actors for membership. Even though Groucho was very well connected, he was both an actor and a Jew. So his appeals to join were continually rejected for over 10 years. Finally, with some considerable leverage exercised on his behalf by board members, Groucho received a letter of acceptance from LA Country Club and immediately fired back his reply: "I'm sorry. But after careful consideration, I've decided I don't want to belong to any club that wants me for a member." Think about it.*
>
> — The Guardian

"The bondage of low Self-Image paralyzes people from truly taking control over their lives and isolates them from the reality that they are the centers of their personal universe. They tend not to learn from their success and positive experiences. And yet if they succeed in doing something, they have no incentive to stop and think and find a better way to do it next time.

"To get out of the trap of low self-esteem, people have to find a way out of the box. If we fail, we have to find a better way to do it next time. Many of us, when we have tasted fear or failure and are pressed to continue on, will often resort to prayer. (As the saying goes, 'There are no atheists in foxholes.') You have to ask yourself, why is it that it takes something absolutely severe to force us to do things that it takes to be successful?

"The choices we make and the Agency we hold onto are the elements that totally determine the course of our lives. We can limit those choices in the future by the commitments we make today—the ones that restrict us and hold us back.

"Once we have recorded the image we've decided to project onto the Screen of Life, we have made one of the most significant choices in determining our life's course. That's because all future decisions will be based upon the Self-Image upon which we have decided.

"Everything we do is connected with Self-Image. It can't be connected with whatever image someone else places upon us—unless we allow it. What we do is take that affect from someone else, plug it into our own self-image to see if it fits and project that self-image outward to the world. No one can force us to do this. It is our choice. It is always our choice.

"Abraham Lincoln once said, 'People are about as happy as they make up their minds to be.'

"In truth, no one can make us do anything without our permission. And how we let it affect us is always our determination to make.

"Michael, I'm here to tell you that there are extremely valuable principles in these discussions we're having…principles that can help anyone to adjust the Self-Image that they project onto the Screen of Life to bring them joy, happiness, success, and peace of mind. They must understand that 'The Past Does Not Exist.' They can learn to speak and act in such a way that people around them can say to them, 'I Like Me Best When I'm With You.' They can learn that the people around them are functioning from the Law of Me, and that what is done to them or said to them is not really about them, but only about the person 'acting out' toward them. They must understand that whenever anyone is angry or judgmental of them they are seeing the Guilt of the perpetrator. Remember what I said earlier, Michael: Anyone working to improve his or her Self-Image must look in the mirror and tell himself or herself that, 'No one ever intentionally does anything stupid.' And finally, they must understand that if anything that occurred which was not their Intention, they can truly say to themselves and the mirror, 'It's Not Your Fault.' (But it *is* your Responsibility.)"

People can actually destroy themselves by their own Self-Image. By the insertion of Guilt into the equation of who they are, they can actually 'de-perfectize' themselves, as it were (creating a lack of perfection). The child, who starts out in life as perfect, goes out and does something he has been trained not to do, and becomes disappointed in himself; so he quickly starts to see himself as something that is less than perfect. So these people become disappointed in themselves; their mask of 'perfection' has been stripped away from them, and they're no longer who they seem to be. (After all, you can't fool yourself.) Suddenly everything they do is an expression of their imperfection. They take on more bad habits. They get bad grades. They let their good credit slide by not paying bills. 'What the hell, let it all go down!' (Their perfection has been marred to begin with, and anything that mars their perfection destroys them.) They feel boxed-in. They feel that it's all their fault, and they can never get back to their perfect state. The whole idea behind knowing 'It's Not Your Fault' is finding a way to break out of that box. Perfection has not been destroyed beyond repair. You can get back to perfection. And it starts here: This is the repair process. Think about it.

— The Guardian

CHAPTER 11

Judgment

Judge not, lest ye be judged.

— Matthew 7:1

"Our next step in the discovery that *It's Not Your Fault* comes in dealing with a concept called Judgment," The Guardian said, beginning the next lesson.

"Judgment!" Michael repeated out loud. "Just the mention of the word strikes a negative chord."

"And with good reason," The Guardian agreed. "Let's start out, Michael, by recognizing that Judgment is an instrument of Guilt.

"Remember, Michael, Guilt creates Victims. And Judgment is the weapon that is constantly used against the Victim as a means of reinforcing that Guilt.

"The concept of Judgment is the result of the erroneous assumption that my evaluation of you should mean something. *Judgment is totally egocentric.* And, despite what we've always been told, it serves no useful purpose.

"It neither 1) makes me feel superior by finding something about someone else that makes them worse than I am, nor 2) detracts from my responsibility to control how I am affected.

"Judgment is immediately predicated upon some false assumptions. First, it assumes that my opinion could or should affect another person. Second, it becomes an excuse to justify blaming someone else for the responsibility that I'm denying.

"Understand this above all else, Michael: *If there were no Judgment, the concept of forgiveness would not exist; there would be no need for it.* Judgment, in truth, supports the false premise of comparative ego enhancement just as it becomes the ultimate excuse to avoid the principle of taking responsibility. Therefore, as a true principle of light, Judgment does not exist.

"At its core, Judgment is an evil concept, counter-creative—the Antichrist! And he from whom *forgiveness* is needed is Guilty of the greater sin—Judgment."

"That's a pretty strong statement," Michael insisted. "Everyone judges to some degree. Isn't that why we have laws?"

"Ah, but Michael," The Guardian said. "Laws are created to administer something called Justice. Justice deals with the basic human concept that says, 'You reap what you sow.' It comes with the establishment of physical laws, and no law has a 'wrong' aspect to it."

"That sounds like a bit of wordplay," Michael said.

"Not really," The Guardian insisted. "Because to establish a sense of *true Justice*, it's essential to remove yourself from a situation as one of the ways of controlling the effect that it has on you.

It is of interest to note that the statue representing justice standing on the steps of our courthouses holds in her hand a balance scale and wears a blindfold. Think about it.

— The Guardian

It's appropriate to be concerned on behalf of others who have not yet learned to control their own sense of Agency (and their own personal universe). But that's a matter of understanding where your nose ends and mine begins.

"That's a simplified summation of possibly the most reasonable concept of Justice ever created—also known as English Common Law. In the appropriate application of Judgment, it offers a very straightforward set of guidelines with one exception. That exception is a moral obligation to protect the innocent from encroachments upon their Agency by anyone who, through misunderstanding or ignorance of the principle, come to wait against it.

"There are two perspectives of, and exceptions to, Common Law. The first relates to Leadership. The leader of any entity, whether he is elected by common consent or as head of an organization (or business) has the obligation to administer the law on behalf of those in his charge—to settle disputes and misunderstandings and protect those who have chosen him to govern. But his jurisdiction, his capacity to judge, is limited to the specific function of the organization or public body in his charge.

"The second relates to his Obligation, in dealing with *the business* of others, to protect the innocent from any infringement by an outside source on their personal liberty, dominion, or freedom of choice—especially in a way that affects or detracts from their own. (These principles particularly apply, as elements of moral obligation, to questions of restraint, intimidation, harassment, suffering, and abuse.)

"Judgment, as it is applied on a personal level, bears no relation whatsoever to what we now come to understand as (social) Justice.

"As I mentioned in the beginning, Judgment is completely centered around the ego. It is the agent of Guilt, and it is used by Victims to create more Victims.

"Victims always have poor Self-Images. Victims or people who are 'self-image' challenged, become masters of giving Guilt to distract from their own feelings of shame. The question that needs to be asked of them is: 'Do you want me to feel guilty? If you want this so desperately what are you feeling Guilty about that you need to distract from?'

"Let's look at an example: You have a husband and wife. The husband, during the later years of employment, becomes somewhat ill, making it difficult for him to work. Although he is apparently unable to work, he's still stable enough to be able to piddle around the house, doing occasional chores, and playing occasional rounds of golf and otherwise leading a normal, though non-working, life. After a while, he becomes increasingly less helpful, starting projects around the house (but not finishing them). Eventually, he begins watching television incessantly, becoming a de facto couch potato and losing any desire to accomplish anything. He grows increasingly critical of everything his wife does and soon takes every opportunity to make cutting statements. His attitude soon becomes one of giving constant 'guilt-trips' and saying things like, 'You don't want me around. You don't want to do the things I like to do.' He's turned himself into a Victim and is using his Judgment of everything his wife does to make sure she becomes one too."

Applications of Justice in our everyday lives take place at the most elementary levels of consciousness (some of them even cellular). In so-called 'primitive societies,' the harvesting of plant life is undertaken with an eye toward conserving the life of the very plant from which the harvest is taken. (Only a portion of the plant is removed. This way it is allowed to renew itself.) What's more, a verbal thanksgiving is extended in gratitude to that plant for providing the gift of life…In the same societies the same rules are applied to the hunting and 'harvesting' of animals. And as they take the life of the animal that is to become their food, they offer their prayers of thanksgiving to this other intelligence that has offered itself so that they might continue to live another day.

To understand this kind of 'cellular application of the law' we point to a couple of experiments performed by Cleve Backster at the Institute of Transpersonal Psychology in Palo Alto, California. A former consultant with the CIA, Backster applied a polygraph machine to two sets of plants to confirm earlier findings that plants are sentient—that they experience emotions such as pain, pleasure, fear, and affection, and that they have the ability to communicate with humans and other forms of life in a recognizable manner.

To reinforce this, Chinese Capsicum plants were divided into two groups—Group One had sensors attached to their leaves and Group Two was left in pots with no sensors. At that point two students were selected—one Abuser, one Caregiver. The Abuser would come into the room, go to the unmonitored plants and abuse them verbally, physically, and any other way they could think of (stopping just short of destroying them entirely). Later, a Caregiver would enter, going to the same plants to extend them every courtesy—nurturing, touching them lovingly and even playing them selections of classical music. After several cycles in this pattern, the 'terrorist' student would enter the room and the polygraph-monitored plants would register high levels of pain and panic, virtually screaming at this person's presence. Conversely, when the caregiver student came back into the room, the plants with sensor monitors would respond with peaceful, calm, low-stress measurements, often calming to lower than normal registrations on the meter.

In other words, the plants responded at very profound ranges of cellular sensitivity to both extreme levels of abuse and tender loving care shown to them. Think about it.

— The Guardian

"There are a lot of cases like that, I'm sure," Michael observed. "There must be hundreds of thousands every day."

"Absolutely," The Guardian agreed. "There's also something called The Dingo Concept. Allow me to explain."

The Dingo Concept

"We're not always as evolved as we might choose to think, Michael. Quite the contrary at times." With that The Guardian drove home his point: "There is a part of us that resembles the mentality of a breed of Australian wild dog called the *Dingo*.

"If one of the dingoes is injured or in some way disabled, instinct dictates that the rest of the pack will turn on it, attacking and usually killing it. This kind of *piling on* is not only present among other animal species but also very prevalent among the species called *Homo sapiens*.

"*Piling on* is part of the mob mentality and typifies Judgment at its very worst. All you have to do is look back in history.

"Gladiatorial exhibitions and 'games' in Rome were nothing more than mass executions enjoyed by tens of thousands of spectators, all of whom had the power of life and death over those in the arena.

"When the Roman Governor Pontius Pilate told the gathering crowd in Jerusalem that he could find no guilt in Jesus Christ, he turned 'this innocent man' back over to the crowd, knowing at some level that their bloodlust and inclinations for piling on would be certain to betray him, ultimately ending in his crucifixion.

"The beheadings in Europe in the Middle Ages were nothing more than spectator sports participated-in by the viewing mob set there to abuse victims even if they had no knowledge of the individuals involved or the reasons for their execution.

"Even in modern times, media hangings and high profile trials (in the press) always draw an element of 'pre-conviction' verdicts by a public that is virtually bloodthirsty in their desire to 'pass judgment' over the accused. Interestingly enough, even when someone's innocence is proven, the expressions of condemnation persist. The damage is done and 'the accused' almost never entirely recovers."

"Then it seems to me that we're not much more evolved in our collective behavior than a pack of dingoes," Michael said.

No Negative Aspects…

"Perhaps not," said The Guardian. "And yet we have every opportunity to evolve if we will. People pass judgment and create victims because they ignore the basic spiritual law that tells us *(in Matthew 7:1) 'Judge not, lest ye be judged.'*

"As I mentioned in the beginning of this lesson, Michael, there are no negative aspects to laws. For example, laws of light state that there is no darkness—only an absence of light. Laws of heat tell us there is no cold—merely an absence of heat.

"Likewise, universal or eternal laws provide specific results as long as you understand and stay in accord with them. If you get out of alignment with the way the law works, you don't fail or get 'un-results.' The laws simply don't occur. To put it in Christian terms, there are no 'un-blessings (or curses);' there is simply a lack of blessings. People know these concepts innately, just as they instinctively know the laws.

"This is why human beings naturally need to know How Things Really Work, so they'll be able to apply the Law that controls all that they desire.

"Remember, Michael, we are the Creators of all that happens to us. So, once you have learned how the laws work, you have to decide what you want to have created in your life. Learn what law contains the promise of that result; then align your thoughts and actions with that law. Once you do that, the results you desire cannot be withheld from you.

"There are no wrong laws; only the absence of understanding of The Right Law and how it works. When we are not in accord with the Laws of Health, we don't fall sick because we are following the Laws of Sickness. We are merely out of alignment with the Laws of Health, and need to return to the path.

"We do that by remembering the gospel of Love—by focusing on the truth that everyone is perfect to begin with. All they have done is fall out of accord with the laws. And they don't need to be judged or condemned for having done this. All they need is a guide to get them back onto the path."

It has been said that 'The Dog is Man's Best Friend.' Isn't it a pity that man can't be man's best friend? But do you know what the difference is? Human beings hold the issue of Judgment as an asset when it is, in fact, their greatest liability—and they use it to limit both their humanity and their human potential to achieve great things. Dogs can be man's best friends because they simply have no comprehension of how to be judgmental. You'd have to walk a very long way to find a judgmental, arrogant, gossiping, egotistical, self-righteous, and righteously indignant puppy. Think about it.

— The Guardian

CHAPTER 12

Approval
The Conditional Love That Destroys

"Approval!" Michael declared. "Seems to be just the opposite of Judgment."

"It isn't," The Guardian corrected. "It goes hand in hand with Judgment. And it's just as toxic."

"But isn't Approval something everyone looks for?" Michael countered. "Every time you get your passport stamped. It says 'Approved.' Your credit card has to get 'Approved,' when you go to pay for something. You are *approved* for membership to a club. You're taught to win the *approval* of parents, teachers, coaches…the list is endless. It's a part of living."

"And how does it make you feel, Michael, every time you wait for that Approval you're talking about? Even though you're pretty sure you're going to get it, even if it's getting your credit card cleared for a purchase, isn't there that little twinge of fear or dread? Doesn't it make you feel powerless, maybe even helpless?"

"Yeah, I suppose it does," Michael answered. "Come to think of it, I've always felt uncomfortable."

"With good reason," The Guardian observed. *"Approval* is the ultimate tool for Fault-finding that parents use to control and manipulate the small child. It's one that immediately tells them something like this: 'If you are to receive my Approval, *you must pass the test.* If you meet the conditions of my Approval (which your self-image and self-esteem cannot possibly survive) you will have been forced to relinquish your freedom of choice and your

Agency to me. You must give this away as a part of the deal *or you will not receive my approval.*'

"Naturally when presented with this kind of choice as a little child, a human being will go into one of two directions: 1) They will either rebel, rejecting your Approval and any influence you may have, or 2) become subservient and lose their identity entirely.

"It's all based in *conditional love.* And conditional love is just another way of inserting Judgment, Fault-finding and Guilt.

"So the child will go one of two ways. He (or she) can sometimes be too good. They center their attention on Approval in order to receive conditional love, rather than doing 'the right things' because they work. So, as the cliché states: They're doing *the right thing for the wrong reasons.*

"The child who attends church to gain his parents' approval will ultimately fall away. The child who learns from the parent that he is attending church because he can learn How Things Work will increase in his desire for each opportunity to learn. The test for the usefulness of any action is whether attention is placed upon performance to receive Approval or performance to get results that work best. It follows the old folk saying: 'There are some folks that look good. And there are some folks that 'be' good. I like the ones that *be good* better.'"

Whose Fault Is It, After All?

"Michael, we live in a Fault-finding society and a Fault-finding world," The Guardian said. "There seems to be this balance in everybody's mind that says, 'If there's a problem, the first thing we have to do is find out whose fault it is. Then we'll try and solve it.' So, why then are there so many questions about any situation that never get answered? It's because as soon as anyone senses that they might be involved, they immediately start adjusting to make sure they're not found at fault. And it takes a tremendous amount of energy, anguish, and creativity to keep from getting blamed. Think of all the misdirected energy on the part of good people when they're suddenly being made to feel at fault when they had done nothing wrong in the first place. That's the legacy of Guilt, Judgment, and Conditional Love.

"*Conditional Love is an enemy to Self-Image.* What's the difference then between seeking Approval and doing things that encourage other people to like themselves best when they are with you? The difference comes with who is in control.

"When you are choosing to elicit the response of another individual that causes you to like yourself better in their presence, you're in control. You have a choice. So, you feel comfortable with your Agency.

"When you feel that they are in control and you have to elicit their approval, you have lost control. In establishing Guilt, your friends reinforce the behavior, which causes you to continue to seek Approval from them and not be able to stand yourself. So, you feel Guilty and can no longer give yourself Approval—and you may not even know the reason why.

"People who are constantly dependent upon Approval from others have lost all control of Approval of themselves. Some people who have lost control of their own Approval live in cluttered environments; and these environments place conditions on any love they receive. As a result, they become incapable of either understanding or expressing Unconditional Love.

"Their minds become jammed up with confused impressions of what 'true love' represents. And this sends them into a downward spiral of disapproval across the board.

"Little girls in a beauty pageant are forced to start lives based upon what the contest judges say about them. Since there can only be one winner, what does that make the rest of the girls? Especially when they notice their parents' response to the fact that their little girl wasn't chosen, they begin to perceive that someone else's opinion of them is the only thing that counts.

"From that point on, everything they do is a matter of keeping score. So they spend the rest of their lives seeking Approval. (Their own Self-Approval, which is truly the most important thing, is pushed aside.) So when their personal law-enforcement system sounds its alarm that some behavior they're being called to perform is not in accord with their sense of correctness, they ignore it because they're now convinced that their own Approval means nothing. But the Guilt remains, and their behavior is now reinforced by the Approval of those around them. They assume an even greater sense of Guilt, becoming more reliant upon (if not, in fact, addicted to) the approval of others, even as they disapprove of themselves more and more all the time. And because people don't understand How Things Work, they pass these sins down from generation to generation, seeking Approval from everyone but the most important being in their lifetime—themselves.

"We speak of Unconditional Love as being objective and 'the ideal.' Then we use every device at our disposal to put conditions on that love. You could then say, Michael, that if God-like love (Christ-like love) is both divine and unconditional, the antithesis of that would be *Conditional Love*. And what defines Conditional Love? *Approval!* 'I will love you, if you seek my Approval. And what is my Approval other than my Judgment of you… whether you're acceptable to me or not?'

Much human activity of a spiritual nature—whether it is expressed in primitive tribes to 'appease the Gods' or in modern religious rules that require us to 'act correctly' or seek the forgiveness and approval of God through prayer and fasting—is more often than not inconsistent with the "unconditional" definition of God-like love. So, seeking Approval (Unconditional Love) of a disapproving God automatically becomes an oxymoron. Think about it.

— The Guardian

"Anytime we do something for the sake of the Approval of someone else, we immediately demean ourselves in the process. And yet there's one thing we, as human beings, can't do, no matter what—we can't lie to ourselves. So it's impossible for us to get away with anything. There's a certain amount of Guilt with giving away our control to someone else.

"We know we can't do it, Michael, because it's our Agency that's been compromised. When we give away our freedom of choice to someone else, it strikes at the core of our existence. That's because *our freedom to choose* is the very definition of who we are. When we give that choice away, when we seek the approval of someone else, we know in our hearts that we have denied ourselves any chance at greatness. (This then, becomes the one sin we cannot forgive in ourselves—that we have, by our very own choices, destroyed our potential.)

"We rebel at someone trying to be in control of us; in fact we become livid. And yet when they succeed, we have to realize that we have no one to blame but ourselves. (Remember no one can truly make you agree with doing anything against your will.)

Even if physical force is applied, an often quoted rhyme, 'The mind that's changed against its will is of the same opinion still,' is still the way things work. Think about it.

— The Guardian

"Competitiveness in sports, as in all things in life, can be a force for good or for evil. The only competitors who can join the contest and come out ahead are the ones who compete with themselves—to be the best they can be. Once they start to see their sport exclusively as a matter of competing with others, they immediately fall into the *Approval trap*. Remember, in life in general and sports in particular, there can only be one winner in the *game of approval*—and it is never the one seeking outside validation.

"The reason that most people have difficulty believing that they can be unconditionally loved is because they've spent their entire life in the cycle of Approval. The bridge between Conditional Love in the Approval game and Unconditional Love is the simple understanding that *'It's Not Your Fault.'*

"So, Michael, what are you saying to somebody when you tell them, 'It's Not Your Fault?'"

"That you don't need my Approval for me to be on your side," Michael finally answered.

"Exactly!" The Guardian agreed. "You don't need my Approval to be loved. What's more, I can prove it. So when I'm saying to you that *It's Not Your Fault*, I'm also telling you that I'm not going to do anything to interfere with your ability to approve of yourself. No one needs to give you Approval for you to approve of yourself."

No One Needs Anyone's Approval

"And when you think about it, no one needs my Approval. And what do they have if they get it? About the same thing they'd get if we established fault in an argument: *nothing*! What is important is how people feel about themselves and their own Approval, and the recognition of their magnificence!

"You never need to overshadow who people are by who you are. If the great ones were to overshadow the lesser ones by who *they* are, what would there be for the lesser ones to accomplish? Remember the Law of Me: *It's all about me. It's not about you.* And you can't make it about me when it's about you.

"When people flaunt who they are or brag about their achievements, what does it say about how they approve of themselves? (On the surface, it would seem that their self-approval is very high, when the opposite is true; they're begging for Approval from others.)

There's an interesting aspect to enthusiastically showing approval. It's a release. But it can also be artificial. Think about the last time you attended a motivational seminar. At the end there's a great deal of applause—maybe even a standing ovation. And some of the applause is for yourself because it's kind of a feel-good feedback you get for having attended the event. But very often applause diffuses the true emotion. What if somebody stuffed that enthusiasm, and actually decided instead to go out and act upon the information they just received? It's a fact that people forget 90 percent of what they hear and see at motivational events within 24 hours. What if they just sat and mentally absorbed what they had just learned. How much more of it would they actually retain? Think about it.

— The Guardian

"When you give a gift anonymously, you don't need applause. The important gift does not require applause. People who give in the true spirit of giving do not need to receive adequate 'thanks' for having done so. That is what Jesus Christ meant when he said that all great masters do their work in secret."

"But what about actors, performers, motivational speakers, anyone in entertainment?" Michael asked. "It seems to me that their whole existence and their entire livelihood is dependent upon the Approval of others. Isn't that why they do what they do?"

"What actually happens when you stand up and applaud somebody who just gave a phenomenal performance?" The Guardian asked. "Aren't you (along with the rest of the audience) saying 'Thank you for paying the price of walking 'the road less traveled' and being self-reliant and self-approving enough to achieve in your chosen field of endeavor that of which others have never dared to dream'?

In reality, most great achievements are the result of the "achiever" stretching his or her skills "outside the box" of conventional thinking (Approval) and being confident in their own Approval of their creativity. Think about it.

— The Guardian

"Sure, you're thrilled about it. But you're not the only one standing up who's also thinking, 'I wish I could be up there singing.' Does that mean you never thank anybody for anything, that you never show your appreciation? Of course not! Just recognize that your appreciation is a mirror reflection of what that artist already has—an Approval of himself."

"It seems to me that people who approve of themselves were probably allowed to do so at a very early age," Michael concluded. "So, Self-Approval and a strong Self-Image all get back to the basics—when you're very young. Maybe they got a lot of Unconditional Love—so Approval from others was not an issue."

"Not necessarily, Michael. Often self-approving achievers have to fight hard against controlling Approval and very Conditional Love (or lack of it).

"But somewhere along the way they found out what really works and learned how to apply it," The Guardian corrected.

Michael felt obliged to add: "Either way, all people need to know is what really works and apply it."

The Guardian elaborated on this and said, "The classic case may be one of dealing with an infant. Let's look at the example you suggested, Michael, of a baby, or a small child. If you apply the principles of *It's Not Your Fault* to that little one, you're exercising Patience and Unconditional Love and you're using it as a bridge across Conditional Love to a place where no Approval is needed (It can still, however, be greatly supportive and appreciated)."

Unfortunately, putting "conditions" on love and approval is so much the rule rather than the exception that very few children have the tremendous advantage of experiencing an early life free of Conditional Love and the manipulation that comes with it. Think about it.

— The Guardian

"Easier said than done," Michael replied. What if the child is behaving badly? He's your responsibility—or *my* responsibility. What if he or she starts throwing a tantrum?"

"It's not that difficult if you really think about it. Temper tantrums are all about control. If somebody feels out of control by being forced to seek the Approval of someone else, they try to take control back by forcing their demands through their temper tantrums or anger. This is often the case with small children who are still in touch enough with their honest rage to express it.

"When you're dealing with a child who's angry at someone (say, his mother), you tell that angry child that it's not his (or her) fault…and you can prove it by the use of a principle called *Distraction by Action*."

The Principle of Distraction by Action

"Action that moves in the direction of the needs a person has will distract them from the sense of being controlled and 'un-faired against.' For a child at bedtime a fun ritual is a good distraction. Bedtime stories, songs, games, special time with mom or dad (that is never missed), hugs, and kisses fill the needs and solve the fears and 'distancing' that are so dreaded. The solution to power control battles is finding distractions that allow the desired behavior to fill the needs of the child.

Here's a test for the next time you get aggravated with having to change a diaper. If you've read this section and understand how these principles really work, you're obligated to immediately make up a sign—no matter how silly you think it is—that says: It's Not Your Fault, and put it up over your baby's crib. If you get that, you've made it nicely to this point. If you don't, you won't be able to comprehend one more word in this book. (So don't mess with me. Just do what you're told.) (☺) Think about it.

— The Guardian

"Think in terms of helping the child, or adult for that matter, to believe that what is being asked of them is not a punishment and therefore you are in essence saying to them *It's Not Your Fault*. And their little Law of Me can live happily ever after. (We will cover the Principle of Distraction by Action in its entirety in Chapter 23.) Here is the thinking that a mother goes through at bedtime: The child (Tommy) is not being told to go to bed because he's being disapproved of, or because his mother (Mimi) is being mean. She wants Tommy to go to bed on time because he's tired and he needs the rest (and that's why he's getting crabby). So she's helping him do what he needs to do. She's applying the proven path that he needs to get his sleep. 'It's not your fault that you need the rest, Tommy. That's just the way your body works.'

"Here's a challenge, Michael. Try to find a situation where, by saying *'It's not your fault and I can prove it,'* to someone, you can still be judgmental toward them. If you apply the principle in the way it's been described to you, you cannot possibly do it. You can't do it because you now have the tools at your disposal to elicit Unconditional Love. So if you choose not to use these tools, any misery you feel from anger, vindictiveness, rage, and revenge fall back onto you—because now it's *your* responsibility.

"So, you see, from this time for ward in your life, anger, hatred, jealousy, and crummy Self-Image are things you can keep in your life. But if you do, realize that you've done it to yourself."

> *Physical contact is extremely important to human beings. There is an old saying that everyone needs at least eight hugs a day. A study with troubled youth indicates that light stroking on the back and touching or a hug with positive brief conversation at bedtime is very calming and establishes a strong, bonded working relationship. Think about it.*
>
> — The Guardian

"Well, I'll make it a point *not* to do it to myself," Michael said. "But what about people who are truly resistant to this? Sometimes it takes more than a couple of good examples for them to get it. Sometimes, you're casting pearls before swine."

"That's true, Michael," The Guardian agreed. "Sometimes with the really hard cases, talking doesn't get the job done. That's because people's instantaneous defensiveness kicks in and they can't even hear you when you try to tell them something. They're so busy thinking about what they're going to say in response that your words are wasted on them. So that's where writing comes in.

"We are so used to seeking Approval, we assume that when we don't get it or when somebody does something that can be interpreted to be against us that they did it *to* us. So, once again, *we're done-onto*.

"It's not about us; it's all about them. But because we're so accustomed to seeking Approval—it's become so much a part of our lives that we automatically interpret everything as being done to us. No one really does anything to us, ever. The past doesn't exist (...unless it's a checkbook). The mistakes that are made are those by people who still believe that, if it's not your fault, it must be theirs or someone else's. In truth, it might not be anybody's fault (and very often isn't). So being exonerated doesn't take proving whose fault it is, it only takes realizing that it's not yours."

"So…according to you, we've made something of a breakthrough!" Michael announced. "Are we pretty well done with my lessons?"

"Oh, no!" The Guardian replied, amused. "In fact, we're just getting to the good stuff!"

There are times when individuals intentionally choose to be mean and behave badly toward you. If there is no misunderstanding for you to clarify it is important for you to understand that their behavior and attitude is never about you and always about them. It would then be wise to remove yourself from the relationship since it would be inappropriate to infringe on their intentional choices. (The Native Americans have an interesting philosophy with regard to impossible situations. They say, 'When the horse being ridden dies the wise man dismounts.') Think about it.

— The Guardian

CHAPTER 13

Unconditional Love
The Cup That "Runneth Over"

"There's been an awful lot of talk about Unconditional Love," Michael said, feeling the need to change the subject. "It seems to me that it's a lot easier said than done."

"Not if you really understand How Things Work," replied The Guardian. Michael said, "Everybody talks about it. But nobody seems to really know what it takes to achieve it. If you're going to truly love unconditionally, it seems that you have to clean up a lot of issues from the past."

"Ah! But we've already established that the past does not exist! Haven't we, Michael?"

"Well, *you* have. I'm not so sure about the rest of us. I think I'll have to learn the fine art of forgiveness."

"Start with yourself, Michael."

"What do you mean?"

"I mean you need to forgive yourself for feeling the way you do about other people—mainly because the anger, frustration, rage, bitterness, pain, shame, and of a little-known concept called *Self-Image Guilt*. Self-Image Guilt is a level of guilt that is so deep-seated and overwhelming that it virtually fills the victim to overflowing—so much so that he or she must project it toward everything and everyone else as a kind of non-stop Fault-finding. And yet no matter how often or intensely it is projected, this Fault-finding is a sword turned inward, because that blade almost always cuts into you and no one else. So you're only hurting yourself."

The reactions we have to other people are judgments that we feel they are causing us to make of ourselves. If you will recall, anger and judgmentalism are both evidence of underlying Guilt. Think about it.

— The Guardian

"I'm not sure I understand," Michael said.

"Of course you do, Michael. You just won't admit it."

"Would you mind explaining?"

"Sure!" The Guardian agreed. He got up to stroll around the conversation chairs as he did so. "I agree that the only things most of us have to work with are past events (which we have already agreed do not exist) because we continue to recreate those illusions as both tangible and real. In fact, they're not, and I can prove it. So, while you're ridding yourself of those illusions, you also have to forgive as well. The paradox here is that you don't need to forgive something that no longer exists. So the forgiveness, if it's needed at all, has to be directed inward by forgiving yourself for the Guilt that you allowed to be levied against you, since so much of Guilt is self-induced.

"He who understands that there is no need for forgiveness understands everything. True forgiveness is effortless and automatic. If we are agreed that the past does not exist—that we can choose not to let it affect a single thing we do in the present—then there is only one question: What is there to forgive?

"Please, if you will, search for something in the non-existent past for which forgiveness is an appropriate response. But before you do, remember no one from the past can do anything to you. That's because the past does not exist.

"When something from the past troubles us it's because we're recreating it; we're giving it a life it no longer has. The only sin, then, becomes the reliving of it. "Often, when people recognize something that has caused them to feel guilty, they fool themselves into thinking they have gotten by it. What has really taken place is the fact that they have merely repressed it. So they're actually recreating it over and over again and then re-condemning themselves for it at several levels, some of them subconscious. That's where the concept of *forgiveness* really kicks in and does its job. Because, above all else, you have to forgive yourself for feeling the way you do."

"So I'm passing judgment on myself?"

"Yes you are, Michael. More often than you realize. And then you're having to forgive yourself for the Guilt that Judgment exerts over something in the past that is, by definition, an illusion." The Guardian continued, *"So, Forgiveness is, in effect, the reversal (or unwinding) of Judgment.* If no one or nothing can affect me except as I choose to allow it (and I can affect no one) what is there to judge?"

"No Judgment. No need for Forgiveness! I get it!" Michael realized.

"I'm glad," The Guardian said as he sat back down in the chair.

Helping and Helplessness…Sympathy and Grieving

"Michael, the concept of Unconditional Love can get tricky, because there are a good many things that disguise themselves as Unconditional Love when they are actually the direct opposite of that.

"*Sympathy and Grieving* are classic examples. Both appear on the surface to be loving, generous, and kind…when they can actually be subtle yet deadly ways of passing Guilt from one person to another. That's because they form a kind of bilateral 'tithing' that victims demand from others as a way to 'drag them down' to their level of predicament. *Grief* in particular is a kind of Guilt-Assessment. So it's an infringement on another person's sense of Agency, or his ability to choose—because he is expected to behave in a certain way that is neither credible nor effective.

"*Sympathy* flings everyone into disbelief in that everything and everyone is caught in an environment that tells us we should behave in a certain way: We should 'empathize,' and be drawn down into an emotional confinement that is not who we are, what we are, or what we want to be.

"Grief is similar to Jealousy, because it is a definite infringement upon Agency, hampering both our ability to choose and the power to have control over our own lives. All this occurs because, 'When there's really nothing more to be said, there's always someone saying it.'

"Think about the last time you attended a funeral service. How much of what went on there was real? Do you remember the statement 'I am not who I think I am, and I am not who you think I am, but I am who I think you think I am?'

"In fact, most mourning is for ourselves. People often talk about *Closure*. (The grieving party is inevitably evaluating what they should have, could have, would have, and might have done, said, or fixed before the loss.) And yet those who are self-confident are not dependent upon others for how they feel about the loss of a loved one and may grieve less for themselves at the loss. Of course, there's a natural sense of missing someone who has died, like they're going on a trip and aren't coming back. But the question has to be asked: To what extent is our identity defined by the individual who is lost?

"The poet-philosopher Kahlil Gibran, in his brilliant book *The Prophet*, wrote:

> *'When you part from your friend, you grieve not; For that which you love most in him may be clearer in his absence, as the mountain to the climber is clearer from the plain.'*

"Kahlil Gibran was absolutely right, of course. And while most people would nod their heads in agreement, very few people can actually view the loss that way. Some who are grieving have a really hard time letting go. That's often because they're angry with the departed for having deserted them in this way. The hyper-dependent wife who relied upon her husband to do everything, the overbearing husband whose spouse catered to his every need, the doting stage-mother or 'jock-obsessed' father whose star child met with an untimely fatal accident all experience extreme levels of Grief that go on for such a long time that they finally revert to what they were in the beginning—a kind of guilt assessment and genuine rage at having been abandoned by their partners in the cycle of victimization."

"I get the *Grieving-Guilt* comparison. But what about Sympathy?" Michael asked. "It seems to me that this is something that comes from third parties. I mean, you go to a funeral, or you're at the hospital when a friend gets hurt. And you try to show that you have feelings for the other person. What's wrong with that?"

"Good question, Michael. So let me answer by asking something in return. Have you ever noticed that when people are trying to *extend sympathy to someone else*, they frequently come out with, 'John (or Mary), I don't know what to say.' Why are we at a loss for words? Is there a message in that? And why, when we do say something, does it always sound so unfulfilling and empty? That's because it is.

"So what is Sympathy? Oddly enough, what people think Sympathy is and what it actually is are two different things. Manufactured sympathy doesn't work. It's the cotton candy of emotions. It satisfies nothing (and causes emotional cavities). *Genuine Sympathy* involves an active emotion called *Understanding*.

"Understanding positions itself in support of someone else. Understanding shows a willingness to take action. So it becomes a useful emotion. (This is where hugs and mirrors come in.) Consider this: People cannot stay distant from us if we hold them, and people cannot watch themselves cry hysterically. It's one reason why we sometimes talk to ourselves in a mirror when we get upset.

"Sympathy without Understanding is useless, and friends who know the difference are worth their weight in gold."

"I think I know what you mean," Michael said, realizing he could cite an instance. "A lady I know recently lost her husband, and shortly after received a visit from a friend who told her, 'I really have no way of knowing how you feel. But I want you to know that I love and care about you. I also know there is going to be a lot of stuff that you're going to have to handle in the next few weeks that you probably won't feel like messing with. So, let's do this. Make a list of what needs to get done—bills that need to be dealt with, errands that you won't have time to run, anything you can't handle right now—and I'll do whatever it takes to get them handled.' After that she gave her a big hug and left.

"Most important, she followed through, starting the next day, with handling the daily stuff her friend needed out of the way."

"Perfect example, Michael," The Guardian confirmed. "By doing this, her friend allowed the woman to deal with her feelings of loss without having to be reminded over and over again of how terrible it must be to find herself in this kind of situation. She did more than that, didn't she?"

"She did," Michael remembered "As time went on, this friend also helped run interference for her by protecting her from other women who'd lost husbands and needed to vent their own lingering grief."

"Action is the language of love that works toward curing the constant run we've had of world disasters. From the devastation of Hurricane Katrina in 2005 to the demolition of most of Haiti and much of Chile in the earthquakes of 2010, America shows its caring by a few words and a great deal of action—folks, food, water, medicine, clothing, buildings, shelter, doctors, nurses, relief workers, laborers, and machines to help them rebuild— that is the Language of Understanding.

"Look at the empowerment you have when you eliminate Sympathy and Grief as human emotions and Understand and Act instead. It makes all the difference. But there's a real danger here too, Michael, because taking action to help someone has to have time limits—generally very short ones.

"It can be a strong point of Unconditional Love to help others. Spiritual teachers tell us that 'Faith (in this case, in the principle of *Unconditional Love*) without works is dead'. Of course, in cases of emergency, giving unconditionally of your time, effort, and perhaps even money is a fine thing to do. The important thing to Understand is that you do it selectively, voluntarily, and usually for someone who would choose self-reliance rather than victimization, if they could.

"You need to realize, Michael, that helping someone habitually always creates helplessness. You become an Enabler, and when you do that you get into the cycle of Victimization. So it's important to keep a couple of things in mind. First, Victims usually don't have any trouble getting themselves victimized and asking for help once they do. Second, the help you're giving someone is usually the right kind *only* if you're empowering them to learn and grow from the experience.

Wants and Needs—The Mentality of Lack

"It's a truth that when you are already in control of all things of this earth, you can create all that is sufficient for your needs. You can create your own reality.

"The excitement of living comes from the realization that anything is within your control," said The Guardian. "And as soon as you realize you can have anything that you want, you almost never want anything. Want and Lack are dangerous weaknesses that creep into the thinking of people. Making someone needful creates dependencies and squelches their ability to create and manifest absolutely. Getting people to set superficial goals, based on avoiding Lack, destroys their ability to take true control of their lives.

"All the bondage that we place on ourselves is based in Wanting. And when resources are seen as sufficient, the bonds of Lack and Wanting are usually released, and all the objects of our wants, whatever item or circumstances, are suddenly no longer 'needed.'

"One of the traps set by a sense of Lack comes with the illusion of total abundance. And it comes when people somehow come to a place where they have attained all they need. People who APPEAR to have all that they need will go in one of two directions. Some will go toward the direction of Approval and try to exercise their influence over others. Others become more caught up in the illusion itself, because they can't actually understand how or why it has happened. (It's an alarming but true statistic that lottery winners often experience this phenomenon, which explains why 90 percent of all lottery winners are broke within three years of winning.)

"Both groups come to be trapped in thinking that having and building increases their stature. In their case, the ego must be fed—the big house, the fancy car, the things that draw the adoration and approval of others. As a rule, people at this level become incapable of being alone. The illusion of their abundance ends up mocking them. And they often end up going into debt just to 'keep up appearances.' (The true master receives joy in his own solitude. It's called peace. Although he loves to teach and empower others, he receives no joy in the Approval of others. Therefore, by definition, the true master is ego-less.)

"When you have a mentality of Lack, it is very much like being constantly hungry. When you are really hungry you want to eat everything. And yet isn't it interesting that, once you've eaten, you don't feel as if you'll ever have to eat again.

"People who are in financial lack want to buy everything, but once they get enough money, their wants and needs diminish almost in direct proportion to the money they have gotten. (Unless, it must be noted, they won or inherited their wealth, rather than earned it.)

"All this is analogous to people with eating disorders (who are also like dogs that only get fed once a day). People (and animals) who eat only one big meal a day very often tend to have problems with their weight. Because of their feeling of Lack, once the food is presented to them, they tend to overeat, often demanding extra-large portions or second servings. By the same token, it has been shown that people who eat five or six small meals a day (like dogs or cats that have food constantly available), will tend to eat less and have less problems with their weight.

"Our wants are directly proportionate, in degree, to our perceived inability to acquire them. People who are in a constant state of financial Lack are the ones who are more constantly obsessed with fine cars, fine boats, big homes, and large wardrobes. And yet once people come into possessions of fortunes or great wealth, their needs often suddenly become simple.

"Those of us who are in a constant state of wanting and needing are ensnared in a Victim mentality. So, when we alleviate the cause, when we get rid of the Victim mentality, we almost immediately come to realize that our needs—our true needs—are much less demanding.

"The way that we can positively affect others is really very simple. We hold a perfect picture of them being in a circumstance that's right for their needs. Not as an appendage of us or an extension of our egos or desires—their motivation should be a direct line between their higher desires and their own perfection.

"In the case of healing, Christ was able to perceive that what the blind man needed to heal himself was the spittle of the master on simple clay placed over his eyes. And after the healing had taken place, Jesus told the man exactly how he would be healed: 'Go thy way. Thy faith (belief) hath made thee whole.'

"Wanting is Victimization because, if we want or lack, it is the essence of addiction. Addiction is a belief that nothing is within our control. Therefore everything is out of our control, and we don't exist.

"To attain the prosperity mentality that comes with Unconditional Love, it is essential for us to hold a clear picture of the perfection of the individual we're working with and strive together to make it happen. And the message to us is to be able, at any time, to give others the tools they need to attain their own perfection.

"Just as many believe God works to help create eternal life and perfection for humankind, it also becomes incumbent upon us to become like Him. In so doing, we become limitless beings and creators. And the way this is done is by giving us the tools by which we can heal our own limitations. In doing so, we basically assist all other human beings, because our work and our progression is to pass the message of limitless improvement toward perfection to all other beings.

"The best way to do this is to attain a mentality of completeness—of prosperity. When you have sufficient resources for your needs, what else is there to work for but the sufficiency of the needs of others? You reach for the Light. And, by sharing your joy and helping others to also reach the Light, you truly become God-like (or Christ-like) in the process."

"So, my ideal role in Unconditional Love is to help others progress by becoming a kind of facilitator," Michael said, thinking aloud.

"Facilitator!" The Guardian exclaimed. "The magic word. And what is God to those who believe but the Great Facilitator. That's why we call God, *The Creator*.

"Let's use the perfect example, Michael: Take the joy of the mother and father who see their child progress and grow and become a responsible, self-reliant adult. There is no greater sense of fulfillment than this. It's the same for you and me, Michael. Whenever we are able to be facilitators in someone else's true progression and growth, we are sharing out of our own sufficiency of needs."

The Law of the Ten-Fold Return

"It's an infallible law, Michael: *The Law of the Ten-Fold Return*. It is the perfect return of energy: the completion of our purpose. And it always returns to us at least ten-fold. If you give away love, you experience a return of love ten-fold. If you give away money, you'll experience a ten-fold return. If you give away wisdom, if you teach, you'll experience a ten-fold return for having done so.

"The Ten-Fold Return doesn't always come back to us from the same source. You won't necessarily get it back in ways that you might expect. Love, generosity, wisdom, teaching—when shared in so many ways—will be returned to you in so many other ways. Wealth you share may be expressed in prosperity and wealth returned to you by someone or something entirely new. Wisdom and knowledge you give may come back in the form of expansion of your own wisdom and knowledge. The Love you give to one person may not be returned in kind by that person, but will come, ten-fold, from someone else. And all these things combine to amplify your being ten-fold.

"The most beautiful aspect of *the ten-fold return* is the fact that you reach a point where you're no longer concerned about how it comes back to you. It doesn't necessarily have to come from an outside source. Becoming dependent upon outside sources for our sustenance soon becomes the extent to which we give away our liberty. So in giving Love, as in giving all things, the ten-fold rule often means that the return comes from within—you become an even greater expression of who you are, the complete self-sufficient human being able to function and love unconditionally.

"In Psalm 23 in the Book of Psalms, the one that begins, 'The Lord is my Shepherd...' David recites the memorable and often misunderstood phrase: 'My cup runneth over...'

With all this in mind, it is important—in the quest for this state—to set the right kind of goals. As is the case with all goals, we have to ask the questions: What is it you want? Why do you want that? Is wealth a means in itself? Or is it just a means of getting something else—perhaps to accomplish something better? The key is an element called Desire, because desire can also cross over into a sense of lack. So you have to ask yourself what the true purpose is for your goals. Once you've done that, release all thoughts and feelings that would limit you: the ones that say, 'you can't have it.' If your goal is abundance, visualize that there are no limits to your abundance. By removing limits, we are able to focus on intention and our subconscious is free to fly to places our conscious mind cannot even comprehend. Do this often enough, and you can master the physical world. So, creating abundance becomes an effortless act. Think about it.

— The Guardian

"That is merely a statement of self-sufficiency that is so complete and so spiritually enriched that the overflow of Goodness, Generosity, and Unconditional Love to others becomes a matter of every day living. The cup that overflows has to go somewhere. And the life well-lived will see to it that it goes into filling others."

CHAPTER 14

Agency:
The Freedom to Choose

"If it's to be, it's up to Me."

Michael thought about everything that The Guardian had laid out for him up to now, and realized how much sense it was all beginning to make. He was starting to experience a kind of resonance—that kind of tingling sensation that all of us feel when Truth strikes a chord inside us. Still, he had questions, a mountain of them. And one in particular.

"You keep mentioning something called *Agency*," he said. "You've briefly explained it, and I think I get it. I realize that it has a great deal to do with your personal identity and your *freedom to choose*. But there seems to be so much more. So, I'm surprised you didn't cover it earlier."

"You're right, Michael. It is *that* important," The Guardian replied. "But Agency is a not a subject you can lead off with, because it's hard for people to catch onto it right away."

"But you said that all the most important concepts are simple," Michael noted.

"They are!" The Guardian agreed. "It's just that we have to empty some of the Trash out of that perfect building before we can get others to understand how clear and simple some things really are.

"Very simply, Michael, you have to get a good grip on *The First Universal Law: The Law of Me*. Once you understand this law–that everything gets back to me, including my need to take responsibility for everything that I do —you can move on to the next level.

"Once you get that, understanding a person's Agency makes all the sense in the world. The basic principle of Agency is that 'I am the captain of my fate. I am the master of my soul.' *I'm the only one who can affect what happens to me and how anything affects me.* And the extent to which you understand and believe that message determines whether or not you find the key to who you are.

"I am the center of my own universe. My Agency is the principle of my liberty, my freedom to choose, my potential—everything I am. So when you mess with my Agency, you mess with who I am. And yet when you get right down to it, no one can do anything to us unless they physically take us and lock us up. Even then, we have within our minds the ability to control everything that affects us.

"Throw some people in prison and they rot and die there. Throw others in prison and they flourish. Mahatma Gandhi was imprisoned many times in his life, and yet he managed to free the second largest nation in the world, India, from British rule. Nelson Mandela was imprisoned for nearly 30 years, and yet he emerged to become president of South Africa and accomplish the 'impossible job' of unifying a racially divided nation. Both men had mastered their Agency, so no one could ever take it away from them.

"Being in command of my Agency means knowing that how I'm affected is always within my control. If it were not so, there could be no absolute justice.

"That underscores the fact that we are creators of what happens to us. So the important issue comes back to understanding that we can't be truly effective as creators until we understand How Things Work.

"Once we understand the concept of Agency—that 'I am the center of my own universe'—we will become who we're truly capable of being. That way, we won't ever again be dependent upon others. And the rest of mankind will be better for it.

"This may seem like an insurmountable task to begin with, but it isn't. It's very much like eating a hippopotamus; the only way you can do it is one bite at a time.

"Michael, there are three things that you do not do: You do not arm wrestle with Superman. You do not sword fight with Zorro. And *you never infringe upon, or get in the way of, anyone's agency.*"

"So your Agency is that important," Michael noted.

"It's *that* important, Michael. Because with Agency, you begin to understand the meaning of Responsibility. Let me show you why."

An Agent on Your Own Behalf

"From the time that a person is born to the time they die, their entire life is determined by the choices they make. Their freedom to choose is their ability to act as 'an Agent' on their own behalf. Their unlimited potential is summed up by the single word: *liberty*. Michael, you can look at your personal Liberty like a bank account that holds within it the entire life experience of an individual. Withdrawals are made from the account and spent as choices. Each choice represents an expenditure, a kind of an *emotional currency*, as a piece of that individual's life. Each choice that is made limits and reduces the amount of Liberty (or life) that remains in that account. Everyone in their heart of hearts somehow senses that they are spending from their life account as they make choices. (That's why some folks break out into a cold sweat even when trying to decide where to have lunch.)

"When you get down to it, there are three ways people choose to expend their life's energy. First, we have *the bank account* of our lives from which we make withdrawals. Second, we have *the currency* (time is the medium of exchange) for the spending of their Liberty. The third element is the one that does the spending (the agent). Tell me, Michael, what the term, *Agent*, means to you."

"Your agent is someone who represents you, making decisions and commitments on your behalf," Michael finally answered.

"So in other words, Michael, *an Agent* has the power and authority to commit the individual or organization he represents to take an action or meet an obligation. Let's look at a couple of examples.

"A ticket agent at an airline represents the airline that sells me a ticket. This obligates the airline to provide me with transportation for the agreed-upon price. On a slightly negative side…an IRS agent is an agent on behalf of the IRS that obligates the IRS to any decisions that he agrees to. Now, maybe that's a bad thing; or maybe it's a good thing. That depends solely upon the 'deal' you, the taxpayer, are able to work out with that agent. So, very simply, an Agent can obligate the individual or organization he represents to the actions or decisions that he makes on their behalf.

"Now, let's see where this fits in your own life plan. In the context of Liberty and Choices, the term, Agent (or Agency), refers to the doer. *When it comes to their own lives, people are in fact Agents unto themselves.* In other words, Michael, you function as an Agent on your own behalf. And as you make choices, you cut down on your options for future choices.

"Let's use a simple illustration, like lunch. Starting this lunch thing from the very beginning. You look at your clock, and it's twelve o'clock noon. That seems to be the time people obey the commandment that says, 'Thou shalt take lunch!'

"So, you're sitting in your office with a number of choices. You can continue working for another hour and miss the lunch crowd, or you can get lunch now. So what do you want to do? At this point you say to yourself, ' Well, I really don't care. But I'm kind of hungry, and I can use a break from taking notes, so let's go to lunch right now, at twelve o'clock noon.' Great! You just made a choice. How long do you think it's going to take us to go to lunch, Michael? Probably by the time we travel to the restaurant, order our food, eat, and travel back, we're going to take about an hour and fifteen minutes.

"As you go out to your car and drive away, you've just committed an hour and fifteen minutes of your life to 'doing lunch.' That means that time is no longer available for continuing to work and getting an extra hour and fifteen minutes of work (or any number of other things like exercising, studying Spanish, or cramming for an exam for a course you might take toward getting your MBA at night school) done. Don't get me wrong. Everybody's got to eat, but you've made a choice here. And the choice is *how you spend the next hour and fifteen* out of the *minutes of your life!*

"So you've carved a little piece out of that account called your Liberty, or your total life, and committed it with this decision to have lunch. You sit down. You order a soup and salad, or a club sandwich and fries. Or maybe you order a chili dog and greasy onion rings, a choice that might up your cholesterol and add additional useless calories that, done often enough, are going to put on pounds and eventually make you fat.

"One thing is certain: Once gone, this lunchtime has been removed from availability in your life's account. Think about some of the choices that people make when spending their time. Every minute you spend keeps drawing down your life's *bank account*.

"There's another thing that most people fail to consider. The instant you are born into any society, you are subject to some choices that have already been made for you. These come in the form of parental rules, social restrictions, school, religion, and your peer group. Government regulations and family traditions also influence parental decisions made about the little child brought into their lives. Some of these decisions are placed upon you in ways that automatically draw down on your Liberty account and completely ignore your Agency.

"Many of these restrictions are temporary. They're set for you until you are ready to choose for yourself. When you're a little child there are very few choices open to you. You have to ask permission to go to your friend's house to play and, until you're old enough to get there on your own, you have to have your mom or dad take you there. Your parents will determine the specific time when you have to be home. You have to hold your mother's hand when you cross the street. Once you learn to cross the street safely on your own, you will be allowed to take back your Agency as well as that portion of your choices when it comes to walking across an intersection and getting to the other side. With regard to visiting friends, when parents are comfortable with your choices of where to go and when to go, they will return your Agency to you. (Of course, some parents are convinced that *their teenager* won't be capable of handling those choices until the time they're 37 years old and married with four kids.)

"Some folks decide to go to school and get an advanced education, and when they do their choices further restrict the remaining Liberty they have for the next four years. It also opens up an entire new Agency where choices may expand later.

"Once someone chooses a marriage partner, they're eliminating a lot of other options. Commitments of marriage and raising a family bring with them tremendous reductions in someone's Liberty bank account.

"People choose employment and, depending upon the requirements of the job, may see large chunks cut from their personal Liberty account when they do so. Folks who spend large portions of their Agency on a career choice will either enjoy or lament the value received directly proportionate to their sense of fulfillment, and many of them come down to an interesting set of new options.

In making choices it is wise to consider, 'whether the view is worth the effort of the climb.' Think about it.

— The Guardian

When people expend their Liberty by committing themselves to indebtedness, the choices they make can become very dangerous. When financial obligations become so great that huge amounts of time and Liberty have to be spent to meet them, it blocks the freedom to make other choices and meet other obligations. This creates a ripple effect that virtually destroys your Agency in other areas.

"Think about it, Michael. How many marriages fail because the breadwinner committed so much of his effort to financial obligations of debt that he had nothing left in his Liberty account (his time) to devote to his wife and children? How often is some child's Agency compromised when the choices their parents make for them are overridden because there is nothing left in their Liberty account to meet those obligations?"

"Seems to me that we use up our Liberty account very quickly," Michael said. "And the farther we go in life, the fewer choices we have."

"And yet this is the beauty of living in a relatively free society," The Guardian answered. "That's the fact that you have more Agency built into our social system than any other place in the world."

"You really think so?"

"I know so, Michael," The Guardian declared. "If you need an example, let's go back to that restaurant where we had lunch and take another look at the menu. Let's say you exercise your freedom to choose by ordering a soup and salad. But what if I told you that you couldn't have soup and salad. Instead you had to have a hamburger…and that was your only choice, whether you liked it or not? How would you have felt?"

"Probably aggravated, because I didn't want that hamburger."

"What if I told you, Michael, that there are some societies in this world where marriages are arranged by the family by the time a child is five years old?" So by the time you and your 'intended' reach the age of 21, you get married. That's it! You have no choice. You are *both* deprived of your Agency, in regard to this large portion of your life, virtually from the start.

"Now, what if I moved you to a country where they give you some tests in grade school to evaluate your capabilities and assign you to the educational path that will create your career path based on those tests when you were a child? Would that bother you? Absolutely! It's ridiculous! And yet there are countries where this kind of educational pigeonholing exists.

"Remember, Michael, you get aggravated when I tell you there are limited choices you have with your life. That's how important your freedom of choice is to you, even at the most basic level. Our ability to spend our liberty (or our lives) as we see fit is the one thing we will defend to the absolute end, because it is who we are!

A unique concept in choices and decision-making known only to Guardians is use of the question: Can you afford to be wrong? A simple example: You are attending an outdoor event. The weather looks like it could be rainy. To carry an umbrella would be a nuisance if you didn't need it. Ask the question "With which choice can I afford to be wrong? If I take the umbrella and there's no rain, I'm wrong, but no problem. If I don't take the umbrella, and it rains, I'm wrong and miserable. So, your decision becomes evident: Take the umbrella. With that choice you can afford to be wrong. Think about it.

— The Guardian

The Hidden Contract

"*Our Agency is the one Universal Law that cannot be violated*—the one law that, if understood, will allow us to literally control our own destiny! We are absolutely creators when it comes to the design of our lives. The frustration comes when we just can't figure out How Things Work.

"It's true that *Agency is absolutely un-infringable.* (Inviolate, if you will!) You can't force people into a mold any more than you can make somebody well just by ordering them to feel better.

Remember the thought that, 'A mind that's changed against its will is of the same opinion still.' Think about it.

— The Guardian

"The challenge, Michael, comes with the fact that people only learn from their problems. Mental and spiritual growth are similar to muscle development. (Weight lifters have a belief-system that says, 'No pain, No gain!') If a muscle isn't pushed to its very limit, its potential remains undeveloped. In the same way, if a person's creative capacity isn't pushed to its limits by stress, worry, anger, and fear his or her potential will never be fully developed. One of the best tools we have to set ourselves into positive motion is Guilt. Provided it's properly understood and used as a temporary stimulant, Guilt can be an excellent motivator to accomplish something better. However, as we know by now, if we don't understand how it truly works, Guilt can be very destructive."

"But thanks to you, we *do* know how it works," Michael observed. "And I've got to tell you that the example you just gave about how we handle our Agency seems pretty unnecessary. It seems to me that all this can be eliminated by understanding that I am the 'master of my fate,' and that we can only become masters of our fate by *taking responsibility* for what happens to us."

"You've got it!" The Guardian agreed. "Responsibility is absolutely the key! *This is one universal law that cannot be violated.* Agency, once it's understood, is the one law that will allow us to control our own destiny. We must take total and absolute Responsibility for everything in our lives, and yet at the same time take the 'I' out of our relationships with others. We understand that we aren't controlled by anyone, anything, or any circumstances other than the ones we choose. When we come to grips with that, we end our limitations. We assume total Responsibility and take complete command of our life's plan.

It is common for people to challenge the idea that nothing can affect them except as they choose to allow it. It is true that someone can punch you in the mouth. Lies can be told about you. You can be placed in prison. Your stuff can be stolen. Your love can be betrayed. Your needs can be denied. BUT you and you alone choose how you allow anything, anyone or any situation to affect you. Think about it.

— The Guardian

"Once you do this, you truly come to understand How Things Work. And your Agency becomes your servant—and not your master."

"Speaking of our freedom to choose…" Michael said. "All this talk of food has made me hungry. I'd like to invest a few minutes from my Liberty account to get something to eat. Is that possible?"

"Of course, lad!" The Guardian replied. "Once you've mastered your Agency, anything is possible. And there's a rather quaint little restaurant that I'd like to recommend…"

CHAPTER 15

The Wonder Hugger
Distance is Disaster
(So the Closer the Better)

If Michael had learned one thing about The Guardian by now, it was that he was always full of surprises. That "quaint little restaurant" turned out to be a diner somewhere in Colorado (where Michael had to admit that the food was pretty good).

Now, here they were, headed back to wherever they had been from a place that just seemed to pop up somewhere in a very pretty part of The Rockies.

The Guardian and Michael had just hopped up on the freeway on their way back from lunch at "Melba's Marvelous Marmalade and Mulberry Pie Café." And though the meal turned out to be delicious, what really caught Michael's attention was what appeared to be a small Colorado range war between the couple in the adjacent booth.

The couple, Jim and Sandy, had gotten into a whispered (but heated) argument that everyone else in the restaurant was able to hear. In fact, Sandy had stomped hard enough in her emphatic exit from the eatery to fracture the heels of her hand-tooled cowboy boots.

"Michael," said The Guardian as he recalled the moment. "Have you ever noticed that when folks get into a little tiff, both parties immediately start distancing themselves from one another? And they do it physically, emotionally, or both. One person may develop the technique of stopping communication: they won't speak to you. Another might take the tactic of physically moving as far away from you as possible—maybe even leaving the area, like Sandy did at the café. Does this reaction look familiar to you Michael?"

Michael nodded. "Oh, sure. When I'm mad at someone why would I want to be around them? So I usually leave."

How People Think Things Work

"When people get angry, there's a natural human tendency to do just what you said you usually do," The Guardian confirmed. "They immediately separate themselves from the other individual. When the emotional separation comes, both people just naturally follow through with physical separation. If two people physically move away from each other, it will very quickly increase the emotional distance. So, here we have the principle *Distance is Disaster*.

The Distance Is Disaster principle is the reason that the technologically advanced communication forms of emails and texting are more devastating to human relationships and negotiations than folks really imagine. The words we use are only a small percentage of our total communication, lagging far behind facial, voice intonation, and body language. (This is why important negotiations must always be done face-to-face.) As a result, true communication is significantly more emotional than logical. It is frustrating to many folks that someone who wishes to avoid TRUE communication will send emails and texts. This practice is often construed to be and often is sneaky and disingenuous. Think about it.

— The Guardian

"You see, Michael, when people get angry they tend to want to stay angry. There is that flaw in the ego that says: 'If I back down first, I lose.' The idea of winning or losing, using emotional and physical distance as a weapon, is *not* the way things work. And yet it does bring up the question: When people argue, Michael, is their intent to destroy their relationship?"

"No," Michael replied. "I'm sure it's not."

"That's right! But what's the issue in losing an argument?" "Well…if I lose an argument, I end up feeling stupid."

"Why? Because you lost? How about if the other guy wins? It proves the conflict was your fault. (So here we are…back to *the fault issue* again.) That's because people think the *Way Things Work* is that there's a big scale of justice that says, 'If it's *not my fault*, then it has to be *your fault*.'

"They move physically away from the other person in the conflict. The message that *moving away* sends is, 'I don't want this fight to be my fault. You're a threat, because to prove that *it's not your fault* you are going to dump on me. To protect myself from the potential guilt, I'm mad at you, and I'm going to get out of Dodge. Shutting down communication or leaving will keep you from passing me the Guilt.'"

Michael gave a knowing nod to The Guardian, but still couldn't help but feel a bit puzzled by what he had said.

The Guardian smiled, and then said, "Look at that pickup truck that just passed us. That's the couple from the café. There you've got Jim, a Colorado cowboy wannabe driving his black-on-black Ford *'Powerstroke'* down the freeway. His sweetheart, Sandy, normally rides glued to his right side a little past center on the bench seat of his 'Cowboy Cadillac'. She lovingly plays with his earlobes and on occasion gets even closer by resting her head on his shoulder. She's become quite an expert at maintaining her place next to him while meticulously dodging the kneecap-bruising shift lever as he goes through the gears. But what happens at the first sign of an emotional storm on the horizon? Sandy instantly plasters herself so tightly against the passenger door that her removal would require the use of a large spatula from Melba's kitchen.

"Now this little cowgirl sweetheart is in for a pretty unhappy ride, and *it's not her fault* because she just unwittingly stepped into a 'bear trap' of human emotions. *It's not her fault* that she moved away from something that she perceived as being unpleasant. The trap is sprung when physical distance is triggered by emotional distance. The principle to learn here, Michael is that *distance is disaster in a relationship*."

How Things Really Work

"If there is understanding of How Things Work, Michael, our little cowgirl can very quickly get cuddled back over where she really wants to be anyway. So let's continue our story.

"The first two years of Sandy and Jim's marriage were relatively rocky. Jim had spent a lot of his off-work (free) time maintaining a strong relationship with his buddies. They were a closely-welded group of weekend warriors and wannabe jocks who spent endless hours involved in every type of city sports league they could sink their cleats into.

"Sandy, and several other wives for that matter, nursed a constant nagging feeling that verged on rejection for having to play second-fiddle to a softball bat and a beer-bellied toothless wonder who played third-string center on the high school football team oh-so-many years ago. Because of this and so many other things, there were constant wars. It didn't take much to start one because Jim's underlying Guilt and Sandy's sense of abandonment fueled every small spark into a firestorm. After the dust had settled, if and when they tried to discuss what happened, neither one could even recall the subject of the war, let alone how it got started.

> *You will often find that, in a heated discussion with another person, they will seemingly have a tendency to not be able to stay on the subject and follow the logic of your arguments. When this occurs they possibly might not be the sharpest tool in the shed, a dim bulb as it were. Nevertheless, in reality they are often feeling Guilt and trying to slip away from the sensitive subject, so they can direct focus away from their discomfort. Guilt can often readily be identified by the misdirection of focus from the path of logical reason. Think about it.*
>
> — The Guardian

"Michael, we have just set the stage for the entrance of the superhero we shall refer to as *The Wonder Hugger*.

"By now, Sandy had heard about the concept of getting close to eliminate the Disaster of Distance from one of her best friends. Her friend was, by the way, a member of the nationwide *It's Not Your Fault* Search and Rescue Team. Sandy decided that the next time a war started, as soon as she sensed Jim pulling away and putting the physical distance between them, that she would immediately make her move. No matter how angry she was (and no matter how tempted to prove her point), she would immediately go over and give him a big hug.

"Sandy had been warned that he might be resistant at first. Nevertheless, she decided that, no matter what, she'd hang on until the ice broke. Given the dynamic of their relationship in the last couple of years, it wasn't long before she got the opportunity. An 'issue' came up—probably something about yet another softball practice—and the battle was on. Almost as soon as it started, Jim plunged into his Guilt-defense mechanism, jumped up from his chair at the kitchen table and stomped toward the garage door, firing off typical, well-practiced, verbal barrages of abuse, combined with accusations and intense denial.

"So, Sandy had her cue. She bounded out of her chair and charged after Jim. She threw her arms around him and hung on for dear life. When she did, he stopped stone cold in his tracks, looked down at her for a split second and was so startled that he couldn't think of a single thing to say. He concluded that he desperately needed to exit the scene of an attack from a crazed woman who had 'completely lost it.' So, Jim continued toward the door leading to the garage, trying, as best he could, to extricate himself from the grasp of 'this thing' that he had previously known as his wife. As he pushed, pulled, and staggered to free himself, he could feel that her grasp was progressively reduced to smaller portions of his anatomy.

"Before the scene was over, Sandy was face down on the floor, holding on for dear life with both arms wrapped around his left ankle. He managed to drag her for about two and a half more steps before he finally stopped and looked down. By now, his argumentative train of thought had completely flown from his mind, and he was able to get the full picture of this scene— a scene in which he was now an unwilling player. At this point, Jim had no choice but to break into uproarious laughter. And it took Sandy a couple of seconds to realize that she could turn off the switch, as Jim helped her up off the floor and warmly returned her *Wonder Hugger* embrace."

> *By becoming a Wonder Hugger instead of forcing Jim to move away from her, Sandy actually enhanced his Agency and made a deposit in his Liberty account, by giving him the freedom to choose another solution to the problem. Instead of growing increasingly angry and trying to avoid blame, he could now offer her a Wonder Hug in return. She had proved to Jim that it wasn't his fault. (It wasn't anyone's fault!) So, Jim no longer felt the need to blame her for trying to limit his choices. Think about it.*
>
> — The Guardian

"It seems to me," Michael observed, "that it took a lot for Sandy to be the one to give in, when it was clear that she was the one who had been abandoned."

"Well, that's the whole point," The Guardian said. "Sandy was able to overcome the perceived blow to her ego and the illusion that she was giving-in by using the concept of *It's Not Your Fault* as a tool.

"When Jim brought up his softball practice, Sandy shifted her thoughts away from the blame issue. Instead she thought to herself, 'Jim *it's not your fault* that you make me feel unimportant, and I can prove it. I know it's not your intent to make me feel bad. (The only one who can do that to me, is… me!) You're just wrapped up in your own little world.'

"It's interesting, Michael, that nothing more was said about the subject of the conflict. It seems to have been forgotten. Jim never did make it to softball practice, and Sandy got a chance to see why she actually married the big lout. Along about midnight, there was a whisper. I'm not sure whether it was from Jim or Sandy, but the words were unmistakable. 'You know what? I really do like me best when I'm with you.'

"You know, Michael, this story is pretty typical. In this case, Sandy is the one who acted to fix this relationship. It's also a little discussed fact that men in America (and just about anywhere else) have to maintain a certain macho image, and not get into that 'touchy-feely stuff.' And yet I'll guarantee you that there are just as many men as women who desperately want their relationships to return to the thrill, excitement, and passion of a courtship that lasts forever.

"There are going to be thousands of guys, probably even millions, who are closet huggers. So let's hope that our little discussion here will give them the okay to come out of those closets and start to understand *How Things Really Work*. But be careful what you wish for… We're in real danger here of having a whole nation of Wonder Huggers running around spreading joy, happiness, and that sense of feeling good until it's almost disgusting. Heaven forbid that two of these newly created monsters should end up in the same family. The results could be absolutely cataclysmic."

Living a no-fault life brings tremendous peace of mind. Giving no fault to another is the greatest gift of all. Think about it.

— The Guardian

"Well," Michael said. "That was quite a valuable lesson. I suppose that the Wonder Hug can work in all kinds of situations."

"Think about it, Michael," The Guardian said. "I bet you've used a Wonder Hug and didn't even realize it. Think about a time when the woman you love felt sad or when one of your kids hurt themselves and started crying. Your first instinct (after fixing the boo-boo) was to go up and give them a hug to let them know that everything was going to be okay. It was absolutely the right thing to do. You became a Wonder Hugger and probably didn't give it a second thought. This way, you just have to think about it a little more and try a little harder. Once you do, you'll realize that the rules are just the same. And the result, *once you learn* How Things Work, will almost always be a good one."

CHAPTER 16

The Big Push-Away!
I Don't Like Me. Why Should You?

Through all these examples that The Guardian had set down, there was an unresolved issue bothering Michael that he just couldn't seem to get over. The Guardian could tell this, of course. So, he waited for a moment or two, hoping his young friend would come out with it. But he didn't.

"Okay, Michael," The Guardian challenged. "You have a question as big as the moon. So get it off your chest. Otherwise, we'll be sitting here much longer than we need to be."

"You're right," Michael admitted. "What about people who still think that everything is their fault? They're the ones who, no matter what you do to break through to them, block everything and everyone that comes their way—even the good stuff. In fact, they're so shut down that they literally drive away all the good things and good people that might make a difference in their lives."

"You've made a direct hit, Michael. And there's a very good name for it." The Guardian exclaimed. "I call it *The Big Push: Away*. It's what happens when people feel so unloved and so unlovable that they just can't accept love from others, even when it's unconditional. That's because they don't trust it, and they certainly don't feel worthy of it."

"That kind of behavior ends up being the ultimate Guilt trip and victimizing everyone involved."

Remember that the significance of the Law of Me is that everything a person does is based on how he wishes to be perceived by himself and others. Notice in that statement that the first and most important perception is of himself. If a person doesn't like himself and sees himself as the Victim of life with no control and no Hope, he can't possibly perceive anyone else liking him and will 'Push Away' to avoid the pain and chance of being reminded of his 'unworthiness.' Think about it.

— The Guardian

"Doesn't that create Victims?" Michael asked. "Seems to me that this

"Well, anything can create Victims if we choose to let it. But remember, knowing what you now know about your Agency, you have a choice—to take on this kind of Guilt or not. And the saddest thing about people who push everyone else away is that most of the Guilt is directed inward, toward themselves. So it's entirely self-inflicted."

"This usually happens to people because so much Trash (Guilt) got dumped into their 'perfect' building at such an early age there's no room left for anything else, certainly not for love."

"Not even for a Wonder Hug?" Michael asked.

The Guardian smiled. "The good news, Michael, is that the Wonder Hug always works. And it works in so many ways. And the other good news is, that by showing them that *'It's Not Your Fault and I can prove it,'* you're giving them a great big *verbal* Wonder Hug."

"So the challenge comes for us to recognize these *Big Push-Away people* for who they are. Sometimes they're not easy to spot, because they often don't look upon themselves as Victims. (Some of them might even be successful on the surface of their lives, but are personally so closed-off that nobody can get inside. Very often, especially if they've achieved some social or professional level of success, they are the very people who are most critical of others—perfectionists, bullying bosses, intimidators, divas, and micromanagers. Usually, however, they're not successful; very often they're a mess. And of course, *It's Not Their Fault—and I can prove it.)*

"These people may feel guilty but would be the last to admit it. And yet

Guilt takes so many forms that you may not always recognize it when you see it.

"The problem with Guilt is that if it's not properly understood, it solidifies the determination to defend because the person feeling guilty needs to find someplace else to transfer the Guilt. In finding fault with another situation or another person, he or she justifies the lie that they're telling themselves. It's impossible for someone to claim they are *not guilty* while, beneath it all, they're actually feeling that they might be lying to themselves.

There are a lot of good counselors and therapists that are very well meaning and help large numbers of people work through problems in their lives by rummaging around in those experiences and helping them 'relive the trauma' in order to relieve themselves of any Guilt in the experience. Human beings are peculiar in that way: anything that causes them pain is immediately evaluated in terms of whether or not it makes them feel as if they 'deserve what happened to them,' and that it may be part of the life plan they have drawn up for themselves. This kind of treatment very often stems from the fact that, consciously or subconsciously, people know that they are truly in control of their own life, and at some point they will have to take responsibility for it. Think about it.

— The Guardian

"We frequently get frustrated because we can't get victims to see the stupidity of their position. But our error is that no one is talking about the true subject, which happens to be Guilt in whatever form it takes. So many folks have so much Guilt dumped (trashed) on them at such an early age they wouldn't recognize it if you made an entire video and *played* it for them."

"But you can't do that because the past doesn't exist," Michael said, thinking he'd hit upon something. "So rerunning old tapes doesn't work."

"Well, you're getting it!" The Guardian noted. "We just have to recognize what the other person is going through and then take them to the next step. But the secret now comes in the recognition."

"The little kid who says, 'You don't love me; you don't like me; you don't want me around,' is actually checking for Guilt. He may seem to be throwing it out to you as a kind of fishing expedition, but what he's really doing is throwing it back on himself.

"Children of divorced parents feel guilty that somehow the divorce was their fault. It's the same with children who have been abandoned. Abused children, abused wives (and abused husbands) are dealing with a tremendous amount of Guilt. People who survive automobile accidents or plane crashes traditionally experience an overwhelming burden of Guilt that may stay with them for years after the event, and the biggest problem for victims of rape is that they feel so much Guilt that they often reject all forms of physical contact, affection, or anything resembling a relationship for a very long time, if not forever. (It is not at all unusual for rape victims to put on a great deal of weight or even become obese as a means of avoiding any future physical intimacy. This is particularly true of victims of childhood sexual abuse. Their fat forms a kind of protective armor for them. Especially in a society such as ours where 'thin is in' and obesity among women is the ultimate turn off, it becomes the last line of defense. They're no longer lovable. They're no longer desirable. And that extra wall of fat will guarantee it.)

"All of these are issues in which it is not only common but also expected that the women, children, and men involved will feel utterly unworthy of love or affection of any kind. And it is the Big Push Away as a major form of expression.

"Whatever the causes, Michael, whether they're extreme or not, the basics remain the same. So what you have to do in all these cases is make the people involved realize that '*It's Not Your* (their) *Fault*. You didn't make your mom go away. (She didn't go away because of you.) You didn't cause yourself to be abandoned.'

"So the Wonder Hug—whether it's physical or verbal—bypasses what everybody thinks is the problem and gets to the real issues. The real issues are, 'How do I like me? How do I like you? And how do we relate to each other and make each other feel best when we're together?'

What would happen, then, if you would do a Wonder Hug along with the declaration that *It's Not Your Fault?*

"So what does all this tell us? It is very simply proof that in almost all traumatic experiences the people who are most severely victimized are the ones who find the most *fault* in themselves. They will continue to ask the (rhetorical) question, first and foremost: 'How could any part of this be my fault?' And yet they believe it is.

One of the most classic cases of The Big Push (Away) comes with an entire movie devoted to the subject: Good Will Hunting. *In the Oscar-winning film, Will, played by actor/co-writer Matt Damon, is a self-educated genius and math prodigy from the streets of South Boston who has just solved one of the most difficult mathematical equations in the history of MIT and yet is a barroom brawler on the verge of being sentenced to prison for his fifth count of simple assault. Instead, Hunting is bailed out by a Fields Medal-winning professor Gerald Lambeau (played by Stellan Skarsgård) with the stipulation that he send the young man to 'counseling'. As ordered by the court, Lambeau runs Will through a gauntlet of a dozen therapists to deal with his childhood issues of abandonment, life in an orphanage, and extreme physical abuse in a series of foster homes.*

After each of his counselors, trying to poke around in Hunting's past, is made a fool of by his brilliant manipulations, Will is sent as a last resort to Lambeau's old college roommate Sean McGuire, played by Robin Williams. McGuire turns out to be as canny, clever, and unorthodox as Hunting is a genius at evasion. And he immediately sees Will Hunting for what he is: A master of repelling everything of value in his life—a loving girlfriend, a six-figure income, and international academic acclaim and recognition (for which he truly longs). After nearly failing himself, McGuire realizes that no conventional therapy will ever work on this unassailable genius. By now, having won Hunting's confidence by refusing to take on any Guilt, projected or otherwise, McGuire simply stands at the threshold of every dark door the young man opens inside himself and tells him: It's Not Your Fault. The phrase, repeated over and over, becomes more powerful every time it's spoken, until Will Hunting finally breaks down (and breaks through)! And yes! The scene ends in a Wonder Hug. Most healing begins and ends that way. Think about it.

— The Guardian

"Until that question is answered that individual will continue to be traumatized. And all of the working through analysis, discussion, and explanation in the world will mean nothing until somehow, some way, that magnificent individual can discover that *It's Not Their Fault.*"

"It seems to me that the biggest temptation for people who push away is the appeal that their victimization is somehow justified," Michael concluded. "So they just might be better at laying on their Guilt trips than the average Victim would be."

"Ah! But remember, Michael, what I originally said about Guilt," The Guardian cautioned. "People can try and give Guilt away. They can try to dump it on you, lay it on you, or transfer it in a dozen other ways. But if you don't accept it, they have to take it back, and that really aggravates them, because then they have to start assuming Responsibility for their actions. This may seem cold, but it is the only thing that really works when you get down to it. Because you cannot become a part of the Guilt-cycle games they're trying so hard to pull you into.

"The best chance you have is to keep repeating *it's not your fault*...over and over, every way you can. *'It's not your fault, and that's okay. Because it doesn't have to be my fault either. In truth, it doesn't have to be anybody's fault, because it's in the past.'* (And we already know that the past doesn't exist.)

"In telling someone it's not their fault, the debilitating Guilt is bypassed and a sense of Responsibility is established. The Responsibility for each person's life belongs to him or her. That Responsibility is entirely in the present. Our life and all that remains of it, begins in this moment. And we are the creators of everything that comes from here on out."

CHAPTER 17

Move Over Casanova and Don Juan, Here Comes Bob!

Before Michael knew it, he and The Guardian were back in that mystical place by the waterfall, sitting across from each other in the "S" chair as if they'd never left.

"Wow!" Michael exclaimed, observing what just happened. "It's magic."

How People Think Things Work

"Interesting you should say that, Michael. Most folks believe in magic. Take love for example. They think that if you like somebody and the chemistry is there, you'll fall in love. Lack of Understanding of How Things Really Work is shown in the use of the word, 'fall.'

"To *fall* is usually an accident and quite unpredictable. If the marriage lasts, it's because the husband is a good husband and the wife is a good wife (whatever 'good' is). If a marriage fails, it was the fault of one or both of them.

"As life goes on it becomes more apparent that if you have friends, you're lucky. If you don't, there must be something wrong with you. It's a puzzle to most folks why they can have a good friend one day and then the next day that same 'friend' acts like they don't even know them.

"Likewise, if your kids turn out well, the parents of problem children or troubled kids openly conclude that you're lucky. Secretly, they wonder what *your* magic is, but they never quite muster the courage to ask for the phone number of your favorite witch doctor. You, of course, are absolutely sure that the theories of parenting developed during your teenage years, in opposition to the mistakes your parents made, have proven correct. When one of your kids goes goofy, you're suddenly clueless. You immediately admit publicly to having only two (not three) kids and covertly canvass the neighborhood for witch doctor emails, phone numbers, and Facebook pages. (You may also set up an endless tape loop to play *It's Not My Fault* 1,487 times while you sleep.)"

"Sounds like you're being cynical,"

"Not at all, Michael. I'm simply setting the stage for you to see the difference between how people *think* things work, and How Things Really Work."

How Things Really Work

"There are two key principles that apply to all relationships," The Guardian continued. "The first is: *To know me is to love me.*

"And the second is: *I like me best when I'm with you.*

"If folks can understand these two concepts, their lives and their relationships would be infinitely easier and a whole lot more fun. Marriages can forever be courtships. Friendships can last as the rule, and not the exception. Kids can actually love and even respect their parents. And parents will never again need to beat on their chests with tears in their eyes wondering all the while, 'What could I have done to keep this kid from being such a dipstick?'"

To Know Me Is to Love Me

"It's truly impossible to get to know someone and not love them. To do that, let's take a typical couple, Bob and Jenny—both upwardly mobile, twenty-somethings who have promising careers and their whole life ahead of them.

"When Bob and Jenny are courting they spend hours sharing their lives with each other. When you learn a person's true Self-Image—his or her hopes, dreams, wants, needs, likes, dislikes, fears, worries, and life experiences—it's impossible not to like them. That's when this seemingly endless process of dating and courtship nourishes the seeds for love to develop and grow.

"After two people in courtship get married, they throw themselves into their own activities. They progress in their individual directions. So Bob starts spending long hours at work. Jenny involves herself with her career or with homemaking and the children. Since they already 'know' each other, there's no need to share the details of what's happening in their private little worlds. Right, Michael?"

"Well, yes. I guess so…"

"Wrong! Once each life partner starts sectioning off parts of his or her life from the other, they start the process of exclusion. They don't really know each other any more. They become strangers. The oneness that they so carefully cultivated during their courtship is abandoned. And the principle of, *to know me is to love me* gets lost. You see, it's quite impossible to truly love someone you don't know.

"When one person feels left out of the other person's life, the message they receive is that they're no longer important. Remember, since folks evaluate everything in their life by the Law of Me, they're going to judge this new detour in their relationship *by how it makes them feel about themselves.*

"Michael, let's pay a visit to Bob and Jenny a couple of years down the road. You'll be able to see how a couple of new principles fit in with some you've already learned.

"By now, Bob is totally into his career at the expense of everything else. Bob goes to work and stays long hours. When he finally drags his body back to the nest, his brain is usually nowhere to be found. (The lights are on, but nobody's home.) He only hears part of Jenny's conversation about the parent-teacher conference that, two hours later, had 'slipped his mind.' He can't figure out, for the life of him, why she would ask him to use a toilet plunger in the downstairs bathroom to clear the clogged kitchen sink. Jenny tries to explain that the only subject of her request was the kitchen sink, but she's quickly interrupted when Bob's cell phone rings, and he has a conversation with his secretary. Bob then proceeds to burn up 43 minutes of what was to be his and Jenny's quality time together.

"You've got to remember that Bob just spent the last ten hours with his secretary. Still, he needs to handle 'some very important stuff.' He then proceeds to discuss in great detail all his feelings and information about his challenges at work. Work is now the place where he invests the largest chunk of his time, energy, and creative effort. What he doesn't realize (and that Jenny has gotten immediately) is that he's talked about more of who he is and where his life is going in a 43 minute conversation with his secretary than he has with his wife in their last six months together."

> *The closeness and time spent with fellow employees in the workplace along with the commensurate distances from family members readily proves absolutely the universal law which states 'To Know Me Is to Love Me'. 'Bonding' will inevitably occur when people share an enhanced understanding (knowledge) of each other. Think about it.*
>
> — The Guardian

"Sounds like a disaster in the making, doesn't it, Michael?"

"It sure does!" Michael agreed. "But earlier you compared this fellow Bob to Casanova and Don Juan—two of the world's greatest lovers. Frankly, I fail to see how this guy is even in the same book let alone on the same page with those legends."

"Well, that's the whole point, isn't it?" The Guardian said. "The secret of all great lovers is that *they know how to love*. That means they know how to make everyone in their lives *feel better whenever they're with them*. Bob has that potential. He had it once before; that's how he and Jenny got together in the first place.

"So let's see how we can get them both back to that very special place in their lives."

CHAPTER 18

I Like Me Best When I'm With You

Love: The Ultimate Validation

"Think about Bob and Jenny in the beginning of their relationship, Michael," The Guardian challenged. "What do you remember most?"

Michael thought about it for a moment before he answered. "I remember that they spent all their time together, literally sharing everything," he said.

"So what happened?"

"They obviously started becoming strangers to one another."

Love others as they deserve to be loved, since you know that it's not their fault. Think about it.

— The Guardian

"Michael, think about Jenny for a moment. How do you think Jenny feels?"

"At this point, I'm sure she thinks, 'Here we go again. He spent all day at work, and *then* when he finally gets home, he spends all his time on his cell phone— with his secretary!'"

"That's part of it," The Guardian agreed. "What evidence does Jenny have now to make her feel better about herself? When they got married, she liked herself best when she was with him. That's why she wanted to be with him all the time.

"You were right on about the courtship. They couldn't get enough of each other—each knowing the other more and more so they could love each other even more deeply than before. From what she knew about him, she liked herself just because a neat guy like Bob thought she made his sunrise and his toes curl. *(That's because she made him feel that 'to know me is to love me.')*

"A lot has changed since then, so let's take another look at what Jenny has to work with now.

"First, Bob spends a lot of time away from home. (Maybe more than he needs to.)

"When he is home, he doesn't hear a single thing that Jenny tries to tell him. (It must not be important.)

"Appointments she makes for them somehow slip his mind. ('Are we on the same page here?' she wonders. 'Are we even in the same book?')

"Outsiders, like his employers and his coworkers, spend more time with him and probably know him better than she does. In fact, maybe she doesn't know him at all anymore. Does he know her either? Of course not; not any longer.

"In fact, Michael, is it even possible for Jenny to honestly say to Bob, 'I like me best when I'm with you?'"

"I'd say no. Absolutely not!"

"Not only is it impossible," The Guardian said, "but by now Jenny has already started to feel that it's better not to have Bob around. She can be happy liking herself as a great mom, a good friend, and a successful career woman or homemaker. It doesn't help to have her nose rubbed in all of the evidence that Bob is now giving her that everything she's doing is meaningless; therefore, *she* is meaningless.

"This is called *taking someone for granted*. If, in courtship, 'to know someone is to love them,' what happens if you don't know them anymore?"

"It won't be possible to truly love them anymore," Michael said.

"That's right," said The Guardian. He added. "And yet, if you ask Bob 'Is your work more important to you than Jenny?' He'd say, 'Don't be ridiculous, of course not. Who do you think I'm doing all of this for? I tell her I love her regularly. I tell her all of this is for us. I tell her she's more important to me than work. I tell her that her opinion of what I do means more to me than anything.'

"Yes, Bob, you tell her. But does anything you tell her mean she receives the message? You've heard the old saying, 'Talk is cheap.' Here's another one that might clarify the picture of how it works: 'What you do, Bob, speaks (screams) so loudly that Jenny can't hear what you say.'

"In all fairness to Bob, Michael, *it's not his fault.* He's only filling the role that he believes life has handed him—as breadwinner, husband, and father. That's the way people typically think it needs to be done. If he does his job well, Jenny and the kids *should be proud of him.* The problem is that *this is not the way things work.* Up to this point, Bob's had no way of knowing this. So, I'd have to say to Bob, 'It's true! It's not your fault.'

"All Bob or anyone else who wants to build and keep a great relationship needs are two principles: To Know Me Is to Love Me and I Like Me Best when I'm with You.

It's easy to learn what makes a person feel best about themselves. They tell you in the tone of their speech, by their appearance and grooming, and by the people and things they surround themselves with. Think about it.

— The Guardian

---

1) How Things Work—To Know Me Is to Love Me

"If Bob would go back and remember how he applied this principle during his courtship of Jenny, how it works would be simple. He would be dragging every piece of 'the dragon' he had slain home for her approval. He'd show off in every way he could think of to get her attention and gain her applause. He'd be letting her get to know him again," said The Guardian.

2) How things Work—I Like Me Best When I'm With You

"All Bob has to do is measure everything he does and says against *what will make Jenny like herself best when she's with him.* A good question for him to use as a guideline is, 'What would I do, and how would I act, if we were still dating?'

"What message would Jenny get from this behavior? The message would be that she and her opinion of him are important to him; she has value. People want to be around and love those who would make them feel valuable. The test is for her to be able to say, 'I like me best when I'm with you,'" The Guardian concluded.

"Seems pretty logical to me," Michael said. "Bob and Jenny just need to get back to where they were when the relationship began, and get back to the magic."

"You're right, Michael," The Guardian agreed. "But first, a few questions…

"First, why do you think parents go to their kids' ball games and dance recitals? Because the parents' support sends the message: 'What you do is important to me.' And the message the kids receive is: 'I like me best when I'm important to mom and dad.'

Love isn't something you can do to someone. It's something you let them feel about themselves by the message you give them that validates their own magnificence. Think about it.

— The Guardian

"What if a wife visited work with her husband just to see for herself the nasty dragons that her man was slaying? Answer: He could show off to her. He'd have a chance once again to win her approval. She could discover that he deserved her applause because she could finally come to appreciate what he really did. The message she sends by doing this is that: *What's important to him is important to her, and he should certainly feel good about himself for what he does.*

"He in turn can say, 'I like me best when I'm with her…or when I have her Approval.'

If each person could honestly say, 'I like me best when I'm with me,' they would have the solution to all problems and the answer to all questions. Think about it.

— The Guardian

"So you see, Michael, How Things Work is quite different from what most people assume. All relationships are tied to these two principles. It doesn't matter whether or not it's a business relationship, friendship or as boyfriend, girlfriend, parent, child, marriage or brand new first time acquaintance, the same rules apply.

"The poet Henry Wadsworth Longfellow understood perfectly how things work when he wrote:

> *'Tell me not in mournful numbers*
> *Life is but an empty dream!*
> *For the soul is dead that slumbers*
> *And things are not what they seem.*
>
> *'Life is real! Life is earnest!*
> *And the grave is not its goal.*
> *'Dust thou art, to dust returnest*
> *was not spoken in the soul…*
>
> *'Lives of great men all remind us*
> *We can make our lives sublime*
> *And departing leave behind us,*
> *Footprints in the sands of time.'*

"That's how relationships work. It turns out that there is quite a simple bridge of understanding between what people do and How Things Really Work.

"Love is like wealth, Michael. If there is plenty, sharing is easy. If there is none or not enough, there is nothing to give. Human beings are natural givers. The love in this analogy signifies a love of ourselves. The only way we can give love is to share the complete understanding of how we get our own. And always love others as they deserve to be loved because you know, *it's not their fault.*

There are four simple rules to follow that will allow folks to like themselves best when they're with you. Rule #1: Let them know that anything they are embarrassed about or guilty about (especially from their past) is not their fault, and you're determined to prove it. Rule #2: Never confront or attack anyone's sense of Guilt by 'should-ing' them. Rule #3: Never infringe upon or override anyone's Agency or freedom of choice. Rule #4: Find and point out every good quality that you see in others. Be completely blind to their weaknesses and faults. (And understand that disobeying this rule will guarantee your relationship a short life expectancy. This particularly applies to double-edged weapons such as 'constructive' criticism and direct accusation, because these are the very things that will punch them in the Agency and kick them in the Guilt.) Think about it.

— The Guardian

CHAPTER 19

The Four Confusions
What People Think When They Don't Know How Things Work

"You've mentioned more than once that we are creators of all that happens to us," Michael said.

"It makes a lot of sense. Is that one of the universal laws?"

"It is, Michael," The Guardian answered.

"It's the Fourth Universal Law: The Law of Creation."

"If that's the fourth one," Michael said, "then aren't we skipping three? What's the Third Universal Law?"

"The Law of Justice," The Guardian said. "There are certain undeniable forces in our lives—like gravity. So, I call it the *Law of Justice*, because it 'just is.'"

"So, there are laws of human behavior as iron clad as gravity?"

"Absolutely, Michael!"

"Then may I assume that's probably the law we're studying next."

"We will shortly, Michael. But before we do, we have a few other things we need to clear up. Call it, 'taking out the last few bits of Trash.' And we have to do that because, for every universal law (as powerful as they are) there's an equal and opposite corresponding misconception that I call *Confusions*. So we have to study the Four Confusions."

"Wait a minute! You mean I have to learn about what's wrong before I can learn about what's right?"

"Well, Michael, I'd say 'you're wrong' about that. But that would just add to the confusion. What we're trying to do is eliminate confusion by recognizing it for what it is—something that needs adjusting.

"So what folks need to do is become lawyers. Concentrate on the things we need to know about how the laws work. We have to get a good grip on what they do and how they pertain to our objectives. That's the only way we'll come to know how the results can be obtained. It makes no difference what religion, philosophies, and knowledge that a person carries with him. If he is in accord with a specific law, he will always get a specific result. The universal and eternal laws are all as absolute as the Laws of Physics and the Laws of Nature.

"There's one I call The Law of Displacement—the law that says no two physical elements can occupy the same space at the same time," The Guardian added. "On the spiritual side of that equation: No two thoughts or dispositions can occupy the same space at the same time. You can't grow and shrink at the same time. You can't love and hate at the same time. You can't praise and condemn at the same time. You may think you can. You may even try to, but one emotion will always consume the other.

---

*There is much concern in recent times regarding **enforcement** of laws. Throughout the history of mankind there has been much issue made of obedience to laws. (Obedience is actually the antithesis of the concept of Agency.) It is the contention of the Guardian force assigned to planet Earth and its human population that true understanding supersedes and obviates the need for the concepts of enforcement or obedience pertaining to the universal laws. If an individual truly understands a law, how it works, why it works, and the benefits of being in accord with the principle there would be true excitement to be in perfect alignment with that law. Think about it.*

— The Guardian

"The objective in embracing any belief system is that it allows a person to be in accord with the highest number of principles within that belief system which are in line with the needs and the development level of the individual at that point in their life. Those who believe in a living God place themselves in direct access to an intelligence that both loves and cares about them—One who provides them with a system where mentors, teachers, and messengers—and ultimately personal inspiration—can help them expedite the learning of the laws.

"Remember: The consequences of universal laws can be viewed only with positive ramifications. There is no such thing as cold, but only the absence of heat; and there is no such thing as darkness, only the absence of light. So also there are no negative or bad consequences of a universal law, just the absence of the positive creative results of alignment and accordance with that law.

"Once people understand the laws, their desire to implement them will put them on the path to making them work. So, a person has a chance to exercise his or her Agency…and they can do it in complete accordance with those laws.

"In fact, it would be ridiculous not to do so. (If anyone with the eyes to see were to walk down a hundred foot path strewn with a dozen or so large and valuable diamonds, do you think they would choose to ignore them? Of course not! They would exercise the 'law of diamond picking,' bend over, picked them up, and put them in their pocket.)

"Once you are able to behold this kind of treasure, the choice to bring it into your life not only becomes easy but also automatic—as regular and unreflective as breathing. So fine-tuning our perceptions by clearing up the confusion between what are the true laws and what causes us to put them into play incorrectly is why we're taking a look at the Four Confusions."

The First Confusion: The 'law of me' vs. The Law of Me!

"The First Confusion has to do entirely with *me!*" The Guardian declared with a smile. "Think about it, Michael. The moment you say the word 'me' in that way doesn't it make you feel a little uncomfortable? It's absolutely true. Remember, in the real Law of Me, people who have mastered the Law of Me *know* that everything is about them, so they no longer need to make everything they do in life be about them. Instead they understand that everyone else is operating in the law without being aware of it, primarily because most people don't know How Things Work.

"When folks don't know How Things Work, they're going to continue to try and justify everything they do. They're going to defend their actions to others to keep from being blamed. They're going to find Fault with others in order to 'beat them to the punch.' And they're going to need Approval from others for everything they do. So they are...what?"

"Completely selfish and self-absorbed," Michael said.

"And people who truly understand the Law of Me already get the fact that it's about them," The Guardian continued. "They realize that it's just human nature that we can only see things from our own perspective. So they become Self-Aware.

"The difference between being Self-Aware and being self-centered is the difference between loving unconditionally and placing conditions on everything. That's because people who have mastered the Law of Me have learned exactly How Things Work. And those who do not are so confused about their own version of the Law of Me that they couldn't find it with a GPS!

"People who have mastered the Law of Me love to teach others and share what they know, but at the same time have learned the rules of *How to Allow*. They let the student find his or her own way through hard work and discovery.

"Those who are still in denial believe that they have to force everything to an issue. They are still reliant upon the opinions of others to influence every decision they make. And they continually extend their love with all kinds of conditions so it becomes a major tool to manipulate others.

"Most of all, they become major players in the Blame game. Their principal motivation in any situation is to find out whose Fault it is. That way they can solve the problem. Millions of confused but well-intended acts of correction are committed by good people on other good people who get caught up in bouts of Fault-finding. And as we know, Michael, finding Fault destroys relationships.

"People who have mastered the Law of Me become the world's best facilitators. They also become the world's greatest lovers—because they are learning how to love all people and all God's creatures unconditionally."

"Does that include romantic love between two people?" Michael asked. "That still seems to me as if it would be the most difficult part of the Law of Me to get into perspective."

"Well, you're absolutely right, Michael. But remember, now we have a few more tools at our disposal than we did when this subject first came up," The Guardian explained. "So let's take another look at this love issue—especially the confusion between love and sex—and see it for what it is."

The Second Confusion: Sex vs. Love

With that idea in mind, The Guardian snapped his fingers, and from what seemed to be out of nowhere there came a strain of The Beatles song, "All You Need is Love," followed by a number of other famous love songs, one after the other.

"Just thought I'd set the mood," The Guardian said, with a glimmer in his eye. "Just listen to the lyrics, Michael: 'Love! Love! Love! All you need is Love!'

"It's the world's biggest theme and the world's most over worked term, because very few people understand how it really works. The place where love most often fails is in the area of romantic love. Romantic love is the ideal, and as we have learned, Michael, people almost always fall short of their ideals because it's so easy for them to get confused over the things that really matter.

"Remember, Michael, I mentioned earlier that making love is the physical expression of unconditional acceptance, approval, and no-fault loving, while having sex can be the ultimate self-deception—seeking approval and never finding it, usually because that approval is counterfeit and often very temporary.

"Basically, romantic relationships between two people move through stages from one to four, and most of them never make it past stage two. The four stages of a love or romantic relationship between two people are *1) ecstasy (or illusion), 2) the power struggle, 3) acceptance,* and *4) dynamic love.* The challenge in most romantic relationships comes with the fact that most people never get past stage two: *the power struggle.*

"If you'll recall, Michael, I said that people tend to believe in magic, especially in a romantic relationship. People always refer to the fact that they've 'fallen in love.' In truth, falling indicates that it was an accident, and things seldom happen by accident. They also refer to terms like 'hopelessly in love,' when true love should be the fulfillment of hope. The question is: what constitutes true love?

"When two people first get involved in the 'euphoria' of initial attraction and nonstop loving, they have embraced the ultimate illusion: *euphoric love*. They're in a constant state of *ecstasy*. They can't get enough of one another. They have to be together every hour of every day for the rest of their lives (or so it seems). Her every move drives him to a point of total obsession. She becomes the goddess in his life.

"She sees him as her knight in shining armor, her rescuer, the fulfillment of her dreams. Everything he does is masculine, powerful, and dynamic. He's in command of his universe (or so it seems). He becomes her security blanket. Of course, she is constantly saying, consciously or otherwise, 'I like me best when I'm with you!'

"He feels the same way, of course. And of course, she's beautiful all the time—even when she's snoring. Everything she says is cute and clever (even when she says something naive and insists that she's right). She is adorable, loyal, unflagging, and supports him 'unconditionally' in everything he does; she is the perfect partner.

"Naturally, during this magical time, they tell each other everything—their hopes, their dreams, their greatest fears, every deep, dark secret from their past, the highest and lowest point in their life up to that point. 'Oh yes!' they rejoice to one another and the world. 'At last, I've found my soul mate!' They choose to be totally blind to any faults in each other.

"Then, slowly but surely, the novelty wears off, and the iron *Law of Familiarity* kicks-in. This is when *the power struggle* begins. And it can start anywhere from two weeks to two years into the relationship, usually after the couple has moved in together and gotten married (or vice a versa). This is when that nasty element called *Approval* creeps into their lives, and suddenly their love has more conditions than either one of them ever thought possible. Suddenly love becomes a negotiation: '*I will love you if...* If you provide us with a bigger house, if you spend more time with the children, if you lose some weight, if you become the trophy wife who fits my image, if you start making more money and providing us with a more secure future, if you do all the things I tell you need getting done over the weekend.'

"Where they once delighted in every little thing about one another, now they don't Approve of anything. What's more, their love gets so burdened with unfulfilled expectations that they start withholding things from one another. He pulls back on being affectionate. She holds out on sex. Suddenly 'making love' becomes a bargaining chip downgraded to the terminology of 'having sex,' which totally turns him off. He starts being attracted to other women, and her sixth sense picks up on it. So she becomes suspicious about his motives, even when he's being considerate.

"Soon enough they start arguing over every little thing. And all those little secrets they shared when they were madly in love at first suddenly become weapons in the struggle for supremacy. And *power struggles are always a zero-sum game,* because for every winner there has to be a loser, and yet there are those struggles for power where everybody loses.

"Usually, it is the Rule of the Power Struggle that whoever cares least controls the relationship. And the one who cares the least can place more 'conditions' on the relationship without any attachment to outcome. So his or her ambivalence actually becomes a power tool—an instrument of leverage—to control the relationship.

"Very often, before a winner is declared, both parties just walk away. Or they just stop communicating and spend their time putting more distance between one another. And as we know by now, Michael, distance is disaster, because couples that grow apart seldom come back together unless they learn the *Universal Laws*. And that's when divorce or separations occur. So, many relationships just become a 'no contest.' By then, though, there are children involved, and all kinds of complications from the failed relationship come into play. Remember, 50 percent of all marriages in America end in divorce. And 80 percent of those take place in families with one or more kids."

"What about a Wonder Hug?" Michael asked. "Seems like a few of those might work…wonders!"

"First, someone has to be willing to just go for it. Usually it's the partner in the relationship who finally gets it, the one who realizes that it's not their fault (or their mate's fault… or anybody's fault), and so they're willing to risk everything. Remember, Michael, half the marriages in America fail. That means half of them succeed. So, is that a bad thing? Or is it a good thing? Is the glass half empty? Or is it half full? Let's take a look at what works in a marriage, and how two people can get back together. And they usually get that way by moving into the third phase of their relationship: *Acceptance*.

"Acceptance usually comes with getting back to the basics of what brought them together in the first place—those qualities they initially loved in one another. Ironically, it often comes in families with children, because little children need and get more Wonder Hugs than anyone. The reason is usually pretty simple. Children, especially infants, are so helpless and so innocent that the parents recognize themselves in those children as well as their significant others.

"So the real Law of Me comes into play. Remember the Law of Me states very simply that, *'Everything I do is measured against how it makes me feel…about me.'* (Or, everything you do is measured against how it makes you feel about…you.)

"Parenting is very often the truest measure of whether or not the Law of Me can kick in for people. That's because it will generally bring up one of two qualities in a man or woman. They'll either become negligent, irresponsible, or emotionally and physically abusive. Or, they'll start to get answers to some of the biggest confusions about the Law of Me: *Who am I? What am I? What is my purpose here?*

"Remember, Michael, animals and small children operate almost entirely from the Law of Me. Infants and small children are perfect learning machines. They sample and test everything. Their world is still one of pure energy. So they know whether or not the Wonder Hug they're getting is genuine, and a smart parent knows that. The small child also gets to receive the Unconditional Love and affection from mom or dad that they're no longer able to give to one another.

"Then something else happens. That mother or father starts to devote Unconditional Loving energy into seeing that their child is able to establish the freedoms they feel have now been denied them. So they again become 'unselfish' in their love. Their natural inclination to teach and share their knowledge takes over. And guess what, Michael? Both partners get to rediscover those qualities in each other—the qualities that they found so attractive to begin with. And they start to *Accept* one another again.

"Having children can often be the starting point that brings couples back together, creating a basis for the final stage of a relationship called *dynamic love*. Dynamic love can take place between two people from the beginning of a relationship and stay with them until the end of their lives. But you have to know, Michael, that this is very rare. Usually it comes when two people really commit to one another and truly understand the Four Universal Laws. And not just the letter of the laws but also the spirit of the laws. It is in practicing the spirit of the laws that we can reach those levels of success that all of us want, but that so few people achieve."

The Third Confusion: The Letter of the Law vs. the Spirit of the Law

After listening to the examples that The Guardian pointed out, Michael remembered that almost every civilization had wrestled with the two interpretations of the law. And yet it only made sense, from all that The Guardian was telling him, that one path was far superior to the other.

"So, Michael," The Guardian challenged. "Letter or spirit? What do you think is the proper path to take?"

"Well…" Michael thought about it for moment. "Since there is no law of right or wrong, (or, as you put it, there is no Law of Wrong), I'm going to go with the *Spirit of the Law*, because that's the only thing that seems to make any sense at all. I mean, isn't the Letter of the Law the very thing that dehumanizes everybody?"

"The Letter of the Law is a starting point, and you have to start somewhere," The Guardian said. "That's how you set things up. It's the foundation. It's never the building itself. And rest assured, Michael, there are examples all over the place.

"Did you know that, according to the *Talmud*, Moses wasn't given Ten Commandments from Jehovah. He was given more than 600. (Imagine the stone tablets! Imagine trying to haul them down from the mountain! He would have needed several wagons and a bunch of his friends to get it all down. On top of that, all those laws probably would have been confusing, and maybe even contradictory. So Moses apparently made the right decision and took the best of the best.)"

"Pretty good decision on his part," Michael thought.

"I'm sure Moses had some help," The Guardian noted. "Maybe he just asked God for the Condensed Version and got it. Even so, those ten created their own dilemma, because inside each one is the spirit and the letter. By definition, the letter of the law is strict, harsh, conditional, and judgmental. (Sound familiar?) It requires Approval. And it limits everyone's Agency.

"So what happened? A few centuries later, Jesus of Nazareth comes along and simplifies those Commandments, condensing them down to two: *Love God* and *Do unto others as you would have them do unto you.* (That's *doing-onto* someone in the right way.)

"Do unto others as you (I) would have them do unto you (Me.)" Golly gee, could this possibly be a concise version of the Law of Me? Think about it.

— The Guardian

"Pretty simple when you think about it—and apparently Jesus Christ put the spirit of the Commandments into practice every day. *Not the Ten; the Two.*

"Understand, Michael, that the letter of the law always deals in a system of Approval, Judgment and Punishment. Judgment always assesses Blame. Judgment finds Fault. Judgment creates Guilt. And Guilt creates Victims. So Guilt by any other name has the same net result. Sin, Fault, Blame, wrongdoing, transgression—they're all just heads on the same monster. And they all make Victims of everyone because some very good people are made to feel guilty because they think that's How (people think) Things Work.

"That's not How Things Work, and Jesus was one of the first to point that out. Remember the incident in the New Testament of the stoning. In *John 8:7*, the crowd had gathered around a woman who had been adjudged to be an adulteress (Apparently she'd had an affair with a married man who was in the crowd getting ready to lob in a few rocks of his own. What a guy!) Seeing that this injustice was coming to pass, Jesus stepped in front of the woman and challenged the crowd. 'Let he who is without sin cast the first stone.' When no one apparently had the stones (every pun intended) to step for ward, Jesus simply allowed the self-condemning mob as individuals to go home and rethink their lives. Of course, He immediately got the fact that virtually everyone in that crowd needed to distract themselves from the burden of their own Guilt by making someone else a Victim—in this case, the woman.

"He also understood that the woman accused of the crime was carrying some Guilt issues of her own. So, immediately after disbursing the crowd, he turned to the woman and said: 'Go forth and sin no more.' And apparently His word alone was enough to cause this woman to repent and amend her life—partly because Jesus, the only man without sin, did not lay Guilt upon her. Instead He just said (in effect), 'Go fix this.'

"So what do you think Jesus did to 'change the game' while He was alive?"

"Is this a test?" Michael asked.

"Well, we've been doing this a while," The Guardian said. "Call it what you like. And, trust me on this: I'm not going to pass Judgment on what you come up with."

To Michael's surprise, it didn't take him long to come up with the answer.

"The main reason for Jesus coming at all was to bring The Gospel of Love," Michael answered. "That's the true Spirit of the Law, isn't it?"

Here is a variation of the concept that is quite revealing of human nature. "The things I find objectionable in you I have in me, for if I did not have them in me I could not recognize them in you." It may be interesting to note that the great masters throughout history found very little objectionable in their fellow man, for they had long since lost those negative qualities in themselves. Think about it.

— The Guardian

"See! I knew you'd been listening!" The Guardian exclaimed. "People don't intend to be out of accord with the Four Universal Laws, and the only way you can guide them along the right path is by employing the

Gospel of Love (Unconditional Love). Ask yourself, Michael, what would happen if everyone were convinced that they were perfect, and that every time they got a little out of tune with what worked it would be easy to get back to true peace, happiness, and joy?

"When Jesus admonished his disciples to 'Judge not lest ye be judged,' He was basically telling them that this was the final indictment on Judgment and the Letter of the Law. When we judge someone, we end up judging ourselves. And almost immediately the sword turns inward."

The Fourth Confusion: "Who Am I?"

"So, how does this apply to the Fourth Confusion about the Law of Me?" Michael asked. "It seems to me that, at this point, *The Law of Me* is pretty clear. So does it really apply for people to continue to ask those questions: *Who am I? What am I? What is my purpose here?*"

"People who try to understand how the Law of Me really works, are able to get a grip on all those issues," The Guardian said. "The problem with most folks is that they just go through the motions."

"*Who Am I? Am I who I think I am? Am I who you think I am? Or am I who I think you think I am?*

Who am I? I am not who I think I am. I am not who you think I am. I am who I think you think I am.

Who Am I? I am who I am. I love whom I choose to be, therefore you can like you best when you're with me."

A wise and wonderful woman who finished her life experience several decades ago, when faced with criticism or judgmentalism would simply respond by saying "Me am who me am." That simple comment alone summarized her own surety of the only approval she needed. Herself! Think about it.

— The Guardian

The Guardian continued: "Socrates once said, 'An unexamined life is not worth living.' And yet how many people, if you asked them the questions we just posed, could come up with an answer? In fact, if you asked most of them they would probably start to get a little uncomfortable. If they were honest they'd tell you that it's something they need to work on. On the other hand, there are those people who can give you specific answers the moment you ask.

"Those are generally the people you can spot right away, because they are the ones who seem to 'have their act together.'

"Answers to these questions, Michael, come in the form of *Goals* and *Objectives*. And that ultimately comes to the issue of our reasons for getting together in the first place. People who have somehow come to a place of Understanding of the Four Universal Laws have also acquired a virtue called *Faith* and are willing to take Action on what they believe in."

"So, the Fourth Confusion is probably a good thing," Michael concluded. "After all, when you come to a point in your life where you are asking questions and you're serious about getting the answers, that's a real breakthrough."

"'Knock and the door will be opened to you,' the Guardian said. "When you truly understand the laws, you also realize that by achieving confusion and admitting that you're confused, you are announcing to the universe that you are ready to listen. In a way, you're surrendering. So you're ready to be taught."

Faith is a most misunderstood concept. It is not dreaming, praying, and sitting around hoping in one hand and spitting in the other to see which gets full first. Faith is an ACTION word. The farmer may have faith that he will have a crop in the fall but he takes action to plow the field, plant the seed, weeds, nurtures and cultivates the crop, all the while praying for divine support. Then when the crop, whether great or small, has been harvested he takes possibly the most important action of all. He humbly expresses gratitude for the bounty he has received. Think about it.

— The Guardian

"'When the student is ready, the teacher will appear,'" Michael repeated the notion to himself.

"Well, there you go!" The Guardian exclaimed. "But remember, Michael, until the student is ready the teacher cannot appear. In fact, it can be said that 'Without a student there can be no teacher.'"

CHAPTER 20

The Four Universal Laws
What They Really Mean

Law #1: The Law of Me

"The secret of any law is that it should be impeccable. That's what makes it a law," The Guardian declared. "Notice the Ten Commandments, Michael. There was a reason they were etched in stone. (And that's where the observation, 'etched in stone,' comes from.) They were unerring, inevitable and impossible to argue with. All true laws are like that. So they're as much physical and practical as they are spiritual and philosophical.

"Take The Law of Me for example."

"I wish I could," Michael answered. "Frankly, I have trouble with that one."

"That's because it's all about you, and you don't want to admit it," The Guardian said.

"Seems so egotistical," Michael found the words coming to him, almost automatically.

"That's just the point," The Guardian said. "The main reason for that is the fact that your Ego doesn't like the exposure. It wants the attention but not the responsibility. So anytime anyone has to stand up and say, 'It's about me,' they get hit with little warning signs that immediately send them into denial. Of course it's about them. And it's about how they're made to feel about themselves.

"Let me ask you, Michael. Do you think these feelings you're expressing are about me?"

"No."

"Do you think they're about the Law itself?" "No."

"Do you think they're about someone else?" "No. No. And again, No!"

"Then, by process of elimination, what is the law about? What are you thinking about right now?"

"I'm wondering if you think I'm learning anything."

"So, you are worried about you, and you're not quite sure how I feel about you. So…you're not quite sure how you feel about you!" The Guardian declared. "So, the Law of Me states very simply that *everything you do is measured against how it makes you feel—about you!*"

"I get that," Michael said. He said it, and yet he realized he was being defensive. "The question is whether or not you accept it," The Guardian reminded him. "And if you do accept it, what's it going to do? It's going to empower you. It's going to open up your freedom of choice. Once you get that it's all about you, it's going to free up your Agency. Why? It's because you are going to take responsibility for everything that happens to you.

"Think about it, Michael. The Law of Me is really about taking responsibility for everything that happens to you. That means no one can victimize you, but you. No one can enable you, but you. No one can "do onto" you anything that you don't want to have happen to you. If you take responsibility, and I take responsibility, and the next person takes responsibility then who can be at fault? When you take responsibility for what you do, guess what? You're going to like you best when you're with…you!

"If you feel good about you, Michael, you feel good about your ability to influence others in a positive way. It makes you a better friend, a better lover, a better husband, a better father, a better teacher, a better mentor, a better coach, a better salesman—a better human being."

"What about the word, *influence?*" Michael asked. "It has a lot of meanings, some of them not so good."

"Everything we do influences everything around us every minute we're alive, Michael," The Guardian explained. "Even the act of breathing in and out influences the trees and grass around us. You breathe out carbon dioxide and the trees breathe it in. They breathe out oxygen and you breathe it in. It's called photosynthesis. It's called life.

"The difference is that when you influence life in that way you accept it as a natural part of your universe. You don't have to think about it. It just happens. Now, let me ask you. What would the rest of your life be like if you just got out of the way of the natural order of things and let them happen?"

"They'd probably be great," Michael said. "And yet you mentioned earlier that we too often equate success with our ability to influence other people's universes instead of our own. You even pointed out the fact that people call it 'freedom of choice' to justify Agency infringement on an unborn child."

"That's true," The Guardian agreed. "If you want true Freedom of choice in that area, where is the choice to be made? It's to be made before intimacy."

"But let's look at true Agency as it relates to the Law of Me."

Law #2: Agency

"There's one thing you need to know about Agency, Michael," The Guardian said. "Once you get the Law of Me and you take responsibility for the fact that it's all about you, you're opening up your own Agency. You'll have a lot more freedom of choice. And you'll be able to offer more freedom of choice to others.

"By truly recognizing the Law of Me, you have virtually gotten free. No one can victimize you, do onto you, enable you, lay guilt on you, find fault with you, judge you, or subject you to their Approval because you have simply chosen not to become part of all that (garbage).

"So that energy *bank account* of your life, the one with all those deposits and withdrawals, has just blocked out a lot of unnecessary withdrawals and given you more life currency to spend. Let's call them credits on your life credit card. So life is rich with choices, and you have much more to spend.

"It's a lot like going into a high-tech store with an unlimited line of credit. You walk in, and all around you are flat-screen TVs, computers, entertainment centers, MP3 and MP6 players, iPads, iPods, smart phones, dig-video cameras, tech games, alternate electronic universes, and every imaginable techno gizmo. You have unlimited funds, great credit, a wealth of experience, and all kinds of electronic upgrades on display before you. All you have to do now is make some smart choices.

"Remember, I also said that, *'When you mess with my Agency, you mess with me, because my freedom of choice is who I am.'* Limit that, and you limit me.

"So what happens when you help open up more choices for me? You're actually building up my Agency. It's like the manager in that electronics store. He knows you want to buy. So, he makes himself available to you by sharing what he knows with you and putting himself at your disposal. Then he gets out of the way and lets you become the master of your fate. That makes him a good salesman. And a good salesman never infringes upon anyone's Agency. He lets you choose for yourself.

"That's the difference between high pressure selling and sharing. People who share new ideas and concepts are actually coming into the lives of others in ways that will enhance their agency. And you can never really sell anybody by forcing them to buy. You share great new choices for them to make, and you let them decide. That's the difference between selling and networking. You're doing it because you want to help and because you're offering something of value. (And at some level they know that.)"

"But what if you have something that people need but don't know they need?" Michael asked. "You want to help them, but you don't want to infringe on their Agency either."

"Good question," said The Guardian. "And it's generally true. The last thing in the world people want to do is make the difficult choices, mainly because it's usually those choices that really cut down the funds available in their liberty bank account.

"And yet anyone who has mastered Agency also recognizes that it involves a lot of responsibility. So they spend their currency wisely. They plan ahead. They realize that those of us who have the most Freedom of choice, also have a Responsibility to those we've chosen to have in our lives. So they become initiators and facilitators. They'll become your partners in the process, and they choose it because it is the right thing to do.

"When it comes to Agency, Michael, people can handle it in one of three ways. The fool has the experience and still doesn't learn. The wise man learns from his experience. *The Master learns from the experiences of others.* It looks as if the human race has a shortage of masters. And I'm not sure that the very wise man has to have the actual experience before he learns from it. (After all, if you wait for your ox to be gored, all you get left with is a dead ox.)

"We know the timeless saying that, 'He who hesitates is lost.' And still people hesitate or worse—they don't make any decision at all.

"We have two different options in our reaction to events and circumstances. One is that the event is out there. Like an 'Act of God' (a misnomer) or a natural disaster, it happens. Life happens, and there isn't really anything we can do about it. And those are the events that so many people lose sleep over. They develop ulcers, wring their hands, and generally believe they are helpless against the whims of fate. (The truth is that we have it in our power to do everything about them. We can plan.)

We can buy earthquake insurance. We can put storm shutters on our homes in case of tornadoes. And if we live in a flood plane, we can choose not to live in that flood plane. We can move to higher ground. We can also have an alternate plan of action. We can and should keep emergency storages of food, water and medical supplies. (We're all aware of our need for these things, and yet less than 1 percent of us are emergency prepared in America, in the richest nation in the world, because the illusion is that it cuts down on our Agency. The truth is that choices such as these, once they're made, expand our Freedom of choices in ways we never imagined.)"

"What about disasters that just happen?" Michael asked. "No matter what we do to prepare, they come crashing down on us anyway. Some strike us very literally like lightning, or a storm that wipes us out."

"We can't do anything about the storm that blew our house away," The Guardian answered. "But we can do all kinds of things about how we let the incident affect us. We can lie down, give up, weep and wail that we've been unfairly 'done-onto.'

"Or…we can realize that what's happened is already in the past. Then we pick ourselves up, dust ourselves off and start all over again. We can start rebuilding, regrouping and move ahead.

"All this comes back to the basic principle of Agency, freedom of choice, who we are and how much we choose to embrace our potential for greatness. It comes back to the fact that 'I am the only one who can affect what happens to me and how I allow it to affect me.' It's the one Universal Law that cannot be violated. It's the one law that, if understood, will allow us to literally control our own destiny."

Law #3: The Law of Justice

"Earlier, you said something about the Law of Justice," Michael remembered. "You said that you called it Justice because it 'just is.' And I thought it might just be a bit of wordplay."

"And then what did I say?" The Guardian asked. But he didn't wait for the answer. "I said that it was an irrefutable law, like *Gravity*. That's because gravity exists and gravity is a force in your life whether you like it or not."

"But you can defy gravity," Michael said. "It happens all the time."

"Now that is wordplay!" The Guardian challenged. "You don't defy gravity. You understand its awesome power and you put it to work for you. That's how we got kites, hot air balloons, airplanes and rockets to the moon. You put these other laws to work for you in the same way. You can't change the Laws, but you can alter the ways that you are affected by them. If you are in accord with them, you'll be happy and life will work well for you.

"If you get out of alignment with one of these laws, the parts of your life connected just doesn't work. Take Gravity, for example (since you brought the subject up). If you know how it works and stay in accord with it, you'll get some great benefits:

"Airplanes can fly. (Gravity keeps the air wrapped around the earth and provides the force to suspend airplanes between the lift of the wings and the downward pull of the earth's core.)

"Golf balls drop in the hole, eight balls drop into the pocket, basketballs get slam-dunked, and footballs get passed down field—all because of the pull of gravity.

"We have muscles and muscle tone because gravity requires that our bodies move against it. Remember when our astronauts are weightless in space, it affects their entire body, muscle tissue, and circulatory system, and they have to readjust all that once they've reentered the earth's gravitational field.

"There are other truths involving all the Universal Laws: you don't have to know the law; you don't have to understand the law; you don't even have to agree with the law; but you do have to have a sense of the law and respect it for what it is.

"All this and more applies to the Law of Justice.

"Call it conscience if you like—a natural sense of Justice.

"I also said that to understand what true justice actually means, it's essential to remove yourself from a situation as one of the ways of controlling the effect that it has on you. It's appropriate to be concerned on behalf of others who have not yet learned to control their own personal universe. But that's a matter of understanding where your nose ends and mine begins.

"Finally, Justice is about control. It's about recognizing the things you have control over, acceptance of all those things over which we have no control, and the good sense to recognize which is which."

"So…" Michael anticipated.

"So, we'll be covering the Law of Justice shortly. It's only…just."

Law #4: The Law of Creation

"Okay! What about the Law of Creation?" Michael asked. "Seems to me that this is what it all comes down to—or comes up to."

"Each law is related to the next," The Guardian answered. "I'm not here to say that there is a level of importance that places one law above the other. But I can tell you this much Michael. There is an order to all things in life. And yes! The other laws lead up to this. So the Law of Creation does complete the quartet.

"There's a good reason that we make this the Fourth Universal Law. You have to learn to crawl before you can walk. You have to learn to walk before you can run. And you need to take the steps necessary to bring you to the last law. (Remember, you're cleaning up that perfect building of yours.) So… once you recognize that it's all about 'me,' once you master your freedom to choose, and once you understand that you control all that happens in your life, you're finally ready for this.

"Essentially, the Law of Creation has everything to do with *Thought*. All great teachers, philosophers and masters throughout history have worked off the variations of the Law of Creation.

"The maxim in Proverbs 23 says that, 'As a man thinketh, so is he…'

"The philosopher Descartes pronounced the premise of an entire philosophy when he uttered the Latin phrase: *Cogito Ergo Sum* ('I think, therefore I am.') So what you think is everything you are and will become.

"Let's put it even more simply: *If you can believe it, you can achieve it.*'

"Jesus used the parable of the mustard seed in Matthew 13:31: 'The kingdom of heaven is like a mustard seed, which a man took and planted in his field. Though it is the smallest of all your seeds, yet when it grows, it is the largest of garden plants and becomes a tree, so that the birds of the air come and perch in its branches.'

"The reason that He did so was to teach us not only how much we are all creators of everything that happens to us, but also how limitless is the scope of our potential.

"If you can think it, Michael, you can find it. If you can visualize it, you can manifest it; and that means everything. Thoughts become Things. That is the Law of Creation. And we were born into this life to be Creators.

"That's the very reason some people write books, paint pictures, compose music, carve statues out of granite, and design skyscrapers. Other people can build networks, motivate people and advertise new ideas to the public in ways they've never seen before.

"There are masters of technology, the internet, electronics, computers and nanotechnology who come up with entire new universes that no one has even conceived before.

"Not everyone has been blessed with those gifts, but each of us has gifts of our own. Some people can manifest money, prosperity, and property. They can, through their business acumen and empire building, create great wealth for themselves and everyone around them. They build businesses, start industries, create jobs, and help make other people rich—and that is a vital kind of creation. It means cars, homes, trips, and lifestyles. And a successful opulent lifestyle is a creation all its own."

"You mean people can create things—cars, clothes, trips, homes?" Michael asked.

"They're by-products of thought, Michael. But yes! With the power of thought you can have anything you ever dreamt of, and the reason you probably haven't received it already is because you haven't conceived it. And you haven't conceived it because you haven't gotten in touch with the power that is in you."

"I'm not sure I have that kind of power," Michael admitted, expressing his doubt. "Not everyone has that ability. And frankly, not everyone is willing to do the work it takes to achieve it."

"Michael, I'm not going to say you're wrong, because there really is no wrong," The Guardian said. "I'm just going to say that you haven't tapped into it yet. And the reason is that you and so many others make such work of it all.

"There are two ways you can put the Law of Creation to work for you. You can think it, focus on it and create it by the power of thought. Or…you can allow it to happen. The miracle of creation is there, and it will take place with very little effort on your part. Just allow it to be."

"I don't get it," Michael admitted.

"Don't try to force it. Just give it permission." The Guardian replied. "Tell me Michael, can you make your heart beat? Can you make your lungs push air in and out? Can you consciously slough off old skin and create new skin every week or so (which you do already)?"

"No. It's automatic," Michael admitted. "It just is…"

"Very good, Michael!" The Guardian replied. "I do believe we're ready to take the next big step."

With that, Michael thought about what he had just said, and he smiled.

CHAPTER 21

A Return to Perfection
You've always been perfect. (You just didn't know it.)

"Perfection is a tricky thing," The Guardian announced. "And we make it that way because all of us are taught at a very early age that it's absolutely something we can't have.

"How many times, Michael, have you heard catch-phrases like this? 'Nobody's perfect!' Or, how about, 'Well, what do you expect? I'm not perfect, you know.' Then there's the ultimate cry of the Victim: 'Anyone who strives for perfection will live a life of frustration.'

"I think English Prime Minister Winston Churchill had the best approach to the issue. 'They say that nobody is perfect. Then they tell you practice makes perfect. I wish they'd make up their minds.' Churchill was right, of course. People can't make up their minds. Life confuses them about the true meaning of perfection. And that's where the dilemma lies.

"Most people will acknowledge the perfect beauty and innocence of a newborn child. And yet the moment that child comes out of the womb that child is slapped with the assumptive concept of Original Sin. (The dark notion that we are imperfect from the first moment we start taking in air.)

"The truth is that we are all born perfect and in perfect communication with our Creator. If we weren't, that would mean everyone was starting at rock bottom. There would be nothing to lose—no hopes, no dreams, no aspirations, and no expectations of excellence. So, when you get right down to it, we are born perfect, and yet we're taught almost immediately how to *de-perfectize* ourselves.

"If you were starting life at the bottom and you were nothing, what would there be to lose? So your movement toward seeking perfection would be something that couldn't really disappoint you. So it must be that, in our heart of hearts, we know that we are perfect. And when we have a hiccup in maintaining that perfection we get depressed, sabotage our Self-Image and fail."

> **De-perfection,** or the de-perfectizing of a human being is not an official word in the English language. But it is a pivotal word in the Encyclopedia of THE GUARDIAN CODE: It's Not Your Fault, since it emphasizes one of the points of critical mass in the deconstruction of excellence. We are working hard on getting the term recognized as a more permanent point of reference.

"I remember that you covered a lot of this when we were talking about Self-Image. And I get that," Michael observed. "So, how does the concept of *'Perfection'* separate itself from *Self-image, The Law of Me,* and all the other things we've covered up to now?"

"In a way it doesn't," The Guardian replied. "The difference, Michael, is that now we've gotten to a point where we understand that Perfection is not only possible, it's inevitable—that it's our God-given birthright! If I had tried to tell you that in the beginning you never would have believed me. Would you?"

"Probably not," Michael admitted.

"But now you realize that all things are possible; not only possible, they already exist. That especially includes Perfection." The Guardian said. "The challenge usually comes with the fact that we don't even recognize perfection until we see it get damaged or destroyed."

"And since, according to the Law of Creation, we are the cocreator of all that happens to us, we are usually the ones who do it," Michael added.

"Or get done-onto," The Guardian confirmed. "Same difference. It all comes down to the greatest contributor to sabotaging perfection in anything or anyone—*Guilt*. We already know how guilt undermines someone's self-image. Guilt over failure to achieve, guilt over having less than perfect thoughts, guilt over not fulfilling a promise or not keeping your word, guilt over taking something you shouldn't have or not getting good grades, guilt about overeating, guilt over not paying your bills on time, over letting your credit rating slip, over forgetting your spouse's birthday—the list of causes is endless. And even though mistakes are always a part of the process of living, we just can't seem to forgive ourselves for them. And this gets really bad once you've gone past the point where (you think) correction is impossible.

"From that point on, you start to think, 'What the hell, let it all go down.' Your perfection has been marred. You hit a point of critical mass, and you just don't care any more. At just about the same point where people recognize their purpose to begin with, they get hit with the concept of imperfection, and anything that mars their perfection drops them into an emotional hole and covers it up. Then through their own sense of Guilt, they lose the ability to climb out of that hole. The whole idea behind knowing *It's Not Your Fault* begins and ends with understanding that you're already perfect to begin with. You get boxed-in by imperfection. Knowing that it's not your fault lets you out of the box. You can get back to perfection. *Perfection is never destroyed irreparably*. But for most of us it does get damaged somewhere along the way. This is all about the repair process—the perfection that is…"

The Guardian paused before he continued. "An example of this is a girl losing her virginity. Until she does, she's looked upon as 'perfect.' So what happens to her? Not only does she lose the perceived physical evidence of her perfection but also the Self-Image of her immaculate virtue. The guilt, the misery and the self-loathing—she's no longer perfect! So that's why it's always easier to commit a sin the second time. That's because it's always accompanied by the belief that we don't have a way back.

"The truth is that there is always a way back. All that girl had to do first was to learn that it wasn't her fault. Second, she just had to know that there is always a way to get back to true perfection.

"Think about it, Michael. When you know you can always get back to perfection, how much more willing are you to take chances—to fall and to fail a second time and even a third? The process, the learning curve of living fully, would become a beautiful experience because you're actually allowed to fail. That means you have permission to learn. So you virtually can never be put into a box that you can't get out of."

And so The Guardian said, "Benjamin Franklin—inventor, patriot and founding father of the U.S.A.—probably understood that perfection also meant having the courage to pursue it when he said: 'I have not failed. I've just found 10,000 ways that won't work.'

The above concept does not allow license to repeat an action already proven to be inappropriate. It's Not Your Fault only applies if the outcome is not what in retrospect would have been intended.

— The Guardian

"When you're having conversations about perfection, people are always making references to Jesus Christ as being 'the only perfect man.' He was born just like any other man. (And how was He born? Perfect!) So what did He do? He set us the example of how to stay that way. He understood and embraced the fact that, notwithstanding the exercises and learning experiences that we have in life, the human being starts out perfect. ('Lest you become again as a little child, you cannot enter the Kingdom of Heaven,' He told us, more than once.)

"So I put the dilemma to you: Do we follow Him, start out perfect and stay that way? Or do we buy into the mythology that we are born in sin and go downhill from there? Does it make any sense, Michael, that God the Father would create any imperfect children? I think not. We are hit with the concept of Original Sin, when the greatest sin is to place that burden of guilt onto the newborn, perfect child.

"Jesus of Nazareth, the perfect man, embraced the perfection in others. That is what he did on a daily basis. He dedicated his life to cleansing the world of Guilt, Blame, and Limitation. In that consciousness, there's absolutely no door to our thoughts, words or deeds that would slam so tightly shut that we cannot open it again.

"If Jesus mastered any aspect of the Law of Me it had to be the one that says, 'I like me best when I'm with you.' Most great modern leaders, motivators and self-improvement gurus imitate that approach to dealing with others. They reveal to others their pure potential by helping them to understand that they merely need to 'tap back into their excellence.' When people are able to say, 'I like me best when I'm with you,' it means that you have allowed them to keep their freedom of choice. They never have to defend against any sense of guilt. So their sense of Agency is allowed to remain intact.

"One of the definitions of a perfect life is one that is guilt-free. To have it said of a person that *they are guiltless* is one of the highest compliments you can pay to anyone.

"Jesus Christ was said to been guiltless. (He is so often described as a 'Man without guile.')

Remember that anger and judgmentalism are the evil Step-children of guilt. Guile is the vicious projection of anger and accusatory judgmentalism. Therefore a guileless person is devoid of the Guilt that spawns guile. Think about it.

— The Guardian

"That's what drew so many followers to Him. And it was the very quality that infuriated the religious hierarchic society of Israel because their stock in trade and their power control mechanism over the people at the time was Judgment and Guilt. A revolution was fomenting over guilt at having been conquered by the Romans. The Pharisees and Sadducees were trying to defuse the guilt they felt over collaborating with their Roman masters. And the presence of Jesus, who spent most of his time preaching the perfection of the human condition, was more than an offense to them; it was a political threat. In fact, they resented Jesus for the sin of being 'good,' and for helping others free themselves of the burdens of self-loathing. So these professional victims and victimizers had to engage in a conspiracy to get rid of him.

"This partly explains why Pontius Pilate acquitted Jesus of any 'Guilt,' to such an extent that he publicly washed his hands and called out to a throng on the verge of riot: 'I am innocent of the blood of this just man; *see ye to it!*'

"So what's Pilate saying here? 'It's not my fault.' (But it was his Responsibility, and he knew it.) 'You guilty people find guilt where you may. I recognize the difference.'

"What Jesus taught, and what he showed us by living an exemplary guiltless life, is what we have an opportunity in modern times to do every day. What we have been given, within the tools in these concepts, is the ability to accept the perfection in our hearts that lead us to perfection in our lives. By eliminating Guilt, Blame and finding Fault in ourselves and others we open up all windows to our potential for greatness.

"We can erase the stress of indecision and second-guessing caused by Judgment and find our way to joy. Where there is joy there is Peace, where there is peace there is Freedom, and with freedom we own our Agency and the ability to accept who we really are—the perfect innocent productive geniuses we were meant to be.

"By definition, *genius* has a Latin root meaning 'divine.' And it originally meant *being in contact with that which is divine in us*. When the human mind has freed itself to embrace a state of joy and peace, it is capable of reaching its true creative potential. And we, as individuals, will be able to accept who we really are: magnificent!"

Jealousy is one of the greatest enemies of perfection. This applies to all elements of life: professional, personal, and intimate relationships such as marriage and divorce. Almost all jealous people conclude that any attraction their mate might have to someone else is a matter of their inadequacy when it may simply be a failure to understand the concept of 'I like me best when I'm with you.' So they almost always drive away the very person about whom they feel jealous or possessive. If they truly understood the concept they would always find ways to give their mates a chance to express themselves freely. So they would enhance the Agency of their significant other and not detract from it. Think about it.

— The Guardian

CHAPTER 22

Is The Pen Mightier Than the Sword?

The Power of the 59¢ Pen!

"So is that all there is to the Law of Creation? That's it?" Michael heard himself asking. As he did, he could see The Guardian break slowly into a smile.

"All great Laws are simple at their core," The Guardian said. "The trouble is that we make so much work…of everything! Remember what I just told you a little while ago? I said: 'We are never *not* creating.' So you're creating at this very moment. Your question is creating an answer. And that answer—and your response to it—creates what you're going to do next."

"So, what if I can't remember it all?" Michael asked.

"Write it down," came the answer. "There's nothing wrong with making lists. In fact, I recommended it when we were talking about Just*ice*. So…go for it!

"The fact is that the pen has a lot of power. It's true that it's mightier than the sword, and it is in more ways than one.

"We know it's really great to use to set goals and objectives. But it's every bit as good when you use it to get rid of unresolved issues from the past."

"Wait a minute!" Michael balked. "I thought you said, 'The Past does not exist.' Isn't that a major part of this lesson?"

"Absolutely correct," The Guardian agreed. "But the past is a funny thing. If you don't deal with it and clear it out, it will remain the biggest issue in your life.

"For that, we have a remedy. It's this little 59¢ writing instrument called a pen. (It used to be 39¢, but that's inflation for you.)" With that he pulled a BIC pen from his pocket and held it up in the air.

"I'm not quite sure I get it," Michael announced. "How is a little pen going to clear up the past for me?"

"Thought you might ask," The Guardian said. "One of the problems about withholding experiences and evaluations in our mind is that we wrap (little emotional overcoats of) feelings around the facts. They're no longer just simple thought patterns but the emotions that we give the thought as we paint them. The various colors through guilt, judgment, denial, fear, neediness, wanting, anger, and love—all these and more will completely, or at least partially, change the pictures on the video that we run through our mind as we repeatedly go back in the past to recreate the experience through memory. We place ourselves at a very unfair disadvantage.

"When we first experience the event, we have a faulty picture of what happened tainted by the emotional state we are in at the time. (This has been proven time and again when people are asked by police to recount the events of an accident or crime. They will almost all give different stories.)

"We are never in the same emotional state twice in our lives. Life experiences, time and distance usually dictate that. So, each time we go back, we re-contaminate the creation of the experience with our present emotional state. We literally never tell ourselves the same story twice. We constantly change the event itself and what it means to us. Over time, we make so many revisions to the actual experience that it tends to impact us over and over again until we virtually become a different person with every rerun. As a result, nothing ever gets resolved!

"Nostalgia is a uniquely human experience. Of course, physical contact is ideal. If we can go back and get with the people who were actually involved in some of the original experiences and have them bring us up to date so we can bridge the time lapse between then and now, we can obtain the greatest relief."

The Guardian continued: "Isn't it interesting how the words, 'relieve' and 're-live' are so similar? When we have an experience about which we retained either good (or nostalgic) feelings or bad (painful) ones, those very same feelings come back to us in more or less the same form. Whenever we feel emotional pain, discomfort, worry, fear, or regret we also tend to experience them physiologically—as pain, nausea, cramping, and even the shakes.

"One of the problems about withholding experiences and evaluations in *our* mind is the overriding power of emotions. Through the filter of emotion, our reactions to life are no longer just simple thought patterns. They're emotions that we give the thought as we paint them with various colors through lenses of guilt, judgment, denial, anger, love, longing, and other needful things that gain greater or lesser importance with each repetition of 'memory.' So much so that, by doing this, we place ourselves at a serious disadvantage.

"Now it's a nice simplistic piece of wishful thinking to brazenly come forth with the concept that if you can do nothing about it then the past does not exist. I can understand how so many people reject the idea out of hand, especially since they're presently experiencing the repercussions that make the past very real.

"It should be quite obvious that we ourselves continue the past by our recreation of it. How would you feel if I told you that there is one answer to the question: 'Can I do anything about it?' And that answer is: 'Yes!' You can do something about how you'd choose to recreate the past. In so doing, you can come to the conclusion that a point in time has taken place and nothing more can be done about it. And yet there are those events that will stay with you unresolved, like undigested food, until you physically do something to remove them.

"Minds are peculiar devices. Sometimes they require some very physical activity to set them free. Some people call it therapeutic writing. I call it 'taking out the Trash,' and doing it in a very physical way.

"So…I recommend writing it all down. And I do mean writing it in longhand. When using writing as a tool for personal development, it is essential to do it by hand, even if you transcribe it later. There is a significant connection between the hand, the eye, the mind, and the physical act of putting it down on paper. When you do this, you create a kind of rebuilding process that is very constructive.

"To get you started out on the right path, Michael, let's try an experiment: Let's say you're looking for ward to a very hectic day. There are a tremendous number of tasks that you need to accomplish. Most people have a tendency to start worrying. They think the first thing that comes to mind and then blow by that one to jump to the next task, and then to the next task and the one after that until they feel completely overwhelmed. It seems to them like their brain is overheating (like an engine that's overheating). They start to get physical symptoms from their very high-speed mental activity—nausea, griping pains, even sweats—all the manifestations of what is popularly referred to as a panic attack.

"Some people respond to this by sitting in a kind of emotional flatline and staring into space or by getting physically ill. They start to feel helpless as if there is nothing they can do."

The Guardian paused for a minute so that his words could sink in before he continued.

"That's the benefit of making lists, Michael. You put things in order. You see them out in front of you, one objective at a time. In black and white on the page in front of you, it's not such a big deal. So, suddenly you're able to put it into perspective.

"All information that we hold in the mind becomes intermingled and blended into an emotional Mulligan stew so that thoughts and feelings become nearly impossible to separate. They all begin to come with the same flavor.

"When we write an experience down on paper we have a natural filter in the transfer from our mind to our writing hand, which takes out the feeling and leaves only the facts. By using our handwriting to filter emotion out of information we present ourselves with a tremendous tool—one that's natural and automatic. When we write down the tasks of the day, when they visibly pop up in front of us, they suddenly seem more doable. (Physically [visibly] they present about one-tenth of the impact they originally had in our mind.)

"When we list the tasks for an extremely active day we find that when the list is finished, we end up with an entire string of priorities:

1) those highest priority items that we need to do immediately; 2) high priority items that we have to do, but with a lesser sense of urgency; 3) those optional tasks that we can do at a time and place of our choosing; 4) tasks and functions that someone else can do. When you set down these options—with pen and paper—the whole day becomes simple.

"The bottom line is that our mind is a very poor place to store reality. It tends to embellish each repeated remembrance of the facts with more and more complexity and fear. Another thing that is *in human nature to overlook is the fact that the present instantaneously becomes the past.* And it does so every minute of every day. In that regard it becomes the only thing we have to work with, and it will stay with us until we get it cleared up and out so we can move onto that other uncharted continent called the Future—which does not exist but is anticipated through that library of thoughts called (you guessed it), the Past!"

"Stop right here," Michael insisted. "I'm confused."

"Good!" The Guardian snapped. "Confusion is the first step on the road to recovery. And there's no need to recover really. Just do something about the past and (virtually) put it out of your mind. And the way you do that most effectively is by making a list and checking it twice. So write everything down, and start today."

"So…how do I do that?"

"Use my Super-Guardian Six-Step Process," The Guardian answered. "And I promise you that it will resolve just about every issue that you have.

The Guardian's Six-Step Process...
to Show the Past Does Not Exist

STEP ONE: Write the experience down on paper.

STEP TWO: Ask the question: Was the experience or event inside my personal Universe—the jurisdiction of my Agency, my choice, my Liberty bank account or my control? Or was it within the Agency and Control of someone else? (If the experience was not inside my Agency then it's none of my business because there's nothing I have the right to do about it.)

STEP THREE: Ask yourself whether or not there is anything that you can presently do to correct or change your involvement in the experience.

STEP FOUR: If the answer is 'Yes,' then do that for which you consider yourself responsible.

STEP FIVE: If the answer is still that you can do nothing or you have already done all that falls within your responsibility, the Past, at least as it pertains to this experience, no longer exists.

STEP SIX: Write down your decision.

Will you understand and accept the fact that the past no longer exists? Or will you choose to recreate it by replaying the memory over and over again, beating yourself up and adjusting your memory downward—all over something that no longer exists? Think about it.

— The Guardian

"There you have it: The formula for working through experiences in your life that you need to resolve, so you can get over this and on with experiencing the joy you came here to have.

"We have emotional ties to all experiences. When they are stressful, we have a tendency to stuff them into our subconscious and even forget them. So many of the facts surrounding those experiences are then abandoned. And in these cases, we just have a funny, gnawing feeling when something reminds us of the *Items* held at the less-than-conscious level.

"Another interesting filter that connects the mind with the hand holding the pen is that remembrances can be drawn back into our awareness. The reason for all this is that the emotional filter allows our mind to be unthreatened by the feelings that caused us to 'stuff' the information away from conscious awareness in the first place. Calling information back into awareness through writing enables us to bring up the question as to whether anything can be done about the experience. We can subsequently follow the procedure of choosing no longer to create that episode and erase that portion of the past from existence.

"If we have an uncomfortable feeling, we can begin to write down the facts and feel the physical process start to free us from the very emotions that have shut us down. We'll be able to bring un-remedied information up in front of us and clear it out so that it no longer affects us without our realizing it. Often other events will be dredged up along with the ones we're working on. So, very often, memories that we might not have even been aware of before are also brought up and swept away at the same time as the ones that we believed caused these emotions to rise up in the first place.

"The beautiful thing about this technique is that it can be done in the privacy of your own mind. Solitude is a teacher, no doubt. But there are several factors you have to take into consideration to see this concept work.

"We've often heard that confession is good for the soul. When you hear that, you have to ask, why? Would it be that, when we describe a 'sin' or transgression to a priest, a minister, a counselor, a spouse or friend that we have a similar experience to that of writing it? The idea behind confession (or counseling, if you prefer) is that we're opening the book, and we're getting it out. We're not trying to soften the blow to the ego. People are often able to be more open and candid with others than they are with themselves. The procedure followed by any good counselor would be to ask: 'How do you feel about that?'"

The Guardian continued, "The next question that same counselor might ask would be: 'What can you do about it?' And if the answer is 'nothing', the next question logically has to be whether or not you choose to let it sit in the back of your mind and fester? And guess what? The confessor, priest, friend, or counselor has just allowed you to do the only thing that can be done: *work out your own problem.* And by doing that, he's allowed your Agency to take over, because the choice is now yours to make. You see, Michael, no one can really ever do anything for us or to us. We have total Control over how we allow ourselves to be affected by anyone or anything outside of our own intelligence.

"Can we see a parallel here with writing the facts about uncomfortable experiences, then asking ourselves whether or not we have a choice regarding the issues? If we do, we have to ask ourselves if there's anything we can do about the situation. Then we can take action. *We do what can be done. We decide whether or not we're going to allow a situation that no longer exists to continue affecting us.* The only difference, it would seem, in keeping our own confidence through writing and questioning is a reduced tendency to water down the facts in order to look good to the confessor or counselor. (Some folks may water down the facts to look good to themselves. It's probably okay to do so. If the past no longer exists, it possibly makes no difference whether we tell the truth to ourselves as long as we accept the fact that this past experience no longer has any kind of a hold on us.)

"*Decision* is an interesting concept. It has a tremendous impact on the mind: the two things people have more trouble doing than anything else in this life is to think and to decide. When the human mind finally comes to a decision it soon becomes very calm and peaceful. Most people will experience a sense of calmness even when the decision is scary."

After a pause, the Guardian continued. "A good example of this comes when you buy a home. When you're deciding between two possibilities it's usually very stressful. People tend to gather more and more facts and get additional opinions in hopes that, through information and insights of others, the right decision will become an obvious no risk issue—a 'no-brainer.' The same thing happens when you're shopping for a new car…as we discussed in The Law of Creation. We price-shop. (That's what people do when they know little or nothing about the product they're considering, hoping that even though they may not get the right car, they'll at least be getting a good deal).

"Why do we go through this misery? We simply don't want to make a mistake. Our parents, our teachers, our preachers, our spouses, our bosses, and our self-images have told us not to do anything stupid. 'Don't make mistakes…don't screw up.'

"And yet errors in decisions are just a part of the process of living. To be alive is to learn by doing. And yet everyone seems terrified of being accused of being stupid. So they just don't do anything at all. (And how 'stupid' is that?)

"The last thing people want to hear from a friend is that they 'could have gotten that for $2,500 less on the Internet.' (The subtext for this is that they messed up, that they paid too much, that they 'got taken.' But it happens. And when it does, the best thing to do is own up to it: *take Responsibility for it*. Laugh it off, if you can, and move on.) "Decisions are invariably dealing with fear of the unknown. And yet it's a fact that for the peace and tranquility of the mind, a poor or wrong decision is much better than no decision. Why do we get caught in the grip of fear about making the wrong decision? It all comes down to the word, G-U-I-L-T. If we make the wrong decision, we feel guilty about it. So we sit in *Judgment* on ourselves for a while."

"I'm starting to see the pattern here," Michael admitted.

"And how each of these facets fit into one another," The Guardian added. "When it comes to experiencing the Past as well as the very brief Present, we use written therapy after we've broken everything down into tiny non-threatening pieces, and we're dealing with pure unemotional facts, it becomes an almost exhilarating experience to realize that we can't really mess up; it's just a part of the process.

"So when the last question comes, as we work through an event that troubles us, it speaks to us in a brand new language: *What is my decision as to whether I choose to recreate that which does not exist so I can beat myself up for the rest of my life, or to make a lovely 'no-brainer' decision?*

"When we ask ourselves that question—when we break it all down into small pieces and put pen to paper—the decision becomes a deliciously obvious one. *We can be right every single time.* Even though our experience from the Past tells us that some decisions would not be ideal, this one is always perfect.

"So by using that little 59¢ pen and getting it all down in front of us, we have retaken Control of our Agency, and we can say, 'I have taken back my Liberty, my Freedom of mind, and my Spirit.'

"Once you can do that, Michael, you never again have to be controlled by things that no longer exist. And you can truly begin your life with new opportunities that you never quite allowed yourself to have. (Are you writing this all down?)"

CHAPTER 23

Justice Versus ... "Just Is"

"God grant me the serenity to accept the things I cannot change, the courage to change the things I can, and the wisdom to know the difference."

— Reinhold Niebuhr

"Basically, *The Law of Justice has to do with Control*," The Guardian announced. "And I know the minute I say that, it becomes the elephant in the room. That's because the word, control, implies all kinds of things, both positive and negative."

"You said that justice in the case of natural or universal law 'just is'," Michael reminded him. "It's a law like gravity is a law. Like death and taxes are considered inevitable—that kind of thing."

"And so it is," The Guardian agreed. "It's the same way with control. There are basically two aspects to control: 1) things over which you have no control, and 2) things over which you have complete control. The real truth, Michael, is that ultimately we may take control of the effect of everything that happens to us by aligning ourselves with the natural or universal laws we have been discussing. We just need to recognize that responsibility—the sooner the better.

"Let's take the present subject for example: Justice. It is generally assumed that when you say the word 'justice' that it means fairness in how you are dealt with in relationships and circumstances. The picture most people have in their mind is the statue on the courthouse steps of a woman who is blindfolded holding the 'scales of justice' in her hand. (A woman is a nurturing figure. The blindfold implies lack of prejudicial influence that could victimize you. And the scale represents the measuring or 'balancing,' implying giving fair weight to both sides as a third-party judgment [outside of either position] of fairness.) This is obviously the first aspect of Justice. The laws here are usually man-made laws of society and may or may not be in accord with natural or universal laws. Once you seek *this* justice you relinquish control of the outcome and can only hope that the judgment is fair. (It is interesting that the language often used for the defendant or the plaintiff is to *'pray'* for the court's consideration.)

"For you Michael, as a gloriously empowered human being, the second aspect of justice, things over which you have complete control, is extremely exciting. All of these laws that we are learning and understanding are just simple truth. When you correctly align yourself with one of these natural or universal laws the result you get *'just is,'* giving you the benefits and results the law provides. You will have just applied a tool and taken control of your life. (So in effect you have 'self-inflicted' justice.)"

The Guardian continued: "Let me give you an example. The law in this case is gravity. (We could use any of the laws, like The Law of Me, 'to know me is to love me,' 'the past doesn't exist,' 'the magic of faultlessness,' or any of the others; but you understand gravity, having experienced the bumps and scrapes of its absolute truthfulness.)

"There once was a stubborn man who loved to sit in the shade of a large rock that was hanging from a rope. One day he called to a master, who was walking along a path nearby, 'See how wise I am to find this comfortable place to sit in the shade of this big rock, protected from the scorching heat of the sun?' The master smiled and said, 'Yes, I see you are very wise, but there is a law that *when the rope breaks, the rock will surely fall.* The rope is already starting to give way. If you are truly wise, you will move before the rope breaks.'

"The man pondered this. 'I don't want to move. This is my place. I found it. I have a right to be here. I have come here to sit many times and the rock hasn't fallen yet. Surely God will not let the rock fall on me.' Having thus comforted himself with what he wanted to make the law become, he decided to exercise Faith that the law would not apply to him. After all, 'all things are possible to him that believeth.' *Then the rope broke.*

"The reason that I prefer the words 'just is' to the word *justice*, for the power and control you are learning for your life, is that once a truth (a law) is stated, it's absolute—no matter what your opinion, attitude, or thoughts about it are. You can agree or disagree with it. It makes no difference. You can prove logically how wrong and unfair you think the law is. It makes no difference," said The Guardian. He added, "You don't even have to understand it because it 'just is.' (However, if you do understand it, your capacity to apply it and align with it improves considerably.)

"What I'm talking about is that by learning and aligning with these natural laws you use choices over which you have control to empower your life and gain the wisdom to be unencumbered by that over which you have no control. In short you control the impact on your life of the things over which you have no control by correctly applying the principles of these personal empowerment laws, which are absolute and predictable."

You can ensure "Justice" in your life by applying the law that "just is." Think about it.

— The Guardian

The Guardian continued: "For example, there are a lot of people in the country who are deeply concerned about weather and 'climate change.' They claim that things are more complicated and challenging than they've been in 200 years with the potential for every imaginable calamity—from crop failures to population growth and shortages. They also acknowledge the fact that this worries them. They worry for their families. They're concerned about ETE (End of Time Events) coming out of every book of prophecy from *Nostradamus* and many other prognosticators to *Bible Revelations* to *The Mayan Calendars* describing time up through the year 2012.

"A lot of other people are concerned with what's happening to our food supply. Our factory farms are churning out GMO (genetically modified organism) foods, and a lot of groups are concerned that they may be harmful to us. We have contamination in our water supply. And every conceivable protein source either has toxins such as mercury and lead or some kind of growth hormone. And if these challenges aren't enough, people grow concerned about the global financial crisis, the corruption on Wall Street, or the highly toxic home buyers' market and fears that a recession may meltdown into a global depression.

"People who dwell in certain parts of the world live in constant fear of tidal waves, earthquakes, and floods. We get inklings everywhere about shortages in the water supply, the loss of glacial mass, acid rain, and statistics showing that our polar caps are melting. Some people actually fret over the fact that this earth's tectonic plates are shifting, and our planet Earth will actually go flying off its axis someday soon.

"Most of the time when the subject of environmental threats are brought up to us, *most* people never really know what's happening for sure, and as long as all these forces of man and Nature aren't touching them directly, they aren't a part of their immediate circle of concern."

Michael considered this and said, "It's easy to get depressed or become daunted by all the things in life that could happen, any one of which could alter the course of your life from that day for ward. There's no way to control any of them. So what I really need to deal with are the things I can control—like earning a living, providing for my family, having loving, productive relationships, and all that small stuff that is so important to us little human beings."

The Guardian smiled a little bit and said, "I know you're being flip about this, when it really concerns you. But you know what? You should be able to handle every bit of this quite easily. When you think about it, all you've asked for is a personal solution to all of the problems that could possibly face the human race for the next five centuries or so."

"Now, who's being ironic?"

"I do understand what you're saying, Michael. The future is uncertain. And there's a lot of information out there that points to the fact that just about any decision you make could be wrong.

"So here's what I suggest you do. Sit down and make a list of everything that you've been concerned about. (If you're worried about food shortages or water contamination, put those on your list. If you've got concerns about the coming financial crisis, write that down.)

"Let's cite some examples: If you live in a certain part of the country, you might be wiped out by a storm. Your house just might flow down a mud slide into the ocean. You could build your home near the edge of the woods and watch a forest fire turn all your dreams into charcoal. In fact there are so many things that could happen, it's humanly impossible to plan for everything.

"You may not have control over whether you're hit by a hurricane, or the economy has a hiccup. But you have total control over how you allow these things to affect you and your family.

"One of the items of concern to you might be water contamination, either through constant pollution of our water ways or an event-induced toxification of our underground aquifers. Obviously, you can't control what's happening underground. But you can make sure your family is provided for by having your own ad-hoc water supply, stores of water, and by setting up your own advanced system of filters. Having done one or both of these things, you have the solution to the problem. And if you have the solution, it's no longer a problem.

The extent to which you are dependent is the extent to which you have given power over yourself to that upon which you depend. Every single fear known to man is prompted by a threat to some dependency. Independence, freedom and fearlessness result from taking control of the threat and its attending dependency. Think about it.

— The Guardian

The Guardian continued, "An example of a very deep concern is one that affects and secretly terrifies us all: financial downturns in our lives. Usually it happens in one of two ways. First is the most common—when we get laid off, fired, or forced into early retirement. For this, the solution is simple and essential. Plan ahead. Save and invest your money and have at least a six months to two or more years of bridge income set aside (depending on your chosen level of security) to allow you to keep your home, your essentials and provide for your family.

> *The majority of people, unfortunately, have gotten away from the tried and true financial principles of living within their incomes and saving a small portion no matter how meager their means. (There is also a universal law called The Law of the Tenfold Return [referred to as tithing in many spiritual belief systems] which would be worthy of investigation by anyone concerned with concepts of abundance and prosperity.) Think about it.*
>
> — The Guardian

"Another more extreme cause of concern for a growing number of people is the possibility of a complete financial collapse of the global economy followed by everything from massive unemployment to food shortages. For these, you also need to have adequate reserves of emergency food supplies, potable water, and possibly even a safe place for you and your family to live for a while.

"Think about it, Michael. In all of these examples, haven't you found a way to take back control over your circumstances?"

"As much as anyone can," Michael answered. "But what if you wake up in the middle of an earthquake, and your house is being broken into pieces? Even if you have insurance, you never get back everything you've lost."

"Then you're at a crossroads," said The Guardian. "You can quit, cry and play the victim. Or you can just pick yourself up and start all over. And sometimes, you end up better off for it.

"A classic example would be the 'victims' of Hurricane Katrina in New Orleans. Many people, those who got wiped out by the Hurricane packed up what they had left, moved away and never came back again. Many others picked themselves up, rebuilt and stayed on as a part of the community. (There is no right or wrong choice here. But the fact remains that you always have a choice about what to do with your life, and those who plan ahead are those who not only survive but have the quickest recovery to get on with their lives.)

Being wise and well prepared can turn a disaster into an adventure. Think about it.

— The Guardian

"It's a vast, random universe out there, Michael, and there's so much of life around us over which we have no control. But you have total control over how you let yourself be affected. When the patriot Patrick Henry said, 'Give me liberty, or give me death,' he was talking about more than his Agency. He was talking about the fact that, without liberty, without that ability to control our lives, living becomes a slow kind of dying."

Debt, the death of liberty

"Liberty is of extreme importance and is essential to the ability to choose how our lives are affected. Every debt we acquire irrevocably commits the portion of our Life-energy necessary to generate payment until the debt is paid.

"Our freedom to choose how that committed piece of our life is used is subtracted from each day's life value. (An example: If you have a house payment of $1,000 per month with an hourly income of $10 and you work an average of 22 days a month. After two hours of your work day has been subtracted for taxes, four and a half hours of every day you work will be subtracted from your life, for the house payment, over which you have given or traded away your choice of control," said The Guardian.

Very simply, with every debt, you literally give away a piece of your life. It would be wise to ask yourself, "Is that sound system, fancy car or too expensive home worth the chunk of my life I am trading for it?" Think about it.

— The Guardian

The Guardian continued, "When you think about it, debt is a kind of death. The bondage that so many people put themselves into with debt, dependency and fear of an uncertain future allows them no liberty. In fact, do they even have a life? There's already a lot in the adventure of daily living that we can't control. The important thing is to gain command over everything that we can.

"Abe Lincoln once said: 'Most people are about as happy as they decide to be.' The good news, Michael, is that the decision is up to you. You can choose to be happy. You can choose to take control.

"So what it all comes down to, Michael, is that you have one of two ways to go about anything. You can recognize that there are life experiences, conditions, and forces of Nature, over which you have no control. And there are those facets to your life over which you have complete control. (Remember that you have the ability to manage the impact on you of everything in your life and complete responsibility for doing something about it.)"

"So…" Michael paused to think about it.

"So now make *two lists,*" Michael. "The *first list,* as I mentioned earlier, would include everything over which you have no control: death, taxes, gravity, natural disasters, catastrophic illness, war, global environmental meltdowns, food shortages, water contamination, car crashes, corporate cutbacks and being New Orleans, or under the Volcano in Hilo, Hawaii).

"After you list these things, add a sub category of things that you can do to plan for them if they do occur. For example: If you live in California, have earthquake and fire insurance. If you're in a career choice that has high attrition (such as advertising, entertainment or overlarge corporations), set up at least two years of gap savings to see you through the tough times. If you're living in some place dangerous, reassess your need to be there. And if it's a regular distraction, move to some place that's less stressful for you and your family.

"The author and philosopher Aldous Huxley once said, 'Experience is not what happens to a man, it's what he does with what happens to him.' So this first segment of the Law of Justice is accepting that all this 'just is' and doing something about it.

"*List number two* should be easier for you, Michael, because it includes all those things over which you not only have control but also for which you have great responsibility.

"Your income planning, your retirement planning, your kids' education, hospitalization, housing, food, insurance coverage for cars, homes, and family health matters—these are all your basics, and every smart adult can and should have these covered.

"The other aspect to this list is a bit more subtle but no less important. That has to do with who you want to be as a human being: your health, your weight, your fitness, your relationships with friends and family, involvement in your community, what you can do to make the world a better place, personal skills you've always wanted to acquire, higher education, languages, ways to be more romantic with your significant other, ways you can make every moment with everyone a better experience.

"This is where you get to apply the other universal laws, Michael: like *The Laws of Me, Agency, and Justice.* Because by now you're beginning to understand that what you choose to do here can affect everything and everyone around you. The great news is that *you get to become the master of your fate* in all of this."

> The above-mentioned lists are handled for you *perfectly* in *My Book of Life*, a target, objective and goal achievement companion journal to *THE GUARDIAN CODE: It 's Not Your Fault* textbook of educational curriculum by The Guardian.

"So, by making these lists and completing them, I'm designing my life," Michael said. "That means I'm building my realities. I'm a partner in creating everything that happens to me. So, by definition, I'm putting the Law of Creation into effect. Am I not?"

"Part of it," The Guardian confirmed. "See! That's why we do these things in the order we do them. Each one is a step leading to the next. But you couldn't even think about being a cocreator in your life without doing a little house-cleaning first. So start making your list and checking it twice…"

"And when I do, does that mean I get to move on to the *Law of Creation?*" Michael asked.

It was a question to which The Guardian could only smile. "Coming soon to a lifetime near you!"

CHAPTER 24

The Law of Creation
You think it. You see it. You be it. You've GOT it!

"The Fourth Universal Law, *The Law of Creation*, works from one spiritual/physical base of power: *Every thought creates itself.* That means everything you think is created—even the uncreated!" The Guardian announced. "You can create anything or any event in your life if you hold it in your mind. In the same way, you can eliminate [or uncreate] negative thoughts and experiences by allowing them to dissipate and vanish from your consciousness.

As you study the depths of creative philosophy within the major comprehensive belief systems of mankind you will discover a concept held in common between them. It is that "all things are created spiritually before they are create temporally." Think about it.

— The Guardian

"There's just one restriction on your powers of creation. *You can't infringe upon anyone else's Agency.* Their freedom of choice is as integral to them as yours is to the definition of who you are. So you need to value and respect their agency (freedom to choose) as much as you do your own."

"Sounds a lot like the Golden Rule," Michael noted.

"Everything worthwhile does," The Guardian answered. "The main issue here is to remember to apply it to yourself.

"Let me give you an example: It's not appropriate to try to use your creative power to make a certain person marry you. It's perfectly correct for you to draw up the specifications for your perfect mate and 'create' that person right into your life. Leave a little open-mindedness and trust in your creative abilities. Most of your creations will come out a lot better than you might imagine.

"There are a couple of things about the Law of Creation that most people need to get, but very often they don't. Here's one of them: *The conscious and the subconscious are one mind.* The conscious consists of thoughts upon which one's attention is concentrated. The subconscious consists of all those thoughts accumulated since the beginning of the intelligence upon which the attention is not focused. Unfortunately, even though the attention is not on the subconscious thoughts, they continue their part in the process of creation. Since Nature abhors a vacuum, as the mind grows still, subconscious thoughts will come to the surface.

"Understand, Michael, that no thoughts go to waste. And what helps to build our creative platform is the realization that all other laws build up to The Law of Creation. The Law of Me teaches us to evaluate everything relative to how it makes us feel about…us! So if failure makes you feel bad about yourself, and success makes you feel good about who you are, there can ultimately only be one thought: that of Creation. Anything else that takes you away from your ability to create becomes an infringement upon your *Agency*. And that *just is* the way things are.

"Anything that takes away from your ability to create also creates an energy of its own called un-creation. When you un-create, it is almost always the result of Guilt, Fear, Doubt, and Judgment that is taking hold in your life. And all these things work to pull you off your purpose."

"Then un-creation is a kind of creation as well," Michael said, giving the concept some thought.

"You're never 'not creating,' Michael," The Guardian answered. "The good news is that you can un-create the negative thoughts literally by removing them from your conscious mind by shifting your mind into neutral and not giving them the energy of thought. That's when un-creation actually becomes a good force that can work for you, because by clearing out the clutter you can get very single minded. Most truly successful people get single minded about what they want to accomplish in life. Some folks call that ruthless. Others recognize it as being focused. (Remember, it's only 'ruthless' or cruel if it infringes on someone else's Agency.)

"When Jesus Christ turned water into wine, he went into the one mode in his mind where the Law of Creation was all that existed. There was no discussion of Guilt or application of 'theory.' The water was just wine. There was no element of Doubt; no question as to whether this creation would work or not. Jesus already saw it as being done, and so it was.

"Most people make too much work of the Law of Creation. First they have to release all thoughts of un-creation. That means eliminating past experience, because if the past does not exist, all memory of failure or emotional debate will disappear.

Maybe the counsel to 'become as little children,' when applying the necessary belief for creation is a valid perception that innocence of a negative history will spawn no doubt of a perfect outcome. Think about it.

— The Guardian

"Even the act of speaking or writing becomes difficult for some people, Michael, because people are constantly evaluating whether or not this sentence or that is going to make the speech hit home or put the main thought of the book across to the reader. Constant evaluation brings doubt into the process and, along with it, thoughts of embarrassment, loss and humiliation. So the past plants seeds of failure. And failure becomes an alternative because we have created that option in our minds.

"One of the biggest challenges to the Law of Creation comes when people are trying to make money or get funding for something. People literally un-create their potential for getting money or building wealth by remembering past loss or by trying to force the issue of funding. That kind of 'experience' thinking keeps most folks out of the one Creative Law. Creating or recreating unhappiness from the past is re-treading the previous experience. (It brings up feelings of embarrassment, failure, and loss.) So the people involved end up trying to force a specific result. And that act of forcing results is bound to land smack in the middle of someone's Agency. So what we are thinking, in these cases brings up so much from the past that we create a framework for limitation—every problem, every blockage, every legal entanglement, every fear, and disappointment.

"What people need to do is release all feelings of concern about where the funds come from. That means allowing the law of pure potential to take hold, and that includes for ward thinking in ways that will keep the mind out of the past."

"Then is the mind the enemy?" Michael asked.

"Only if it's still dwelling in the past," The Guardian answered. "And I'm the first to acknowledge, Michael, that it's much easier to talk about leaving the past behind than it is to actually do it.

"Still, that's the whole idea of the Law of Creation. Remember, 'As a man thinketh, so he becomes.' We know that 'thought creates things.' If those things we are going to create are to be perfect manifestations of the Law they should come without baggage. That means all thought has to be for ward. *Forward thinking is the secret.* And if it's left unshackled it will bring us every physical reality we ever wanted in our life. And the Law of Creation goes beyond just stuff. You can create your own realities—every goal and objective—jobs, dream places to live, ideal relationships, a better world."

"There are limits to what I can do physically," Michael insisted. "If you say so," the Guardian replied.

"I mean, I can't bend the steel and turn the bolts to create a Corvette."

"You probably could if you really set your mind to it. But the truth is you don't need to. You're a more powerful creator than that. You think the thought, and all the details are handled in the automation of your creation. You either create what you want in your life or allow it to happen, by default (which is not something I recommend).

"Let's take a simple example of the Law of Creation, and one that is actually within most folks range of accomplishment—buying a car.

"Let's say you just made the decision to get a car. Some folks choose the make, model, color, engine, upholstery, comfort system, sound system, and wheel covers. Then they visualize that particular vehicle in their lives until it manifests. That's called creating what you want in your life.

"Unfortunately, people often envision what they want, then turn right around and buy a car by default. You check the Internet and the paper. Then you hit a few dealerships. You find a salesman you can stand. He asks, "How can I help you?" And the insanity begins. You try to sound like you're a well-informed, know-exactly-what-you-want buyer. (So don't mess with me with your sales techniques.)

"You also must broadcast a very important message to this guy on the other side of the table—Leroy, the car salesman. That's because right now, he's trying to fit you into the fluorescent pea green (Army fire engine colored) one-and-a-half ton, two-wheel drive, three-on-the-tree underpowered pickup with the mini compact car engine that somehow slipped through engineering specs and onto the showroom floor. To juice up the matter even further, it's last year's model, so Leroy's going to make you a 'deal.'

"You kind of like the notion of a pickup, even though it wasn't what you came in for, and you somehow manage to get yourself talked into buying it, mainly because you don't have a clue about what a pickup truck really needs to put it at the top of the line. But the whole thing comes down to price, and you've just been convinced that you got yourself a super-bargain, when it was something you never wanted in the first place. Welcome to living by default. (It might not be all that bad. You never know when the Army might need someone who has an Army fire engine-colored pea green truck with just enough power to coast downhill with the critical five gallons of water needed to finish off the last smoldering embers of a burned out emergency road flare.)

"So rather than that dream car you've always wanted, you end up with somebody else's castoff creation, a definite lemon, and a classic case of buyer's remorse."

"So that's my creation? I can do better than that! You say every thought creates itself," Michael confirmed.

"That's right," The Guardian answered. "It also means taking responsibility for what you're thinking. If people could read each other's thoughts what a different world it would be. A lot of guys who couldn't find the Law of Creation with a GPS would spend half their day getting slapped by pretty women who overheard what they were thinking."

"But by now I do have at least a basic understanding of the Law of Creation," Michael announced. "So, for those of us who do, why don't we have perfect relationships, dozens of fancy cars, two or three homes, millions of dollars, and no problems in our lives?"

"Do you recall that I said 'All thoughts aren't themselves'?" The Guardian asked. "More or less, yeah," Michael remembered.

"That's because some thoughts and the people who think them are what I call un-creators," The Guardian said. "People so often start out with specific goals and dreams in mind, and then almost immediately fall off the path with doubt, fear, second-guessing and that dirty demon of denial from the past called 'rationalization.' That's because, even though all thoughts aren't themselves, all thoughts do create themselves."

"So what's the difference?" Michael asked.

"Let me give you an example, Michael. Do you remember when you were driving past the Auto Mall last week?"

"I do."

"Remember the brand new black Corvette the lot attendant was just pulling onto the showroom floor?"

"I sure do. It was something special." "Tell me all the thoughts you had."

"It was really sharp —state of the art. I thought about how nice it would be to own it. I wondered what it would be like to drive up to my house and take my sweetheart for a ride. I thought about how my friends at work would react to it. Mostly though, I just felt the rush I would have from owning it."

"Were those all your thoughts?"

"I think so. Nothing else comes to mind."

"If I'm right here, if every thought creates itself—and every one of yours becomes reality—how come you're not driving that black beauty?"

"I don't know. If your Law of Creation is really accurate, all those thoughts should get it for me, unless…there's a flaw in the Law."

"The Law of Creation, like all the universal laws, is flawless, Michael. So, you need to do some scrolling back into your mental Rolodex, and when you do, you'll realize that you just left out some very important thoughts. So let's take a closer look at some of them and see what we come up with. There was a guy standing at the side when 'your car' was being parked. What was he doing?"

Michael had to think about it for a moment, then he remembered.

"Probably waiting until he could take a closer look, get in, and see what it feels like to sit in the drivers' seat," he said.

"So what did you think?" The Guardian asked.

"I was a little jealous."

"No, I mean physically—did you feel a little queasy? Maybe more like a kind of nostalgia?"

"Come to think of it, I did," Michael recognized. "It did seem kind of goofy for me to do that."

"Not at all," The Guardian corrected. "I call it 'window-shopperitis!' And it's a passive form of depression. Folks come down with it when they think about something they would like to have but at the same time think the hopeless thoughts that they can't get it. So…tell me your hopeless thoughts, Michael."

"I knew I couldn't fit the payments for that lovely toy into our budget," Michael admitted. "So I resented the fact that the guy kicking the tires could."

"At least you assumed he could," The Guardian noted.

"Yeah. I felt crummy about my employment and thought my income wasn't up to the challenge. There were a lot of things we needed and bills that I had to pay before I could feel the least bit good about this executive toy. Besides, the 'Vette' is very definitely a two-seater. So it's not much different than having a motorcycle for a family car. I don't have the cash. So I'd have to make payments. No way! In fact, I probably couldn't even afford the insurance."

"Okay, that's enough!" The Guardian said. "In fact you've made up enough excuses to un-create just about anything. Don't get me wrong. It's nothing unique. We see these 'contra thoughts' all over the place.

"As soon as you said: 'I can't believe it's possible based on my past experiences,' you'd already lost it. These, Michael, are only the thoughts that you are consciously aware of. Frankly, you have ten times as many thoughts and feelings that you've stuffed out of sight, out of mind, and into your subconscious. And even though you've logged them away somewhere in your memory, these thoughts exist just as powerfully.

"The most powerful thoughts are often those we have stored away in our subconscious. They're stuffed away there because they're not very nice to us. They don't make us like ourselves better, so we hide them. And yet the fact that we hide them won't make them go away. Sometimes they just sit there in the deep recesses of our mind, building muscles and getting stronger. So, when you get down to it there's only one of two things you can do with them. First, you can try to ignore them. (And that just doesn't work, I can tell you.) Or, number two, you can learn how to defuse them and turn them into creators that actually work for you. (We'll get to that in a minute.)

There is a really simple trick to bypassing the un-creating, negative conscious thoughts and the reverse feelings that bubble up from the subconscious. When you set a goal or objective, visualize and think only of what you desire and why you want it. Never give any thought to how or whether you will obtain the objective. The universe is much more capable than you are of figuring out how to fill your needs. Don't fumble around and get in the way of your own creation because "How" thinking is a petri dish for growing the slime of doubt and depression, the great un-creators. Don't work so hard. Learn to sit back and enjoy the magnificence of your power to create. Think about it.

— The Guardian

"First, let me answer your questions about why you don't have abundance by the ton raining down on you at this point in your life.

"The answer is obvious, Michael, in your thoughts about the Corvette. Look at the number and power of the thoughts that started creating your ownership of the car. (Did you see yourself closing the deal? Did you envision it in your garage or yourself behind the wheel?) Then look at the 'un-creator' thoughts that you inadvertently generated. When you do, I think you're going to see that you undid it even faster than you did it.

"If you want to know how things work in the Law of Creation, well here it is: *Those who are successful and prosperous think more significant thoughts that create than thoughts that un-create.* And truly powerful people have cultivated focused, positive, creative thinking into an art form; virtually no negative thoughts creep into their mind, and if they do they're treated with the same kind of dismissal as a sneeze.

"Some people are about average in their joy, status and prosperity of life. They not only think a lot of creator thoughts, but also think about an equal number of thoughts that un-create. So they tend to cancel each other out.

"People who fail simply un-create more than they create. In fact, they are so good at un-creating they have all but lost the ability to create anything but failure, disappointment and defeat."

If every thought creates, it can be concluded that everyone creates and un-creates constantly. The difference between success and failure is the determination to simply create more than is uncreated. Think about it.

— The Guardian

"So, they're failures," Michael added.

"Only if they quit," The Guardian corrected. "As long as there is hope and a desire to make changes, success is always an option. They just need to learn How Things Really Work. The question is: Have you learned?"

"I'm getting there."

"Good! Getting there is half the fun. Just remember that virtually all the Universal Laws apply to everything you do. And knowing what they are and how they work is the secret to taking responsibility for everything in your life."

"So, does anyone ever reach a level of complete mastery?" Michael asked.

"Not a large number, but more than most folks would imagine," The Guardian answered. "Complete mastery is perfection. Perfection in the human arena is a difficult challenge; and perfectionists who don't understand how things work as I am teaching you are almost always miserable. Successful people know that and just do the best they can until they are ready for their next teacher to appear.

"The multi-millionaire who runs an international corporation and owns cars, homes, and all kinds of things that money can buy may *probably* need to work on his 'creation' level with his wife and kids. He may need to spend more time with them, be a wonder hugger, and a more compassionate, considerate husband and father.

Fear of perfection, or our inability to achieve it, is one of the principal blocks to understanding the Law of Creation and applying it. People can't seem to get it that failure is just a stepping-stone to success. Many get so frozen with fear that they just don't try at all. The best remedy for that is just to do simple things first. Set small goals and objectives, and once you've mastered those, you can move on to something bigger and better. Remember one of the Four Agreements (by Don Miguel Ruiz) is: 'Just do your best.' The rest will follow.

— The Guardian

"A man who is great with his own family may need to work on his people skills with his coworkers or get his act together financially. People are all pursuing their self prescribed educational process to get better, and by learning the Four Universal Laws, they can.

"Hall of Fame football coach Vince Lombardi once said, 'Perfection is impossible. But on the way to seeking it, we can capture excellence.' And isn't that what makes life worth living? (That's an answer, not a question.)"

> **The Four Agreements** are based on the Ancient Toltec *Wisdom Book* and yet include lessons in conduct that very much apply today:
> 1) be impeccable to your word;
> 2) never take anything personally;
> 3) never make assumptions;
> 4) just do your best.

Once you reach a certain level of understanding about the Law of Creation, you get to realize that every thought you have creates... something. So it's important to release all negativity and blockages in your life—every negative thought, every notion of rejection, failure and especially Guilt. One of the best ways to do that is through meditation. And three times daily is recommended. Most of us have about 18 waking hours in our average day. If you take about half an hour three times every day to get still, clear the clutter from your mind and get in touch with what Abraham Lincoln once called 'The Better Angels of our nature,' you'll be amazed at what you can actually create. Some people might call that making contact with the Holy Spirit. You may call it what you like. The secret lies in trusting the good forces in your life and allowing them to come in. And don't feel guilty about the feelings of joy and fulfillment you get when you do. Instead, start out with a profound sense of Gratitude for everything that you have. Life is a gift. Celebrate that gift. And don't forget to say "Thank you." Think about it.

— The Guardian

CHAPTER 25

Goals and Objectives: The Power of Faith

Visualization, Spiritual Creation and other Important Things

"The important thing, Michael, is to recognize that opportunities are everywhere," The Guardian announced. "Once you've applied the Four Universal Laws, they open up horizons of opportunity like the one you see before you. The secret comes in learning how to take advantage of them. And the best way to do that is to recognize what you want and go for it."

"But what if you want something really big, something that's such a huge dream it almost scares you to think about it?" Michael asked.

"How do you eat a hippopotamus?" The Guardian asked, reminding Michael of their earlier conversations.

"One bite at a time," Michael remembered.

"And you do that by setting down a list of goals and objectives, and having the faith (deciding) to follow through with them."

"Follow through…" Michael thought about it. "One can only hope…"

"Not hope, Michael, Faith!" The Guardian corrected. "Hope, as we have mentioned, is a passive word. Faith is not passive—it's active. Hope has wishful expectation. *Faith has decision and intention.* And intention is where accomplishment begins…"

"But not ends," Michael interrupted.

"Agreed!" The Guardian said. "But every great journey begins with the first step. And faith is what causes us to take it.

"The word, Faith, has such power in it, Michael. And yet it is often the most misunderstood and misapplied word in the English language.

"The word itself is a call to action. We often hear such things as the biblical quote: 'Have faith, and faith will be given to you.' Oliver Cromwell, a British military and political leader, encouraged his troops to, 'Put your faith in God (but keep your powder dry).' Faith, in a way, is always a call to Action. Faith puts a pair of pants on hope, and gives it the courage to surge ahead.

"Basically Faith consists of three elements: *1) vision, 2) single-mindedness,* and *3) action.* The first is spiritual, the second is mental, and the third is physical. So Faith is the integration of all three of these things as it guides us to achieve all the things we choose in life. It's important to emphasize all three elements because they are linked in a chain of Responsibility that we all have to accept if Faith is to work at all.

"Examples of Faith and how it drives us to excel always come best in every day life, just as there are examples everywhere of how it might be interpreted incorrectly.

"Take the case of Harry, a man working as a small business entrepreneur, selling door-to-door, an in-home salesman if you will. Harry disliked traveling and all the hard work of finding people to approach. So, he was at home studying the Scriptures when he came across a quote from Matthew 6:28:

> *And why take ye thought of raiment? Consider the lilies of the field, how they grow. They toil not; neither do they spin. And yet I say to you that even Solomon in all his glory was not arrayed like one of these...*

"So it was there that Harry decided, if he was any good at applying this thing called Faith, he should be able to free himself from the distasteful aspects of his chosen profession and dump the Responsibility for sustaining a livelihood for his family on God—saying, in effect, 'It's not my fault' (i.e. Responsibility).

"Unfortunately, Harry made the very common mistake of implementing only the first two aspects of the Faith principle. He had his vision and a focused mind. He even stayed home a couple of weeks to fast and pray, keeping his attention riveted on what he hoped would be the miraculous appearance of the means to sustain his family and pay his obligations. Nothing happened. Why? He had missed, as so many do, the third element of Faith—action.

"After having spiritually and mentally created his objective, Harry had failed to act by placing himself on the path of the avalanche of prosperity he had started to create in his mind. Without the action of searching for the right people, telling them his story and making himself available to write their orders, nothing happened. All the hoping, dreaming and wishing in the world wouldn't move potential customers to seek out his home address in order to mail orders to someone they didn't know for products they had no idea existed.

"The first two elements of Faith—vision and single-mindedness—include the intention of what we want to accomplish. And most people assume that this is where Faith fulfills itself. It's that assumption that leads to the quote that reads,

'The road to hell is paved with good intentions.'

"Faith—of hell-bent intention fame—is the ecclesiastical result of trying to sit on two legs of a three-legged stool. And *that third leg amounts to doing the deed.* Remember that Biblical quote from the book of James: 'But wilt thou know, O vain man, that faith without works is dead?'

"Did the scripture mean that Faith is actually dead? Of course not! Faith doesn't die, but it truly can be stillborn. So it will never express itself if you just sit there thinking about things, and you don't take Action on them. That's because you're mistaking Faith for hope, and they're two entirely different things.

"Remember Faith takes Action. And the Scripture was directed specifically at those misguided with the impression that it's only necessary to hold a beautiful vision of their objective, not allowing their mind to be distracted while sitting in a lawn chair sipping lemonade waiting for a miraculous manifestation. And on their tombstone it shall be written that, 'It's not my fault. I visualized. I concentrated. I prayed. I guess Faith doesn't work.' No, Melba, it's not that your Faith didn't work. It's just that *you* didn't.

A classic case of how Faith really works comes with the story of the man whose house is caught in a flood that virtually engulfs his entire home. Desperately, the man scrambles to his rooftop while the floodwaters come right up to the edge. Sitting on his roof peak, the man puts a prayer up to heaven.

'Dear Lord,' he prays. 'I place my faith in You. I know You will come and save me in my time of peril.' Convinced his prayers have been heard, the man waits for the miracle when a fellow comes along in a motorboat and offers to take him to safety. 'No, thanks,' the man on the roof says. 'I put my prayer to the Lord and He will save me.' So the motorboat motors away, and the man on the roof continues to wait.

A couple of hours later a large rescue barge comes along with hot food and Red Cross relief services and offers to take the man on the roof aboard. 'Oh no thanks,' the man tells the barge Captain. 'I put my prayer to the Lord and He will save me.' By now it's several hours later. The water continues rising, and the man is clinging to his chimney top when a helicopter comes overhead and drops down a ladder. 'Grab hold!' the helicopter pilot calls down to him. 'Oh, no thank you,' the man replies. 'I prayed to the Lord and I know the Lord will save me.' Shortly thereafter the floodwaters rise over the man's whole house. He loses his grip and drowns. But since he's a decent man he goes to heaven. When he gets to the Pearly Gates, he expresses his disappointment to St. Peter that his prayers to God weren't answered, and that he was left to die. Surprised, St. Peter checks his log and says: 'I don't understand. It shows right here that we sent you two boats and a helicopter.' Think about it.

— The Guardian

"The application of only the first two elements of achievement is a common practice that victims use to justify their victimization. They say: 'I see the vision of a better standard of living. My mind is totally focused on a better financial situation.' They think this is where Faith ends. They ignore the requirement that life places upon them to act. Instead, they seem to think that enough of something had been done for them to whine, 'I tried, but nothing happened, It's not my fault.'

"Where most folks seem to drop the ball is the single-mindedness (mental) portion of Faith. Keeping one's eye single to the goal is very much like the horse wearing a bridle with blinders. The blinders are intended to shield the horse's vision from distractions. Originally intended to keep the horse focused on the objective ahead, blinders don't work if the horse is easily distracted. Human beings, it turns out, respond to distractions even more easily than some horses. And yet saying, 'He's wearing blinders,' very often means that someone is unaware of the world around them.

"So the perfect counterpoint to help you perpetuate your 'active' faith is this: *You can fool your mind into doing now what all the experience from the Past says you can't do.* We're going to teach you how to 'con yourself' into success: It's called *The Principle of the Distraction of Action.*

"Perhaps you've tried it yourself, Michael, and might not have even been aware of it."

Michael thought about it for a moment, and realized that he had.

"I think I know what you're talking about," he said. "My first inkling of what you call 'the distraction of action' came while I was a traveling salesman. I checked into a motel in a brand new market one night. I knew no one in the town I'd come to. I needed an income—because like most salesmen dealing with market variances, I was living day-to-day, and occasionally hand-to-mouth. There were some mornings when I'd wake up, look at the tiles on the ceiling of my motel room and wonder what it was going to take to cover the check I'd just written to buy my groceries the day before.

"At that point, my plan was simple: First, I'd get on the telephone and figure out who among the thousands of people in this new market that I was going to call (none of whom I happened to know personally). I knew I had to call enough of them so that I could find the ones who wanted to hear about my product. I had to figure a way to bring up the subject so that someone would want to talk to me.

"Next, I had to figure out how to talk to them in a way that they'd like me, trust me, and begin to trust in what I was telling them. I had to set at least five appointments each evening, working around their schedules of softball games, TV shows, shopping mall binges…whatever. And of those five appointments, I expected at least two of them to fall through. Of the remaining three, one or two might turn into complete presentations. Of those one or two, I had to hope that one might actually be able to afford to make a purchase. (This might not sound like much to some people, but if you've ever been in a sales situation it can be a pretty daunting experience.)

"Many mornings, I'd just lie there in bed. (Many salesmen do that from time to time.) One morning, after a particularly difficult evening, I woke up to a spectacularly beautiful morning, threw back the drapes to my dreary motel room, and looked out at the birds singing and the flowers in bloom and, rather than get caught up in the grind, took off for a brisk half-hour walk. As I did, I noticed that I was able to put my fears, worries, and anxieties on hold and get downright distracted—by life! I was distracted by the trees, the birds, the sunshine, the way the goofy contractors had poured concrete onto the building driveway next door— everything!"

"So what happened next?" The Guardian asked.

"I came back into my room, and just threw myself into calling like crazy," Michael remembered. "And I discovered that as long as I was doing something that was totally focused on the mental portion, step two of the faith principle, being single-minded about what I wanted to accomplish, I didn't get caught up in the 'paralysis of analysis.' I didn't fall prey to the worry, fear, and anxiety of wondering how, why, or when I could do it. I just did it!"

"So what did you learn?" The Guardian asked.

"I learned that just by doing the thing itself, the power will come," Michael answered.

"Then you learned a very important lesson, Michael. Another way of saying it would be that *repetition is the mother of skill*. But it works best if you do it with a new attitude. And that's what the power of focus provides.

"The world of sports is full of examples like this. Babe Ruth, the true home run king of baseball (before juiced balls and juiced players), also holds the record for the most strikeouts. And yet Ruth never let the strikeouts keep him from his main goal—hitting home runs. There were some games in which Ruth would strike out all four times at bat, and yet he never let it keep him from taking full cuts at the ball. And that 'action' was the distraction that kept fear out of the equation.

"Ricky Henderson, the all time base-stealing record holder, also holds the record for the most times being thrown out as a runner. Ricky never thought about being thrown out; the action was the distraction. (In fact, he thought of himself as scoring every time he got on base.) As a result, he was simply the most effective leadoff hitter in the history of the game and rated one of the five most effective ballplayers of all time in Major League Baseball.

"Perhaps the story of English miler Roger Bannister is the most poignant expression of the action/distraction of faith. Born in England in 1929, he was severely burned as a toddler, a disfigurement so severe that physicians of that era gave him virtually no chance of walking normally, much less running at any level of competence.

They knew how to measure physical dynamics but not those of the heart (spirit). In answer to their grim predictions, young Roger began crawling at an early age. He would work his way to a fence in his yard, use his arms to pull himself up onto his feet, then slide along to strengthen the legs that had suffered the brunt of the damage. As the years went by, young Roger learned to walk, then to run, and then to race; not only race, but race magnificently. When he first started, he ran almost incessantly, never once allowing himself to be distracted by the injuries or the medical naysayers and 'sports experts' who wrote that it was physically impossible for any human being to run a mile in under four minutes.

"Soon enough, Bannister ran for his college at Oxford in England and for the English Olympic Team in 1952. Then on May 6, 1954, during a track meet in Oxford, England, Bannister became the first person in history to run a mile in under four minutes, clocking in at 3:59.4. His record was broken one month later by Australian John Landy in a time of 3:58 (3:57.9). And yet it was Bannister who proved his dominance in August 1954 by defeating Landy head-to-head with a winning time of 3:58.8. (Landy, "distracted FROM action," looked back while Bannister passed him on the right.) Dr. Bannister retired from competition in 1955 to practice medicine. And in 1975, he was made Knight Commander of the British Empire by Queen Elizabeth II to become Sir Roger Bannister.

"In each of these examples it all boils down to a simple principle—*single-mindedness, focusing on the goal or objective.* In other words, to exercise Faith you need to get a clear picture of what you're doing, getting it firmly in mind, and then making an unwavering decision to 'just do it.'

"The best way to do that is to make a hand written statement of the goal or objective. (But be careful not to get bogged down in the 'paralysis of analysis' I described earlier.)

The Guardian continued: *"Vision and single-mindedness form the blueprint* for the creation of what is going to happen. The important thing to do at this point, once you've created the moment, is to move on. Do not under any circumstances dwell on the issue so that you have time to 'un-create' whatever wonderful things you've set in motion.

There is a very effective way to eliminate the unwanted in the image of creation. In other words, you can eliminate 'un-creation' before it has a chance to work its wicked little will on your game plan. And you can do that by the following: 1) Distracting–belief in something or someone outside yourself. 2) Psyching oneself up by joining the group dynamic, including prayer, meditation, rallies, meetings and chanting and other means of group expression. Most motivation 'gurus' use this means of meeting and pep-rally gathering to help get people focused. And this is especially effective in sports, using the team concept to get people motivated and focused on the game or event. 3) Eliminating flaws in the picture by releasing the anti-creation images in your success projection.

This third step involves something called "The Steering Wheel Concept of Management." It is very much like the way we drive our car to a destination. We know where we're going, and we know we'll get there. Still, we steer the wheel back and forth across the directional intention of our car through little acts of overcompensation, even as we're guiding our car toward our destination. We already have a perfect understanding of what we want to accomplish. We know we're going to get there. So we don't bother dealing with all the little reasons why it won't happen. Think about it.

— The Guardian

"What many people don't understand is that in the process of 'doing' with the vision and the mindset, they become entitled to receive inspiration in regard to the blank spots of their action plan. Action brings understanding and perfects the plan of achievement. The Action is the distraction from all those elements, those experiences that would otherwise suggest that what we want to accomplish can't be done.

"If we keep our concentration totally on the pros and ignore the cons, is it truly possible for most of us to accomplish great things with amazing speed? The answer is absolutely, yes! But the key lies in sidestepping the negative mental traps all along the way. Think of the quotation from the comic strip Pogo, 'We have met the enemy and they is us.' How many times have we heard winners in many fields of endeavor tell the world that the secrets of their success came with this statement? 'I finally learned to get out of my own way.'

"So, when in doubt as to what to do, the best counsel is to start trusting in the process of doing. It is the third element, and taking Action is the final act of Faith.

"In the film series *Star Wars* the clan of intergalactic knights, The Jedi, become living examples of faith into action. They accomplish their amazing feats as pure spiritual warriors by eliminating mind (and doubt along with it) from the equation of their success.

"In the words of the immortal Jedi master Yoda, as he trains the Padua learner, Luke Skywalker, he admonishes Skywalker to take on the next assignment. The young apprentice replies: 'I'll try.'

"'No!' Yoda answers. 'Do or do not...there is no try.' That is the final leap of Faith."

CHAPTER 26

Failure as the Pathway to Success

"Success is going from failure to failure without a loss of enthusiasm."

— Winston Churchill

"Now that we've come to understand that we're perfect, we're going to take a look at failure," The Guardian announced.

"Wait a minute," Michael balked. "I thought you just said that once we understand the Four Universal Laws, we can't really fail."

"That's true, Michael," The Guardian responded. "I also said if you understand that you are born perfect, failure is not an option. At worst it is the greatest teaching tool that life has to offer. At best, it is merely a postponement of success. Either way you just have to look at it for what it is: a step in the process to perfectly mastering your personal universe.

"The question we want to deal with here is this: Why does the concept of failure terrify so many people? In fact, most folks are paralyzed by it. Some Asian societies teach that it's an almost fatal 'loss of face.' In Japanese culture, failure is such a horrific notion that people in power have committed *hara-kiri* (suicide) over having failed at something—a government, a business, a military campaign, an education, a marriage.

"By the same token someone once said that, 'the only failure is a failure to try.' And they were right. C. S. Lewis noted that, 'Failure is just a signpost on the road to success.' And some of the greatest successes in modern times have experienced failure and rejection on a grand scale.

"Actually, some of the most successful people in the history of this planet have failed spectacularly! Milton Hershey, founder and originator of Hershey's Chocolate, started and failed with three candy companies (and even had to file for personal bankruptcy) before finally creating the company that he became famous for. Can you imagine starting three companies that all failed?

"Author J.K. Rowling was rejected by seventeen publishers before one small London house took a chance on her *Harry Potter* series. (Even then they told her not to quit her day job.) Now, she's the first author ever to border on becoming a billionaire in her own right.

"Steven Jobs, Founder and CEO of Apple, first built his company designing computer boxes in his parents' garage. And yet by the time he was 30, his own board of directors fired him because they decided he had nothing more to offer the $2 billion corporation that he had helped create. So what did Jobs do? Rather than wallow in self-pity and live off his royalties, he went on to build another billion dollar company called Pixar—creator of such animation masterpieces as *A Bug's Life, Monsters, Inc.,* and *Toy Story*. In fact, so striking was Jobs' success with Pixar that in 1996 his old company Apple came groveling back to ask him to return as 'interim CEO.' Ever hear of the iPod, iPhone and iPad? (Apple now has a stock market cap value of more than $222 billion, making it even larger than Microsoft.)"

"I get the fact that there are so many people who have failed several times before they succeeded," Michael admitted. "What I don't get is the fact that they appear to be the exception. They had all succeeded at something before. And they all seemed to like what they were doing. They had passion and focus."

"Those are very important ingredients in using failure as a platform for success, Michael," The Guardian agreed. "But there are others.

"One of my favorite examples is Abraham Lincoln. We now look upon Lincoln as perhaps our greatest U.S. President—certainly one of this nation's three greatest. No other president in American history was faced with more challenges and yet guided his war-torn country through its most difficult time. No U.S. President, in retrospect, is more beloved or more revered than this man. But did you know that he faced incredible difficulty and frequent failure at nearly everything he tried before he got elected to the highest office of this land? He only had a year and a half of formal schooling before he was forced to work as a young man and was, in fact, self-educated. In his early twenties, he failed at his retail business and had to file for bankruptcy before he finally put himself through school to get a law degree. By the time Lincoln eventually ran for President, this nation was so divided the Southern states had already declared that, if Lincoln won, they would secede from the Union.

"By the time he took office, Abe Lincoln was hated by half his constituents. His military generals often defied or ignored his executive orders. He was facing a near bankrupt U.S. Treasury. Members of his own Cabinet tried to sabotage him (and steal the office out from under him), and more than 22 attempts were made to assassinate him in office before John Wilkes Booth finally succeeded in 1865.

"In his personal life, he was plagued by a marriage to a bipolar, extravagant wife who nearly led them to financial ruin, the death of three of his four children before the age of eighteen, and his own imperfect, irregular health.

"And yet this same man was so single-minded when it came to saving his country from ruin that he literally gave his life in the service of his cause, freed the slaves, fashioned a strong return to peace and unity and restored the principles of a newly formed Republic. So strong was his influence that, by force of his brilliance and personality alone, he saved his nation from the most ruinous conflict in its history."

"Well, in every example you've given me, you're talking about people who are extraordinarily gifted," Michael said. "If anything, it makes me feel worse, because I'm not sure I have the same kind of genius, dedication and discipline of these people. I don't think any of them ever saw failure as an option. I'm just not that... powerful. (I'm not sure anybody is.) What does all this do for ordinary people? Failure presents an entirely different challenge to the rest of us."

"Actually, they all have more in common with the rest of us than you might imagine, Michael," The Guardian answered. "Of course, they all had disappointments, painful experiences, and faced the terrible prospect of starting over, just like everyone else. But remember what we talked about earlier? It's not failure but how you respond to it that determines what happens to you. And the only real failure is if you quit.

People tend to learn very little or nothing from the easy times of their lives. Struggle, difficulty, and failure force people to do what they won't do when life is easy. The thing they won't do without being hit between the eyes with the proverbial "two-by-four" is to think and decide. If necessity is the mother of invention then terror is the father of pure inspiration. Think about it.

— The Guardian

"Too many people confuse failure with quitting. Failure is and should be a temporary state of being—a period of incompleteness that requires further learning, developing and improvement. By definition, when you quit something, you abandon or leave it, and it implies a state of permanence. When you quit a job, you're not coming back. When you quit on a marriage or a relationship, it usually means you've given up on it.

When you quit on life, trust me, life will quit on you. Think about it.

— The Guardian

"Don't get me wrong," said The Guardian. "I'm not trying to make light of failure. Everyone has failed at something. It's part of living. And, no matter what you're trying to do, it's devastating to fail. People who fail at something still have to deal with the harsh consequences of that failure, such as financial ruin, homelessness, putting food on the table, etc. And yet that's what separates winners from quitters.

"Quitters will run, will give up, will go on the dole, start drinking, start doing drugs, put on about 100 pounds, grab a grocery cart, load it up with personal items and hit the streets—or a combination of these things. Winners will sit down, analyze how to fix their situation, and set about a game plan to overcome their problem.

"The fact is successful people don't quit. They don't allow failure to block them from pressing on. They have a vision for their lives, and use their failures as stepping-stones to get to their ultimate goal."

Failure often inspires the redirection from an incorrect path to the correct or intended goal. (The universe is always able to provide a better path to an objective than you can imagine on your own.) Think about it.

— The Guardian

"It's very much like the hurdler in the track meet. The losers always see the hurdles. The winners only see the finish line. (And of course the runners have clipped or hit hurdles [failed] a thousand times during training on their way to running their race *perfectly*.)

"We all learn by doing. Winners will determine what they did wrong and start to fix it. There is a formula for doing that. Still you're responsible for recognizing it and putting it to use. Start by making a list of all the things you were doing to accomplish it and subdivide that into two categories—things that work and things that don't.

"*First of all, take Responsibility* for whatever has happened up to this point. Accept the fact that, for whatever went wrong in your life, you are the architect of your failure, and usually you did it through some failure to plan. So, just as you designed all those things in your life that haven't worked up to now, you can create an entirely new blueprint for all the things that will.

"*Second, list what you want to accomplish:* in a goal, a business, an invention, a product, a relationship, or any of a thousand other things you might want to accomplish.

"*Third, list all the steps necessary to achieve it.* (Come on, you already know, or if you don't it's probably the reason you crashed in flames to begin with. So, find out!) You should also list any steps here that you missed or didn't take, and determine how you can adjust your actions. When you have thought of all you can and still have holes in your plan, don't worry about it. The universe will fill in the blanks. What you have to do is get started, and then follow through on what you began.

"*Fourth, implement your plan of Action.* And ask yourself the difficult questions along the way: Have you clearly defined and visualized your objective? Are you willing to speak of, and see yourself having already obtained your objective? Have you made certain that you have reciprocal desires with everyone you've engaged in the process?

"*Fifth, follow through*—and do so on a daily basis. (Visualize, in detail, having achieved your objective at least two times daily.) Success in anything is a matter of daily application. You have to tend, refine, water, and grow *any crop*, business, marketing strategy, science project, family relationship or romantic involvement— if you want them to flourish. If you do and if you've done your homework on what does and doesn't best serve your objectives, success is inevitable.

"*Sixth, refine, polish, and protect.* This requires an attention to detail and an understanding that perfection is a matter of constant diligence and never taking anything for granted.

"*Finally, let go of your attachment to outcome.* Once you have done your absolute best to make something work, release it to a higher source. Ralph Waldo Emerson once said that: 'Once you make a decision, the universe conspires to make it happen.' The important thing is that you allow it."

> *The most important step toward any objective is to decide. Everyone has heard the statement that 'leaders make decisions quickly and change them slowly and followers make decisions slowly and change them quickly.' Think about it.*
>
> — The Guardian

"So, there are no failures," Michael concluded.

"On the contrary, Michael, there are tens of millions every day. The important thing to recognize is that it's not the end of the world. People who have failed and rise again to succeed have a complete understanding of this. Those who haven't, those who have quit, understand nothing. And they never will until they learn that all failure is the very first step on the path to success.

Whatever your goal is, there are some inner qualities that lie within your power to help create the dynamics of success: 1) Decide. Most people fail because they fail to make a decision about what it is they truly want to do. Once you do decide, you'll sense a shift of energy in your favor that you can virtually feel. 2) Have a strong Desire to accomplish your objective. Your decision is only as effective as the mental, emotional and spiritual energy that fuels it. 3) Visualize. You should see yourself having accomplished your objective. Embrace all aspects of it. See it as already done. And do it at least twice every day. 4) Concentrate. All success is based upon the ability to focus one's energies magnificently. There's a universal law that says in effect:

'Whatever commands the majority of your attention expands.' If you focus and concentrate on the completion of your objective, success will be the result. 5) Willpower is often the difference between success and failure. Vince Lombardi once said: 'The difference between a successful person and others is not a lack of strength, not a lack of knowledge, but rather in a lack of will.'

People with true will power never quit, and because of that, they seldom fail. 6) Usually will power is the twin of a quality called Self-Discipline. All the visualization and concentration in the world will accomplish nothing unless you discipline yourself to accomplish what you've set out to do. 7) Persist. The greatest achievements in the world were often accomplished by people who others thought were too dumb to quit. President Calvin Coolidge once said: "Nothing in this world can take the place of persistence. Talent will not; nothing is more common than unsuccessful people with talent. Genius will not; unrewarded genius is almost a proverb. Education will not; the world is full of educated derelicts. Persistence and determination alone are omnipotent. The slogan "press-on" has solved and always will solve the problems of the human race." Success always comes with a plan, failure with excuses. Think about it.

— The Guardian

"The main thing to understand is that this failure is fertilizer: a growth medium for success. (The great success coach Denis Waitley refers to failure as the 'fertilizer for success.') And you can use it not only to plant the seeds of success but also to create the blossoms of perfection in your life. But first, you have to recognize it and learn from it."

If failure is the fertilizer of success and farmers fertilize their crops with manure, then when you are wading through the crap life dumps on you, you must be growing. Think about it.

— The Guardian

"Hey Guardian! How is that for quotable?" "Don't quit your day job yet, Michael."

The Hidden/Forbidden Zone

"So…" Michael thought about it. "It seems to me that, if I'm just able to apply the lessons I've learned here and take responsibility for every aspect of my life, I can achieve anything. The sky is the limit."

"Absolutely, Michael," The Guardian agreed. "By now, you've learned the Four Universal Laws, and you know how they apply to everyone. You understand that you are perfect (that you are that perfect building), and that every failure you experience holds the seeds of your success."

"And yet I can't help but feel like something's missing," Michael added. "Most of those we've talked about are more or less normal people. In some ways, we've stayed away from extremes on both sides. So, I guess the final question for me is what about that hidden world that people don't talk about? I mean, people who are abused or victimized in extreme ways, or people who go through extreme depths of addiction, or circumstances that seem beyond repair or redemption—what about those?"

"You're right. There are hidden places, Forbidden Zones, most people either can't accept or refuse to acknowledge," The Guardian confirmed. "And yet, if we're really going to cover every aspect of your training, we have to recognize them for what they are. The good news about some of these hidden places is that not all of them are negative, or what we often refer to as 'bad.' Some of them involve secret worlds that we often take for granted or have simply allowed to escape our notice. Once we realize what they are, we might even look upon them as buried treasure: the good, the bad and the ugly, the controversial and uncharted lands, magical worlds and wretched places—all of them serve to enrich our understanding of this amazing journey of life. And finding out everything you can about them will help complete your education.

"As the philosopher William Blake once said: 'Joy and sorrow are woven fine.' The important thing is to approach the journey with an open mind… and a willing heart. So…what do you say, Michael?"

"There's only one thing to say," Michael responded. "Let's do it!"

CHAPTER 27

Gratitude
The Application of All the Universal Laws

"Well, Michael, we've covered a lot of informational territory in a short period of time. We talked about how things work, how perfect people really are, the misconceptions people have about who they are, the Universal Laws and a whole lot of principles connected with relationships and how people get along with each other… or not.

"A little bit ago when I asked you what you thought about approaching this journey with an open mind and willing heart, you said 'there's only one thing to say: Let's do it!' With that great attitude, Michael, I guess it's just about time for me to get back to The Guardian Council and for you to leap off the branch and take your solo flight into a new life of faultless liberty, freedom, joy, happiness and peace of mind. Thanks for giving me the opportunity to be your teacher by being the student ready to learn."

With that The Guardian wriggled into a pure white duster (a full-length riding coat for those unfamiliar with Western wear) picked up his Stetson (it's a cowboy hat, for crying out loud) from the S-shaped chair, and fit it on his head. With a two fingered touch to the brim in Michael's direction he smiled then turned and walked away into the setting sun.* As the dust from his footsteps, blown by a gentle breeze, swirled furling the

---

*Just for your information, the waterfall described earlier was in the opposite direction from the path taken by The Guardian in his (attempted) exit from Michael's presence.

coattails of his duster you could hear the long and lonely whistled notes of the theme (song) from *"The Good, the Bad and the Ugly"* (the classic Clint Eastwood Western) echoing through the canyons.

The whistle was lost in the deep hiss of the rising breeze and a voice rolling off the surrounding hills like thunder announcing:

> *"This is the Guardian! He is the eternal witness. He is the messenger. He is the sound of one hand clapping. He is…"*

"Wait a minute! You can't leave me like this!" Michael ran and caught up with The Guardian. The Guardian stopped, turned to Michael and very impatiently said, "What do you want? This is supposed to be my 'riding off into the sunset' scene. They couldn't find a pure white horse, but never mind. You have completely ruined the effect. Besides, I think I was just getting a handle on where that 'rolling thunder off the hills type Guardian announcer voice' was coming from."

"You can't go yet! I've got all of this unbelievable, exciting knowledge, wisdom, understanding and stuff that I don't think anybody's ever heard before rattling around in my brain without a clue about how to put it to work! I can feel that it's all true! You told me how things work and more important you've explained why they work. This is valuable stuff but how do I get it all put together in a usable plan for my life? It's almost worse having all of this understanding and being uncertain of how to get it going than it was running around with my finger in my ear not knowing any of this."

"Michael, are you saying that you were happier being blissfully stupid? Haven't you learned anything? That's about as silly as the people who say ' What you don't know can't hurt you,' when in fact the only thing that can hurt you is what you don't know because if you knew you wouldn't let it hurt you. (In the vernacular of the day 'Well, duh.')"

"Well, Michael, let's go back over to our private little conference center and wrap up a few loose ends. I know exactly what you need." Just then three glorious musical notes rolled over them that seemed to emanate from the clouds hovering over the distant throat of the canyon. Michael spun to face the source of the sound. Turning toward The Guardian, Michael asked, "What, where and why is that beautiful music?"

The Guardian did not respond. He was standing motionless, face tilted upward toward the clouds, eyes closed, the middle finger of his right hand touching the center of his brow. Out of courtesy and respect Michael sat down on 'his' side of the 'S'-chair and waited. After a short time The Guardian relaxed, opened his eyes, smiled, and walked over to sit with Michael.

"In answer to your question that was the 'fabled' music of the celestial spheres. As you just experienced it's not so fabled after all."

"What was it for?"

"It was notification of a message from my sweetheart. Kind of like when your cell phone rings only in this case it transcends all time and space. Ordinarily you would be no more able to hear it then any other person (that's why it's fabled) but we were still connected on what you might call the telepathic 'Guru Line.'"

Michael sprang to his feet. "Wait a minute, what do you mean, 'sweetheart'? You've got a sweetheart?"

The Guardian leaned for ward, narrowed his gaze as if to look right through Michael and with that familiar little chuckle in his voice said, "What did you think? I come to you because you want to know How Things Work. I teach about relationships and how perfect people are. I tell you the best thing you can do for anyone is to give them a No Fault. If you love someone Unconditionally they can say about themselves that 'I like me best when I'm with you.' You've learned 'distance is disaster' and 'to know me is to love me.' Do you think quotes like 'Neither is the man without the woman nor is the woman without the man' and 'The man is the head of the home but the woman is the heart' are nice concepts that we Guardians teach but have no experience in application?

"How do you think we first learned How Things Work and then were able to go beyond typical thinking and teach *why* they work? Is this an exercise in 'those who can't do, teach?' I think not!!!

"The reason you are here on this path, following the curriculum you wrote into your book of life, is to experience the incontrovertible laws by which the universe and all creation functions. You are on this path that you might *know*, rather than imagine their truth and return to your childlike perfection only this time with the magnificent wisdom, power, and unconditional goodness that is your natural state.

"This learning and experiencing has to have progressed significantly for a master to be able to learn and progress by reading about the experiences of others. It has to have progressed quite well for a wise man to learn from observing the experiences of others. But, until people have broken out of the bondage of indecision, denial of responsibility for their condition, and the whining black hole of victimization, they will just have to (forgive me for this) continue to pee on the electric fence.

> *This little commentary on the electric fence issue has been stated in its shorter form from earlier in these discussions. Think about it, again.*
>
> — The Guardian

"The reason that students become ready for their teacher to appear is that they have progressed on their personal path of learning to the point where they need outside input. The 'readiness' might be brought about by harsh difficulties, enlightening experiences, emotional attachments, or any of the infinite range of life's circumstances that require a person to realize it when they *need more*."

> *The 'a-ha' of a truth, for which you are ready, will be so familiar, even though previously unknown, that it feels like a remembrance. Think about it.*
>
> — The Guardian

Michael asked, "How do you know when you are in the presence of wisdom that you need at any given point in time?"

"Simple, Michael. Every human being has the power to draw exactly what they need to themselves at exactly the right time if they are open to their teacher when he, she, it, or they appear.

"The way you recognize 'your truth' is when you feel an immediate connection, exhilaration, and sense of understanding that what you *know* fits who you are and your circumstances.

"Remember, as you learned each of the laws and principals that we have encountered, how each one made so much sense and you could 'feel and know' it would work for you. You wouldn't have heard, seen, or understood it (or even been here) if it wasn't exactly what you needed. You made the choice, even if you didn't realize it, to put yourself 'in the way' of the wisdom you needed.

"Well, Michael, I guess you are ready for this teacher to give you the final piece of the great puzzle of life which is the application and the key to all the laws and principles that people need for their progression. (Besides, the other part of the message I got from my lovely companion was to quit "messin' witcha" and finish our work.)

"There is a principle that will enable you to understand and apply all the laws and principals we have discussed. It is the weather vane, the litmus test of whether you are on the path to greatness in your quest to become the magnificent you that you deserve. It is the principal of Gratitude."

Gratitude... the Attitude to Live By

"Michael, I'd like you to try a little experiment for me."

"Sure, what do you need?"

"I want you to sit down, relax, and concentrate on trying to think of being selfish and grateful at the same time."

Michael closed his eyes and was obviously focusing. A frown crossed his forehead and his eyes squeezed tighter and tighter shut, evidencing his increasing determination to succeed in the task.

"Don't hurt yourself, Michael. I just wanted you to experience the impossibility of thinking those two thoughts at the same time."

Michael relaxed, opened his eyes and said, "You're right, it's absolutely impossible."

"Got another one for you, Michael. Try to think of being arrogant and grateful at the same time."

Again Michael focused, this time for a shorter period. Then, with some exasperation, he said, "That's impossible, too."

"So what do you think the lesson is here, Michael?"

"Well, I guess Gratitude is such a positive attitude that selfishness and arrogance can't exist in its presence."

"Absolutely correct. In fact, if humility and selflessness are virtues, they can be best maintained by an attitude of Gratitude.

"You will discover that most people have difficulties when they focus outside themselves (which they are accustomed to doing in order to deny Responsibility for their conditions and circumstances). If an individual were isolated on a desert island where no one could see what they do, hear what they say, or know what they think they would probably never experience Guilt. They couldn't be Victims with no one to blame for their victimization. They would live the true Law of Me perfectly with no one to perceive the image they were attempting to convey of themselves through approval seeking. They would waste no time arguing the Fault or Blame of what happened. With no ego to defend, they would simply get on with fixing the problem. They would never judge or be angry with anyone since there would be no one before whom to feel Guilty. (I think you can see where I'm going with this, Michael.)

That blissfully isolated individual we have just described would face each experience with the innocent, wide-eyed, childlike joy exemplified by the character of Jethro (of "Beverly Hillbillies" fame)... or Tarzan (of ape relations fame). Think about it.

— The Guardian

"'Lack Thinking' is the greatest failure mechanism known to mankind, Michael. When someone thinks that they don't have enough and, in their failure to accept responsibility for their Condition, blames 'the luck of the draw,' outside influences, and the 'haves' (successful and prosperous people) for their plight, they are participating in the extremely destructive practice of 'lack thinking.' They believe that there is only so much prosperity to go around. They think if someone else makes a lot of money there is that much less for them. In their guilt at not being all they wish they were, they resent those who are prosperous. They're the ones we've talked about earlier who believe life is a game of chance. Instead of studying what others do to succeed (which would imply that they 'should' be able to succeed also) they conclude that some people are simply born with a 'silver spoon in their mouth' and if they had a rich daddy they could have the 'good stuff' too. They have been innocently born into a miserable condition for which they should probably go home and punch their daddy in the mouth. The other favorite way the 'poor in spirit' look at the success of others is that they must be crooks or that they had some sort of magical advantage not available to the 'common folk.'"

Most successful people have been broke (or short on money) many times before they reach true success and prosperity. However, they never allow themselves to be 'poor' in the vision of how they see themselves. Think about it.

— The Guardian

The Guardian continued: "The terrible thing is that 'lack thinking' is often made into a self-fulfilling prophecy by those who feel unjustly 'lucked,' 'silver-spooned,' and 'crooked against.' They really want it, so they decide to fake it because they have no clue as to how to make it. This is why you have business owners who steal from and cheat their employees, salespeople and distributors. They believe there is not enough for everyone so they make sure they get 'theirs.' People steal, embezzle and counterfeit because they don't know how to make it, so they fake it.

"Here is an interesting concept for you Michael. Lack thinking says 'I don't have enough and I will never have enough because there is only so much in the universe and those rich jerks already have it so I have two choices. I need to resign myself to being 'poor' and never have enough, or I find some way to cheat, steal or con what I 'deserve' (because I have been unfairly done on to) out of what they, I'm sure, have 'stolen' from my share of the universal prosperity.

> *If folks put one half of the effort and creativity into the success and prosperity principles taught in and by thousands of self-help and success books, seminars, Scriptures, gurus, parents, Masters and summarized in these discussions I have brought you from the Guardian Council, that they put into cheating, stealing, conning, crime and unethical schemes, they would invariably richer in a very short time than those from whom they steal. (It is truly a sorry commentary on the human race that some of the greatest minds can be found in prison.) Think about it.*
>
> — The Guardian

"Here is another exercise for you, Michael. Try to think of yourself *lacking*, not having enough and resenting someone who has more than you do at the same time you think of being grateful for all you have, who you are, and what you are capable of."

Michael focused on these thoughts as he had before, trying to smash the concept of lack thinking and the principle of Gratitude together and concluded 'this doesn't work.'

"I can't fit Lack and Gratitude into the same thought."

"Absolutely correct, Michael. Gratitude totally eliminates lack thinking and all of its vicious stepchildren."

"Now, Michael, we have all the pieces to the puzzle. So let's take a look at the principle of Gratitude and how it is a simple application of all the principles that we have discussed. (This is similar to one-size-fits-all, but in this case Gratitude is one principle that 'encompasses all' of the principles.)

"Gratitude is spiritual tithing. The giving away of a portion of one's earnings (usually 10 percent) is a widely accepted principle of prosperity universally recognized in success, religious, and personal development teachings.

"There are two mentalities in tithing. One says I will give because I am promised a tenfold return. (This is basically lack thinking and amounts to playing a bargaining game by giving a dollar and hoping to receive $10 back from the big slot machine in the sky.) The focus here is usually on money rather than inspiration regarding the means to obtain it.

History is replete with dictatorships and totalitarian governments being established by encouraging the resentment that "lack thinking" creates in the minds of the have-nots against the more intelligent and prosperous members of society. When the thinkers and the doers are eliminated, the poor unfortunate "lack thinking" are doomed to the true endless "lack" of servitude to the purest lack thinkers of all the political elite who produce nothing and steal everything. This is not intended as a political statement. We Guardians don't involve ourselves with such foolishness. This note is only intended to exemplify the terrible ultimate extreme of "lack thinking." Think about it.

— The Guardian

The Guardian continued: "The second perspective on *tithing* is abundance-based. It says 'I am grateful for that which I have (however great or small) and in gratitude for my abundance I choose to share and give back a portion.' In accord with the principal stated earlier by Plato and Emerson, 'that for which one is grateful cannot be denied,' the tenfold return on shared abundance will be realized. Gratitude is a simple means of correctly applying this universally recognized principle of prosperity.

"There's a principle in setting goals and objectives called 'acting as if.' Simply stated, you set a goal and then you act as if you had already achieved it. This tells the universe, and the subconscious mind, that the goal has already been obtained (or created). This helps the individual avoid the 'un-creation' of the objective through doubt. The beautiful thing about Gratitude is that it takes a step further ahead of accomplishment of the goal, looks backward at the achievement, and expresses thankfulness. So gratitude is acting *as*, and there is no *if* involved. Expressing gratitude for that which is not yet achieved is the same, in universal law, as gratefully paying tithing on income not yet received. If no doubt or un-creation is allowed to enter the mind, the object of gratitude cannot be denied.

What if one was to use the principle of gratitude in prayer? What if gratitude were expressed rather than a request made in prayer? Gratitude for a need having been filled (even before it has) is a considerably different creative state than praying and asking for the need to be filled. Think about it.

— The Guardian

"You know, Michael, giving is a perfect form of gratitude. It says I have plenty; therefore I share and give to others that they might have also.

"Can thoughts of mental flagellation, discouragement, and depression exist at the same time in the mind as gratitude for what you have, who you are, and what you can be? Go ahead try and think 'I'm stupid and useless' at the same time you think 'I am grateful for who I am and what I can do.'

It is highly probable that if you think about it guilt is the result of ingratitude. (There are scriptures indicating that God considers ingratitude the greatest sin. The parents of many modern teenagers may have a strong tendency to agree.) Gratitude is an attitude—and the lack of gratitude is the greatest offense. Please understand: you can fix a mistake, but not an attitude. But interestingly enough, if you maintain the attitude of gratitude you will not make mistakes. Think about it.

— The Guardian

"Remember, Michael: We said earlier that any time you run into anger or judgmentalism you are always looking into the eyes of Guilt. (You could probably have guessed that I would get around to this sooner or later. So here we go.) Try being angry and judgmental (not giving an 'It's Not Your Fault' to someone) and being deeply grateful at the same time. 'Neener, neener, neener,' you can't do it can ya?

"An awful lot of the discussion here has been about relationships. We talk about How Things Work and how to fix them. But the biggest failed relationship for most people is with themselves that's called the Self-Image. Your Self-Image determines everything about how you relate to the outside world and those around you. It's pretty commonly recognized that there is a serious epidemic of 'lousy self-images' (that is a new Guardian clinical term) throughout all generations but very strongly evident in the younger generations.

"The bad Self-Image is almost the 'Murphy's Law' of emotional psychological behavior. It takes credit for addictions, criminal behavior, depression, abuse, failed marriages, and an endless litany of aberrant and stupid behavior. Here we go again. We've already tried to think 'I'm useless' and be grateful for who and what I am at the same time. It didn't work then but you can give it another shot if you want to. So, gratitude is a solution to the crummy self-image epidemic.

Take each of the principles from the table of contents along with those from the various discussions and match them with Gratitude as an application. It's all about relationships. Look at the desert island concept. No relationships, no problems. The principle of Gratitude is most probably the solution to all human problems. This is pretty simple. But after all, shouldn't life be simple enough so that everyone can live it in peace, joy, happiness, love and abundance? If people didn't make life so hard and were simply grateful for who they are and the magnificence of all they can be they could joyfully achieve the full measure of their creation. Think about it.

— The Guardian

"A crummy self-image is the antithesis of prosperity and abundance. The good news is that right next to it sits the perfect opportunity to "put The Class back in."

SPECIAL KEYS TO THE GUARDIAN CODE

THE ZONE!

All who enter here...
Prepare to Learn More About What Really Matters in Life

ZONE A

Baby, It's Not Your Fault

Little Amy, keep it simple.
Grown-ups are communications impaired.
And Understanding (or a lack of it) is the problem.

"Michael, let me pose a question to you: What if all your communication, everything you wanted to say, every feeling you could convey, would have to be expressed in a single word? What if you were in a kind of emotional partial paralysis where all you could do was open your mouth and blink your eyes? Your five senses would be as alert, as would be your mind. You would just have no voluntary control over your extremities. This would mean you wouldn't be able to use any signals to express your feelings such as nodding your head, or shaking it, or wiggling your fingers to gesture for something. So you would have no physical means at your disposal to supplement your one-word vocabulary.

"So…let's assign you *the word*, Michael."

"Okay," Michael laughed. "But it better be a good one."

"How about, 'Ah!'?" The Guardian suggested.

"Wait a minute!" Michael protested. "'Ah' isn't even a word!"

"That's okay. Your choices at this stage of your life are limited anyway. So, 'ah' is going to be about as good as any. Now, Michael, I'm going to give you a tummy ache. As a baby, you have no idea what a tummy ache is. You just know it's very uncomfortable. So what do you say, Michael?"

"Ah!"

"Very good. What kind of response do you think that gets?" "Probably not much reaction at all."

"So now you have to turn up the volume, intensity and repetition until you get the desired results; or at least some results. The problem is that you don't know what results you want."

"So, I just keep going 'ah' until something happens," Michael said, making note of the obvious.

"That's right," The Guardian agreed. "And you do that until Mommy shows up. Usually, that's a good sign. You're delighted to see her because she almost always means something good. She checks your diaper. It seems to be all right. She feels your forehead. That seems to be all right as well. Another 'ah' gets you a binky plugged into your mouth, and a blanket pulled over you. So, what do you have to say about that?"

"Ah, ah, ah, ah!"

"Still not quite sure about what you've been attempting to tell her, your mom picks you up and rocks you, trying all of the 29 ways she knows to burp you. You settle down for a little bit because things got a little more comfortable. This doesn't last long though, because she isn't getting around to solving the real problem. You know you're not happy, and things are going to get resolved if you can somehow get her to do something. And she does not understand your 'ah,' Michael, because it's the only tool you have. So, let me ask you. Aren't you getting a little frustrated by now?"

"You bet I am!"

"And not only are you getting frustrated, Michael, but she is starting to feel Guilty because, after all, she is your 'Mommy,' and so (you both think) she should know what's wrong with her baby. But the truth is she really doesn't have a clue about what needs to be done. So she's starting to get exasperated. She's had a long day and feels like it would be nice to have a little bit of time to relax on the couch and watch TV.

"At this point, two things are happening to your mom that nobody handles very well. Your mother has unwittingly gotten into the area of something called the *no touch-'ems* of life, Guilt and Agency. First, she feels *Guilty* for not being able to figure out what her baby needs. Her love for her baby requires that she make the unhappiness go away. The longer her little one suffers, the more she becomes angry with herself. And until she figures it out, her sense of responsibility demands that all wants, needs and choices in her own life are overridden by the needs of her infant child. And second, though she isn't able to recognize it at a conscious level, *her freedom of choice* has just become severely infringed upon. Her own precious baby has just stomped on her *Agency*, and her 'liberty bank account' has just been drained of funds. (This might be okay for one occasion, but over a prolonged period of time, it's going to pose some serious problems where the mother and child relationship is concerned.)"

Michael listened, and finally exhaled a little sigh of relief.

"I've got to tell you," he said. "That was an eye-opening experience. I felt helpless and completely frustrated. I'm sure glad I've got a vocabulary of more than one word."

People can get pretty goofy sometimes when it comes to communication. Ask any blind person. They either get yelled at as if they're hearing impaired, or else others around them overcompensate for their blindness, and start to behave as if none of their other senses work either. Think about it.

— The Guardian

"Now just having lived (or relived) that experience, Michael, you can see how mothers can get angry and possibly even abusive because the infringement on their Agency becomes so extreme that it completely blows up their tolerance levels. All she knows is that her baby is suffering—maybe even crying. She should be able to stop it. (After all, it is her job.) But she can't. So she's riddled with a sense of guilt and anger that she can't quite define. At this point, she starts to feel 'done-onto.' All she knows is that she wants the problem solved, and she wants to shut off the child alarm, even for a while. But rather than address the problem, she tries to force the issue. Need overtakes reason, and suddenly her crying baby starts to resemble the high-pressure salesman who doesn't know how to close the sale and yet still refuses to stop. He tries to make the people buy to fill his own needs and then makes unreasonable demands for payment.

"So what happens next is a great deal like the guy who smashes the buzzer on the smoke alarm rather than look around to find the actual source of the smoke."

Hands and Booties are for Shaking. Babies Are for Holding.

"Never forget one thing," The Guardian continued. "Especially when dealing with children and small animals—the helpless creatures of the world. *The Law of Me* will always override everyone's emotions. That especially applies to the 'adults' involved in the relationship.

"Deep down inside, most folks feel that everything that causes them aggravation is all about them and is being 'done-onto' them. The greater their sense of helplessness, the more stress they feel placed upon them. And the more helpless they feel about something they know is their responsibility, the greater the degree of guilt. The greater the guilt, the stronger the tendency to feel victimized. The more they feel victimized the greater the potential for one of two things to happen.

"So what you're dealing with is a kind of victimization that is laced with Guilt, Frustration, Anger and sometimes even Rage. (And that's where the danger to the baby comes in.) One of the worst aspects about this is the fact that the parents often feel as if they had absolutely no choice in the victimization. So their Agency absolutely takes a broadside.

There is an absolute law that states the following: "Whenever you see anger or judgmentalism you are always looking into the eyes of Guilt. (This is true even if the anger is righteous indignation. The Guilt is the result of frustration at the inability to fix the situation.) Think about it.

— The Guardian

"When folks feel that 'done-unto' it's because they believe that events have caused them to totally lose control. Forget the Russian roulette of contraception; a lot of children get born despite the best efforts of the couple not to get pregnant. So they often look upon their sudden parenthood as a kind of birth control failure (and resultant victimization).

Then again, there is the young bachelor who falls into lust for a single mom who happens to have a very young child. She's got a kid, so he realizes that this is a package deal. Later, when they develop a relationship, he's watching NFL football on a Sunday night. The Redskins are making a goal line stand, and the game is on the line. With a sinister sense of perfect timing, the girlfriend's baby starts to cry. The boyfriend is done-onto. The night is ruined. And 'the kid did it!' This begins a recipe for disaster. Think about it.

— The Guardian

The Guardian continued: "So the little infant becomes a symbol of their self-induced loss of freedom. Often, in cases such as this, the little child becomes a Nemesis set in their lives to punish them for their uncontrollable lust and soon to become the single reason for their loss of youth, freedom and sense of invulnerability.

"So Baby, *It's Not Your Fault* that your little tummy might be hurting and you only have a one word vocabulary. So you can't be held responsible for the fact that we can't understand what you're trying to tell us. You might be hungry. You might be cold. You might be downright scared. Or maybe, just like the rest of us, you just might need a cuddle once in a while.

"The important thing that everyone—parents, grandparents, and sitters alike—need to do is make a little sign that says: [Amy], IT'S NOT YOUR FAULT. And they need to put it up over the little baby's bed. *It's not your fault that we can't understand what you're trying to tell us.* They should also put up a little checklist that includes all the reasons that they don't entirely understand what is going on in that little baby's universe. And they need to employ some qualities such as patience, understanding, and unconditional love.

"This particularly applies to sitters or caregivers who don't necessarily comprehend the situation surrounding this tiny creature in their charge. If they could just read and understand this very important sign hanging over the crib, they would understand their role a lot more clearly—and miracles would happen."

"I'm not sure I understand. Are we in need of miracles where babies are concerned?" Michael asked.

"Well, that's the whole point, isn't it?" The Guardian answered. "The thing we have to recognize about this strange forbidden world of the infant is that they are emotional sponges for everything that happens to them. They feel every sensation— every sound, every noise, every touch, every caress, every trauma."

"Are there traumas?"

"More than you realize. In fact, there is an ugly phenomenon of modern society called Shaken Baby Syndrome (SBS). That's the major point of helping everyone understand the underlying importance of *Baby It's Not Your Fault*. It's not only meant to save relationships. It's meant to save lives."

"Sounds pretty serious," Michael said. "What do you suggest?"

SHAKEN BABY SYNDROME (SBS)

How to Recognize it. How to Prevent it.

- Every day in the United States, eight children under the age of five will die or become permanently disabled because of SBS.
- 50,000 cases occur every year in the United States alone, many of them fatal.
- Approximately 5,000 babies die each year due to SBS.
- Victims range in age from a few days old to around five years of age.
- More than 70 percent of the perpetrators are male (usually the biological father, step-father, or boyfriend).
- The majority of females who injure babies are caregivers or sitters.
- It doesn't take much to permanently injure an infant or small child. No more than two or three seconds of violent shaking causing the baby's head to whip back and forth is enough to cause irreparable damage such a spinal cord damage, spasms, brain damage, paralysis and death.
- Less than 10 to 15 percent of all shaken babies ever completely recover.

Key Prevention Points to Remember

- It is never ever okay to shake a baby. Make sure that all the people who care for your baby know this and understand the repercussions of doing so.
- Never leave your baby alone with someone that you know has an anger problem or violent temper. (That includes members of your own family.)
- Have a plan of what you will do if your baby keeps crying and you become upset or angry. There are things you can do and people who can help you (including physicians, family counselors, and trained professionals).
- Make sure you and those caring for the infant understand that crying is normal behavior for babies. It is one of the few ways they have to communicate. Crying does not mean that they are being naughty or demanding your attention. Much of the time, it is the only way they can deal with their immediate universe.
- If you are employing the services of an outside caregiver, nanny, or baby-sitter, it is important that you vet this individual (check them out). And it's even better if this person is vetted as a certified caregiver.

"Understand that everything that happens to the baby is reliant upon a simple rule: *Happy, confident, loving babies get their best start with happy, confident, loving mothers,*" The Guardian pointed out. "And an important part of the 'loving' comes with looking out for the child's best interest in every aspect of the relationship.

"Remember how to empathize. Get back to that experience we just went through, Michael. Put yourself in that little baby's place for a while and realize that you're going to be hit with an avalanche of sensations the moment you come out of the womb and start taking-in air—and you're going to be helpless to do anything about it, except to interpret it and respond to it in very limited, often endearing and occasionally irritating ways.

"That means every adult in every situation is going to have power over you, is going to influence you, and is going to make their imprint upon you.

"The loving mother, the stressed-out father, the fascinated older brother, the baby-sitter who just came into the room after having recently had an argument with her boyfriend—all are going to impress you with their love and nurturing, their curiosity, their fatigue, their stress, their anger, and anxiety. In that way, you're often given over to the 'kindness of strangers' and there isn't much you can do about it. So, as a parent, an adult or a caring family member what would you do for that child?"

"I think I would vet everyone around that child," Michael answered. "I would start with making sure that I send my best energy to that very special little soul. I would convey the best of energy, and make sure that anyone else around her or him would be the same. Especially the men (since they pose the most emotional challenge) would be people I would be most careful to qualify."

"That's a good start," The Guardian agreed. "And did you know that they now have certifications for qualified caregivers—nannies, baby-sitters, nurses, and those in the profession of looking after infants and the young? And with regard to happy mothers having happy babies, Michael, your Daddy was quite a horseman and he used to say 'a switchy mare will have a switchy foal.'

"This is a very special place in the Forbidden Zone, Michael. And because it is, it's also perhaps the most crucial. Everything starts here. Life continues here, and impressions made upon that little life are among the most powerful they will ever encounter.

"So, even though we can't guarantee that everything will be perfect for those tiny, life-changing souls that have come into our lives, we can make certain that they'll be protected, free from harm, and able to see the friendliest face that life has to offer. And we can do it early and often!"

ZONE B

The Abandoned Child
Don't Worry, Little Guy. It's Not About You.

"It seems to me," Michael said. "That it all begins with the little child." "Ah… but not where it ends," The Guardian said.

"I'm not sure what you mean." "Come with me, and you'll see."

Before he knew it Michael found himself walking alongside The Guardian in a new state-of-the-art shopping mall, interwoven with escalators, a high, domed ceiling, and shops on three different levels. The Guardian motioned toward a nearby bench just outside a children's clothing store, and invited Michael to join him there.

No sooner had they sat down than Michael noticed that The Guardian's attention was drawn to a mature lady with a young boy, four or five years of age. She was carrying a shopping bag in one hand and using the other to expertly guide this exuberant, bouncing young ball of energy in her charge. In fact, the little fellow was pleading his case with great determination to lead her on a pilgrimage to Nirvana, Valhalla, Shangri-la, and the State Fair all rolled into one: The Toy Store.

The woman was obviously the five-year-old's grandmother. She was smiling as she gently admonished the boy, suggesting that if he could be patient just a little bit they went home. She also took the opportunity to remind him that—if they did find anything to buy—it would be great if he could remember what a great 'sharer' he was. Michael read this as an obvious political campaign on the part of the grandmother to reinforce a behavior that the little lad was apparently having some difficulty with.

The grandmother's comment must have sparked something in the boy, because as the two passed close to their bench, the young lad became suddenly serious, and Michael could overhear him say, "Grandma, am I a bad boy?"

With that, the older woman's smile wilted into an expression that was both compassionate and sad. And through a voice that was laced with kindness, and perhaps more accustomed to smiles and laughter, she answered. "No, Timmy. You're a very good boy."

At that point, the little guy pulled himself up tightly against her, looked straight up into her eyes and said, "Then why did Mommy leave?"

The lady knelt down, scooping him up into a big hug and said, "Timmy, your mother's going away had nothing to do with you. *It's not your fault.*" Then, as if to emphasize the point, she held the lad for a little while longer, then gave him one more squeeze, and said. "Remember, Timmy, that you're a very good boy. And none of this is your fault."

A short time later, the grandmother got back up, took Timmy's hand, and led him straight into the toy store, which had now taken priority over all her other errands...obviously for a very good reason.

Michael glanced over at The Guardian who responded to the question he was about to ask by saying, "That's Timmy and his grandma. There is a valuable lesson to be learned here, Michael. Timmy's mom, Brandy, left when he was about two years old. He felt like every other child of divorce or abandonment—guilty that her leaving must have been about him. To his four-year-old sense of logic, if she was going to do that to him, then she must have thought that he was a bad boy. For pity's sake, if your own momma doesn't even want to be around you, what does that tell you about your worth? He needs to hear, '*It's not your fault, Timmy,*' and he needs to hear it often. Of course his grandmother got that right away and made certain that she said it. Now, wouldn't it be great if he could hear it from his mother too?"

"But put yourself in the child's place," Michael insisted. "If you establish the fact to Timmy that it's not his fault, he is going to conclude (and who wouldn't?) that his mother is to blame. At this point, I get the fact that we're supposed to conclude it's not her fault either. But how do you get that across to Timmy at his tender age?"

"You make an interesting point, Michael," The Guardian agreed. "In this zero-sum game that we're taught to play at a very early age, most people will rush to judgment and immediately assign blame. Certainly Timmy's mom is the logical candidate. But as we know now, that's not how things work, because *The Law of Me* prevails. (And children are the honest masters of this.) So Timmy's only concern is with what his mother's leaving him has to say about him. Remember he asked, 'Am I a bad boy?' His honest child's point of reference is that it had to be about him.

"Then, if it's not Timmy's fault (a given), and it's not his mom's fault. Whose fault is it?" Michael felt obliged to ask.

"I see, Michael, that you are still itching to prove blame in spite of the fact that it won't do a thing to fix Timmy, the past doesn't exist, no one ever does anything intentionally stupid and everyone functions only from the perspective of the Law of Me," The Guardian challenged. "You have to remember that a constant theme of our discussions is that finding fault or assessing blame accomplishes nothing. Timmy, like all of us, functions totally from the law of me and will only respond to his own conclusions as to how he 'should' feel about himself. Laying blame at the feet of his mother won't heal him. Only finding ways to help him prove his worth to himself will mend his broken 'self-picture'."

ZONE C

It's Not Your Fault for Dogs
Life Lessons That Cut Across All Species

Before Michael even realized it, he and The Guardian had left the shopping mall and were once again back in that mystical space by the waterfall, sitting across from one another in the S-shaped chair that had now become so familiar to him.

"Wow!" Michael found himself thinking aloud. "That was quite an insight. I suppose you finally come to a point where you realize that the philosophy of *It's Not Your Fault* cuts into all human relationships."

"And beyond that, Michael," The Guardian added, "it virtually cuts across all species."

"It does?"

"Let me introduce you to, *'It's Not Your Fault for Dogs.'* And we'll use a classic of life experience to do it: We'll call it Buck's Tale.

"Buck was a half German Shepherd and half whatever came down the street at the right time. He was a confident rascal. His tail was always up, his ears were always perky, and he perennially wore that special kind of canine smile on his face. He was ready to play at the drop of a hat. And he absolutely thought the sun rose and set on his (human) buddy Fred.

"Fred and his family, of which Buck considered himself a part, lived on what is referred to, in 'urbaneez', as a *farmette*. There was just a big enough lot under his house to be more than anyone with any sense would want to mow and take care of, but it wasn't enough of a spread to become an agricultural source of income for Fred and his family. Fred's little piece of the world did have animal rights, however. So they did have a few chickens. There were 14 hens laying fresh eggs daily that also provided enough nuisance value to make Fred aware that his 'cottage' egg industry was probably more trouble than it was worth…Sound familiar?"

"You'd better believe it," Michael declared. "That was my family. That's the world I grew up in. So you're going to go back to my life experience to use for an example?"

"What better place, when you think about it?" The Guardian replied, and he continued.

"As you recall, for quite a while Fred had been hanging on with white-knuckled determination to resist his inclination to get his oldest daughter a horse. He knew that those beautiful rascals were nothing more than four-legged money pits. (Fred's daddy had always told him never to own anything that eats while you sleep.)

"Still, there was some merit to acquiring a horse for his daughter. She was a teenager. He thought that a relationship with, and a responsibility for, an intelligent being might help keep her attention on the good values for her life. Michael, do you remember what your daddy used to say?

"I do," said Michael. "He said, 'If you're going to ride a horse, you've got to be at least as smart as the horse.'"

"That might be a good idea for most teenagers today," The Guardian added. (By the way, I noticed that you ride a motorcycle. I wonder if there's a message in there someplace.)

"Anyway, back to old Buck… Fred would go to work, and his wife would need to run some errands. So, just to be on the safe side, she would tie Buck up to the tree just beside the house. As soon as she would start to drive away, Buck would set up a woof and a howl that would put the screaming of the proverbial long-tailed cat in a room full of rocking chairs to shame. Fred would usually get at least a couple of complaints from the neighbors that were both aggravating and embarrassing.

"Fred also had one other problem with Buck. His wife usually got home from picking up the kids and running errands sometime before Fred got there. While she was in the kitchen fixing supper, she would turn Buck loose so he could stretch his legs and wander around the place. Now, Buck had an uncanny sense for knowing when Fred was coming home. He seemed to be able to hear Fred's truck long before it came around the curve in the road about a quarter of a mile from the driveway.

"Just before Fred's truck would actually appear, Buck would position himself toward the back of the house right beside a big bush—the perfect ambush position. It was directly across from the chicken pen, where this 'cunning predator' would wait. So, when Fred's truck actually pulled into the driveway that was Buck's cue. He'd slink down close to the ground, pressing himself as flat as he could (like one of those World War II combat dogs). Every muscle was coiled and tensed. His concentration on the flock of 14 egg-laying hens was absolute, watching their oblivious pecking and scratching with a sinister kind of delight.

"All of his senses were raw and on alert. He was all of the perfect predators rolled into one—the leopard stalking through the pampas, the Cheetah by the water hole, the wolf crouched at the edge of the forest clearing. His concentration was so perfect that he didn't have to take his eyes off the chickens to see the truck. He could hear the familiar scrunch of the springs as the Dodge hit a pothole half way up the driveway. (That was his trigger to leap into action—the 'beast of blood and horror' unleashed upon the world.)

"Buck sprang from behind the bush. With eight fully extended bounds and one triumphant leap, he cleared the chicken fence and catapulted himself into the flock of hapless, unsuspecting chickens. He was a vicious ball of black and tan fur and fang, claw, snarl, and snap. The chickens were horrified to think that their fate had been sealed. They ducked, dove, and flapped in every possible direction to escape this terrible ferocious beast. Convinced that the end had come and they would be dinner, these traumatized Leghorns screamed, squawked, and beat their wings so hard that the feathers flew off their bodies in every direction.

"Now, Buck would never really hurt any of the chickens. However, just to prove that he could if he wanted to, every once in a while he'd get a mouthful of feathers from the south end of a northbound chicken. (He didn't do it too often because the feathers stuck to his tongue.) Nevertheless, even after he was back out of the pen and on his way to greet Fred, you could tell he was really quite satisfied that he'd terrified the chickens."

"I remember that," Michael said. "And the chickens (who are dumb as a box of rocks anyway) were so intent on getting out of the pen that they'd plunge through the chicken wire up to their wishbones and often got themselves stuck.

"I also remember that, after Buck had leapt out of the pen, he'd trot very proudly about half way toward Fred's pickup with a big silly smile on his face and a look of superiority to every other creature on earth. Buck had also learned in situations like this that discretion is the better part of valor. So when he got about half way to the truck he'd start to change his attitude.

"Fred always took a stance of being aggravated with Buck and kept his fist propped on his left hip while he leaned on the hood of the truck. Sometimes, if Fred was in a particularly good mood, he actually thought it was funny the way Buck went through his antics. But most of the time, it was just irritating because he couldn't get that silly dog to stop chasing the chickens.

"It also brings to mind, at this point, that Buck would go through his hangdog routine, drop his tail to about half mast, shift his brazen saunter into the purposeful crouch of repentant resolve. He'd walk right up to Fred and just kind of say, 'Okay. I'm guilty. I did a no-no and probably deserve any kind of swat you give me.' And even though his behavior made Fred mad enough to want to punt Buck's backside all the way to the house, there was something about this kind of submission from a dog that makes you feel like not punishing them—and Buck had this concept down to a science.

In any animal/human relationship you have to ask yourself this question: Who is really the master here, and who has who trained? And how well are they trained? The dog goes to the door and barks once. The 'master' immediately gets up and goes over to open the door. So, when you really get down to it, we're observing 'one command' obedience here. How many folks have ever had a dog or a kid that was that well trained? Think about it.

— The Guardian

"So I guess it has to be pretty obvious what the problem is: Buck is aggravating the daylights out of Fred with all his yelling and howling when the family is gone and all the chicken-chasing when Fred comes home. And, of course, he's doing it to get attention. So, I guess we have to ask how to fix it. And I have to remember how it got fixed."

"Well, this is where 'It's Not Your Fault for Dogs' comes in, Michael," The Guardian replied. "Once again, you'll notice that *It's Not Your Fault* and the statement that comes in behind it, *and I can prove it*, both help us see through the other person's eyes. It's about the only way we can truly apply the principle that 'to know me is to love me,' and understand it.

"As we talked about many times before, no one ever intends to do stupid things. It's just that every choice people and animals make is relative to how they feel about themselves. So, if we can step in, get a glimpse of life from their perspective and adjust the way we feel about them as we do so, we can help move the relationship forward without having to play judge, jury and executioner.

"Once again the fact remains, that I can't say or do anything to change you. The Law of Agency states specifically that you are the only one who can change what you do and who you are. That's your freedom of choice (and your responsibility) and nobody else's.

"In Buck's case, Fred got the (not your fault) idea and realized that if Buck came to understand that he was a person too, it just might work for him as well. So what did he finally do? He waited until Buck went through another one of his chicken-chasing routines followed by the usual bites of 'humble pie' repentance, then he knelt down on one knee, took Buck's head in his hands, and looked him straight in the eye.

"'Buck,' he said. 'You're driving me nuts with all the barking and howling when we're gone, and with all that chasing of chickens every time I come home from work. But Buck, I know *it's not your fault…and I can prove it.*'

"In this case, since Buck couldn't speak English and had only a dog vocabulary, Fred had to play both sides of the conversation in order for the *INYF* formula to work. So he continued…

"'Buck', Fred said. 'When you bark and howl when we're gone I know it isn't your intention to make the neighbors mad at us. So I know it's not your fault that I got humiliated and got in Dutch with everyone who lived within a three-block radius. So, obviously you're trying to tell me something. I know that you're a pretty intelligent pup and that you get bored, so obviously you can't think of anything else to do to let us know you're not happy. You're not able to say to me that you hate to sit on the end of this leash for four hours while the family is off on errands, and there's nothing at all for you to do.' *(I can't even go lay down in my favorite place. I can only go to the end of this chain.)*

"'It's not your fault, Buck, that you're just like a kid. And just like any kid the moment someone tells you there's something you can't do, it's the first thing you want to do.'"

The Guardian continued: "Now, Michael, the reason people get upset at animals or children is because they actually feel as if the irritation or embarrassment those very honest creatures are causing them is (somehow) intentional when nothing could be further from the truth. And what Fred came to realize about Buck was that it wasn't about Fred; Buck loves Fred. Buck was howling and carrying on because he felt restricted. His Freedom of choice and subsequently his Agency had been shut down. So this was the only way he had to express his sense of helplessness."

"It's a lot like the infant with the one-word vocabulary," Michael realized. "Only Buck's 'Ah' was a bark or a howl. But it's basically the same frustration."

"And more," The Guardian added. "As we said earlier, Buck's sun rises and sets on his relationship with people. (Who else does he have to relate to…certainly not the chickens?) So Fred found himself in a very interesting situation. At this point Fred was smart enough to realize that it wasn't his job to solve his problem with Buck. Fred's problem was to help Buck solve Buck's problem—boredom, loneliness, a sense of abandonment, and probably a lowered self-image.

"We already know that no one can do anything to us unless we allow it. And Fred had to realize that it certainly wasn't Buck's intention to victimize him. Babies don't intend to victimize their parents by crying and yowling and making them feel guilty over not understanding their needs. (Babies don't know how to assess guilt or blame. Only we can do that to ourselves.) So, by now Fred had been able to assess and solve Buck's howling when the family was gone.

"Now he had to deal with the more complex issue of why his favorite dog was chasing the chickens. So, he had to get with him and say, 'Buck, we've got some chickens out in the yard who just looked like they backed into a Weed-eater™, not to mention what it's doing for egg production (or a lack of it). Needless to say it has me mad at you just about every time I come home. Now, tell me. Was that your intention?'

"So, Fred has had to put himself in Buck's place once again. And the feedback he got from Buck was something like this: 'Shucks, I don't know anything about egg production, although from what I understand they do a lot to add great flavor to those pancakes I love so much. (Believe me, I would never do anything to jeopardize any of my snacks.) As far as the feathers are concerned…well that's a kind of challenge. All of us dogs still have a little bit of the hunter left in us. And at some level I'm actually pretty proud of the fact that I can still catch one of those little rascals. But, Fred, the most important issue is that I want you to be proud of me. I'm trying to show off a little bit. After all, I like me best when I'm with you, and I want you to feel the same way. That's why I do the hangdog stuff, because I know that you're not entirely happy with me when I play *chicken-tag*. It's just that I'm trying so hard to please you that sometimes I make a mess of it, and this is the only way I have of apologizing for my actions.'

"So, Michael, this isn't a lesson in animal psychology. But it is definitely one in problem solving. And this was the day that Fred was able to fix his problem with Buck.

"What he learned from his wife was how frustrated Buck got when he was tethered to that tree whenever the family left him home alone. To solve that dilemma, Fred just put some chain link around the yard to protect Buck from wandering out too far. So, after that, Buck didn't feel lonesome because he wasn't bored any longer. He could go about sniffing in holes, lie down in his favorite spot and check out the chickens, singling one out for his next little practical joke. Since Buck wanted to please Fred at all times, Fred and his wife concocted a plan to channel his energy more constructively.

"Knowing that Buck loved to chase a Frisbee whenever Fred found time to throw it, she picked a time when she knew Fred was coming home from work. She'd keep Buck in the house for a little bout of snacking and anticipation, until a couple of minutes before she knew Fred would be coming up the driveway in his truck. And in that very brief span of time before the pickup pulled into the driveway she'd let Buck out the front door of the house (rather than the side where the chicken coop sat in full view). Then she'd cut loose with a deft toss of the Frisbee right at Fred as he got out of the truck, and just in time for Buck to intercept it. Of course, Buck was so tickled to chase his favorite disk that it only took a couple days before he forgot all about the chickens. A new kind of game had been invented, one that involved them all. And Buck's days as a problem pooch had finally come to an end.

"Now in this case, you'll see a similar chain of connection to all those that take place in every instance of the *Not Your Fault* principle. Every individual is given the opportunity to solve his or her own problems. In this case, you might say that Fred solved it, but Buck is the one who proved it: Once you have the solution, the problem disappears. He's the one who gave voice to his difficulty with the only tools available to him. And if Buck hadn't expressed himself, nothing would have worked. So you were right on with your observation, Michael. With the animal, just as with the little baby, that one word vocabulary, the bark, enabled those in the limited world of adult communication to finally address the problem that needed to be solved.

"You could also say that the experiences of Buck and Fred follow another interesting principle with regard to Laws and Legislation. One of the basic premises that we've learned in our Four Universal Laws is that you can't legislate morality. It's something that has to come from the individual's innate desire to do the right thing.

"Fred initially had a set of rules for Buck: 'You don't bark while we're not around, and you don't chase the chickens.' But it was unenforceable because Fred originally set the boundaries with incomplete information. And laws made for the wrong reasons are impossible to enforce. Only when it became Buck's choice, when he discovered his needs would be met if he took the high road, did the law get complied with. So that's the way it goes: *If it's your law on me, there's no way you can enforce it. And if it's my law that I can accept, there's no way you need to enforce it.*

"You might say, Michael, that this is a bit of a stretch. And yet it really isn't, when you think about it. If you consider, in any society, if the laws are in accord with the Laws of Justice that we innately know to be correct, the individuals subject to those Laws will not only follow them, they'll conduct their lives in ways that actually raise the standards for everyone."

ZONE D

Addiction

"You can't decide what will come into your head, but you can decide what will stay there."

"We come at last to the closing issue of the Forbidden Zone, Michael," The Guardian announced. "Can you guess what it is?"

"It would probably be Addiction," Michael said.

"Good answer!" The Guardian replied. "And why do you think that would suddenly jump to mind?"

"All of our talks about victims and victimization dealt with addictions of various kinds, but we never really talked about the subject itself. And it is a major topic."

"More than you realize," The Guardian agreed. "And it comes in so many forms. "Did you ever have an occasion where you wanted to jump out of your skin? We've heard that term used before, usually by someone in a state of desperation.

Sometimes the statement is said in jest. Other times, it's said because of an addiction.

"At first glance, most people think of addictions that are physical dependencies—drugs, alcohol, nicotine, food, sex—when they're not necessarily. I grant you those are the most common forms, and the ones that get the most attention. The truth is that addictions take many forms, and all of them are bad. That's because almost all addictions are another type of denial.

"Frankly, Michael, the way most people fail to take responsibility for their lives is through denial…and blaming everything and everyone else for their situation.

"Addictions are one step even further down into the rabbit-hole than when we blame someone else for our problems. Addictions are our ways of hiding from life, and any circumstances that you would have to think about and even go through (like the slightest bit of judgment to determine your responsibility for them) are a means of escaping totally.

"Addictions have a way of taking more forms than we can imagine. Sex can be an addiction, and is for many people. So are work, art, games, sports, shopping—things you might not first take into consideration. All these and more can be ways of escaping from your responsibilities for your life. These aren't necessarily bad things, but when they become obsessive and all-consuming they can have devastating effects.

"What we have in this insidious cycle of addiction and denial is a victim mentality. Those who get caught up in it are making a judgment that something is wrong and are placing blame on something or someone else. They aren't taking responsibility. Instead, they're doing just the opposite, and they're shrinking or stepping away from responsibility. Most addictions don't even allow you to recognize that there's a responsibility to be taken. It's a hiding from the realization of the rational judgment required to take charge of our lives.

"If someone is involved with sex as their addiction, for example, they would want sex as often as they can get it because when they're in the process of having that sexual relationship the world goes away. The physical gratification allows the escape. (It even releases endorphins into the system so you get a serotonin rush.) It provides something else—a pleasure target toward which to draw the mind. Some people develop chemical addictions because they release the mind from responsibility. They literally numb all feeling, and all pain along with it. And it doesn't just involve illicit drugs either.

"Talk to someone who is very confident, who acknowledges his or her obligations, and who is willing to take responsibility for all their circumstances in life. Ask how they'd feel if their tongue was thick, their fingers were numb, their vision was blurred and that they'd have to concentrate very hard just to comprehend the world around them. Ask them if they'd prefer that experience.

Forget heroin, cocaine, and marijuana. Most of the painkillers, stress-relief drugs and antidepressants are now sold by prescription in the billions of units. Brand name drugs such as Prozac, Zoloft, Paxil, Vicodin, and Lexapro are legal and yet can often become ticking time bombs. People who think they need them often get prescribed antidepressant cocktails that are variations of these formulations. And because they're issued under a doctor's car, people take them regularly by the billions of units a month. The result is that they have become victims in the Great American Prescription Drug Culture. In fact, once many patients get hooked on these antidepressant cocktails, their physicians literally cannot allow them to quit cold turkey because the two most frequent side effects of withdrawal are deep-depression and suicidal tendencies. Think about it.

— The Guardian

"Talk to someone who is very confident, who acknowledges his or her obligations, and who is willing to take responsibility for all their circumstances in life. Ask how they'd feel if their tongue was thick, their fingers were numb, their vision was blurred and that they'd have to concentrate very hard just to comprehend the world around them. Ask them if they'd prefer that experience.

"If you put the question to them, of course, they would categorically reject the notion as ridiculous. In fact, most people in control of their lives are entirely focused on the importance of it—so much so that if they had to undergo an operation they'd probably prefer the least amount of drugs and painkillers possible."

"On the other hand, the ultimate victim would opt for almost any mind-altering experience, longing for the 'high,' yet whining because it didn't happen to be their addiction of choice.

"People who know themselves would reject any 'unnecessary' influence on their consciousness. They long ago came to realize that they can't hide in a bottle, in a bedroom, at the end of a needle, inside the office, or with any of the other seemingly subtle addictions that lie in wait.

"Of course, the workaholic says, 'I have to be there. I have to concentrate. I have to spend eighteen hours a day to properly do my job.' Totally immersed in their addiction, workaholics look upon their job obsession as a safe haven because, after all, 'Who can condemn you for working?' It's the old-fashioned American work ethic in all its many forms. And yet it's also an addiction.

"Any addiction, however benign, is still the antithesis of who you are, and it's a total rejection of your individual power to create.

"Gambling is a common addiction. There is the story of the woman in Las Vegas some years ago who played the same dollar slot machines every time she'd go into a particular casino. Day in, day out, she would sit with racks of silver dollars posted at the same machines and never vary her routine. Finally it became apparent that the woman wasn't really playing the slots for the money. And when one of the other patrons of the casino asked her why she always did this, she openly admitted, 'I gamble because I'm bored.' Gambling was her escape. It had become her addiction. "We all recognize what a universal addiction gambling can be, and yet 41 states in the United States have laws that not only permit gambling, but also encourage it—with casinos, state lotteries and weekly Powerball drawings specifically designed to lure the addict and the disenfranchised of the world. Talk about an oxymoron: Governments spend tens of millions of dollars getting people off narcotics and alcohol and then turn right around and try to sell lottery tickets to the recently recovered.

"Addiction is the worst form of victim mentality. How do you stop it? Again, the total control over how we deal with what we allow to affect us is based upon what we have chosen as our *self-image*. The only way people can deal with an addiction is to accept responsibility for everything in their lives. They are the creators. What they have to ask themselves is why they created it in the first place."

"But what about physical addictions like tobacco, alcohol, sugar, chocolate and caffeine drinks? If those are your addictions and you want to get yourself free, how do you work through all of that?"

"It's an irony of human nature, Michael, that the body is constantly able to permit the mind sudden and unexplained corrections. How do you explain such mysteries as spontaneous remissions of cancer? No one can determine the reasons, and yet it happens every day. Why is it that one day, some women decide to quit smoking due to pregnancy or health issues, and then they are just done with it? Yes, we have different gene pools, different genetic encoding, and different chemical make-ups. But who inhabits our bodies? We do. And whose responsibilities are they? Ours!

"Who has total control over how things affect us? Do you think the individual who is in total control would have a problem giving up some behavior in an instant? Of course not! It's all mental, because you *can overcome any physical condition or circumstance* with the mental power you already possess. There are millions of people who smoke for twenty or thirty years, and then one day decide they've had enough. They realize it's a stupid thing to do, and they just quit. They quit because *they decide to.*

"This is very often the point of critical mass that junkies arrive at when they hit 'rock bottom.' When any addict hits rock bottom, they can go no lower. Or else something scares the daylights out of them, and they stop. And who stops it? They do. Not the therapists, not the counselors; not the parents; they do.

"Something gets their attention. So, they become the student. They see what happens to their friends or other addicts. Or else a spouse decides they've had enough of their antics. The causes may be many, but somewhere along the line a two-by-four of reality smacks them between the eyes, and they quit their behavior—period—cold turkey, 'never gonna go there again.'

"Now, some people will ask what the difference is between addiction and obsession. Obsessions are very often the beginning of addiction, or they may be addictions themselves. But usually obsessions bring their own warning signs and happen very suddenly.

"For example, you might hear something like, 'He's obsessed with playing basketball every night after work, but he's not addicted to it.' This might be okay if it goes on for a few days. But addictions often tend to take on a life of their own. And the biggest warning comes when the habit becomes a priority over everything else in someone's life. That's when it becomes the addiction. When basketball takes precedence over something that this person would normally choose, they are becoming addicted.

"If that person chooses to play basketball, ignoring a family commitment, it could be an addiction.

"If the snowmobiler 'has to go out in the snow' every weekend or they'll just burst, that's addictive behavior. This is especially true if the obsession overwhelms that person's normal obligations—those things in life they know they should be doing but just can't find the power to do. Picnics, birthdays, anniversaries, even household chores—you know what those things are. But your passion, your obsession, your addiction to some other form of behavior takes priority.

"As we've noted before, Michael, addictions take many forms. Substance addicts, such as alcoholics or crack-cocaine users, realize at some level that their actions are interwoven with the cause. And yet the greatest addiction in society today is Victimization.

"Victimization is particularly insidious because victims truly believe that they have little or no control over all the awful things that are happening to them. Welfare families, for example, can't seem to get out of the rut they're in. Government entitlements often make the rut deeper because the recipients get hooked on the benefits and actually become afraid to retake control of their lives for fear of losing them. So this victim/enabler addiction becomes the ultimate vicious cycle. And that addiction leads to many others. We develop habits, which may or may not become addictions. We become compulsive in some of our behaviors. Think about some of the habits we observe in others that could be related to victimization—biting nails, overeating, obnoxious behavior, loud talking, picking our noses, picking our teeth, poor hygiene—the list never ends. True victims look for behaviors to help them escape whenever and wherever they can. And yes! It's true that all addicts are Victims. And conversely, all Victims sooner or later can become addicts. The important issue to remember is that victimization, like any other addiction, is something each individual has the power to quit. It is a matter of making the decision to so do, and then taking Action.

"Addictions are always important things to consider because we are all susceptible to them, often without realizing it. And they are one of the ways we give up our liberty, our freedom to choose, our gift to create. Like all of the topics within these pages, they intersect with each other. 'And it all becomes one thing.' To regain our Liberty, our Agency, we first have to fight off the addictions that attack it.

"Knowing *that it's not your fault requires accepting responsibility.* Not only accepting it, Michael, but embracing it. Responsibility, like Faith, is an active term. And all the people who have quit their addictions have finally gotten the message— to take action, to create change, and to become better.

Addictions cannot survive in responsible people. Responsible people have made a covenant with life. And they're the ones who have finally learned that, 'I like me best when I'm with me.'"

"So once I take responsibility for everything I do, what can I expect?" Michael asked, knowing the question made sense. "Let's just assume I woke up tomorrow morning and started applying everything you have taught me here. What would my life be like from that moment on?"

"You would not only discover but experience the magnificence of who you really are. The bottom line, Michael, is that the propensity to avoid addiction is directly proportional to the individual's willingness to assume responsibility for their entire life experience.

"Think about it, Michael," The Guardian said. "Imagine the great day you would have. In fact, don't stop at imagining, **decide** to have a great rest of your life."

My Book of Life

(Now that you've got it, just do it!)

"My counsel to you, Michael, is that you make up a 'Playbook' for your personal game of life that shall be titled My Book of Life.*"*

Thinking about all that he'd learned from The Guardian in the past few hours or days (time was relative, at this point), Michael sat back and tried to put it all together.

"All I can say is, 'Thank you,'" he said. "I just hope I can make it all work."

"Of course you can, Michael. But let me suggest something: Set out a *game plan* so that you can put it all into place."

"You mean, like a final exam?"

"Nothing that severe Michael. Let's just call it a workbook. Better still, why don't you call it *My Book of Life, THE GUARDIAN CODE* "Playbook."

"There's a famous quote by J.D. Salinger in *Catcher in the Rye* that says, 'Life is a game. And you play according to the rules.' So, how do you learn to win at the game, Michael? Any game?

"First, you learn the rules then you put together strategies. In sports, they're referred to as *plays*. And you use them to accomplish your objectives, to reach your targets…and win! That's your Playbook.

"Michael, you have just studied all these essential principles and laws— all the elements of *THE GUARDIAN CODE*. You have learned that the principle of gratitude encompasses the application of all of this wisdom. Now your ongoing work and opportunity is to systematically put this all into practice in your lifetime Journal that you, Michael, will write called *'My Book of Life.'*"

"Of course, *My Book of Life* is in reality 'Your Book Of Life.' What is amounts to is a small, pocket-sized, daily use, companion journal to *THE GUARDIAN CODE: It's Not Your Fault*, master plan.

"Your assignment, Michael, 'should you choose to accept it,' is to perform the daily exercises in this little journal for a period of six months. And here's how it works:

"When your first six months Journal is completed, you will then refresh and renew your commitments, objectives and targeted accomplishments for the next six months. I promise you Michael, that if you will take a little time each day to create your future and document what you have experienced and learned you will fill your life with happiness, joy and unimagined abundance and prosperity. Your '(My) Book of Life' will ultimately read as a great adventure to both you, in retrospect, and those who follow you as the students of the teacher they are ready to have appear."

How It Works (...Is How Things Really Work!)

"*My Book of Life* is made up of Three Sections or 'Journals of Creation.' It may sound like a lot of work. It isn't. In fact, once you've mastered The Guardian Code, these three tools help frame what will become almost a kind of "automatic excellence" in your life.

1) "*My Gratitude Journal.* Remember the Emerson/Plato quote: *'For that for which I am grateful, I cannot be denied.'* Start here, and the rest falls into place. So, My Gratitude affirmations are the master keys by which all negative, doubt, fear and "un-creation" can be either controlled or entirely eliminated. Virtually all of the true principles taught here in *THE GUARDIAN CODE: It's Not Your Fault* textbook are implemented through this magnificent all-encompassing principle."

2) "*My Creation Journal.* The creative tool by which you turn 'thoughts into things'. Michael, after you have listed all of the objectives or targets you wish to obtain and achieve, you need to follow this simple system of affirming visualizations for each desired item 'as

if' it has already been achieved or is in your possession. You have learned that every thought creates its physical form when you put out a clear statement and mental (creative) picture of it already being in existence. You can follow the instructions in this journal to create your future 'as if' it already exists."

3) *"My Journal Of Knowledge And Reports* is a documentation, essentially a diary, of the knowledge and understanding you have obtained along with the objectives and targets achieved. Michael, this is an exciting chronicle of the rewards you have received by practicing the creative principles that you have learned. As you read and remind yourself of what you have accomplished you build an ever more powerful belief in who you are and your power to be master of your destiny.

"Michael, the reports in this journal tell you how well you are doing at consistently performing your daily creative exercises. By recording your actions each day you become accountable to yourself for the results you achieve.

"Michael, as you work with your 'Book of Life' make sure you have a fun and exciting time. Most problems people have come from taking life too seriously. It's not serious. But it is important.

"So let's open it up and see what happens."

The Guardian Code Formula for creative living has very ancient roots in logic and application. About 1200 years ago, the Philosopher Lao Tzu observed: 'In dwelling, live close to the ground. In thinking, keep to the simple. In conflict, be fair and generous. In governing, don't try to control. In work, do what you enjoy. In family life, be completely present.' Pretty good advice! Think about it.

— The Guardian

Michael took the little "My Book of Life" Journal from the Guardian and curiously ruffled through its pages. He turned to the journal's introduction, scanned through it and then carefully read the instructions to the gratitude journal. He accepted the "$.59 pen" offered by the Guardian, paused briefly in thought, and then Michael started writing, feverishly making lists as if his "My Book of Life Journal" was automatically writing for him. He started to pause to ask The Guardian a question or two, but realized that every question that came to him became an answer almost as quickly as he'd started to ask it. The Guardian had settled comfortably into his side of the "S-shaped" conversation chair, closed his eyes, and drifted off to that delightfully beautiful timeless place where Guardians repose while waiting for their neophyte students to surface after being immersed in the "everlasting waters of truth and light."

Michael finally finished, realizing that he had been practically mesmerized by the process of creation. Looking up, Michael could see that the green field, rolling hills and the waterfall were there. So was the 'S'-chair. But the man that had been sitting in it, The Guardian, was gone.

Had he left? In fact had he ever really been there, Michael had to wonder as he felt his consciousness roll back from open wonderment to the focus on the world around him. And yet somehow he knew that The Guardian had been with him all along.

"The Teacher appeared because I was ready," Michael smiled to himself. "But what to do next, and how do I go about recreating that perfect day?" He realized that a question, when asked, often becomes the answer in itself. And he realized that he already had the answer. "All I have to do now is find the way back home, and I can put all this into practice."

That's when he realized he was home, settled in the comforting clutches of his souped-up La-Z-Boy recliner. His little pocket-sized "My Book of Life" Journal was now firmly fixed in his left hand while the "$.59 (mightier than the sword) pen" dangled loosely between his first and "bird" fingers of his right hand.

Michael absently let his fingers do the walking to the "My Gratitude" section of his Journal. As he did, he realized that he still had many more things that he was grateful to list. He flipped forward to the "My Creation" section and noted how many objectives and targets that he still needed to list to be created. Michael quietly said to himself, "I thought I had an idea of how things worked—that life was a game of chance where some were lucky and some were not. But I really don't have to be limited to just what life happens to throw my way. The glorious exciting fact is that there is more, unbelievably there is so much more."

As he said it, Michael could feel that somewhere nearby The Guardian was smiling. (And somehow he could hear him whisper.)

"Yes, Michael. You're right! There is so much more. And that's where the real fun begins…"

Acknowledgments

It is with joy and gratitude that I acknowledge those who have made contributions to this book…and who have supported me on this new journey…

Sherry Jane Shenk: My lovely, late, wife of 33 years. Sherry, through the magnificence of her life, is the reason that the understanding and the wisdom brought forth in the book *THE GUARDIAN CODE: It's Not Your Fault* was made possible. She took a husband who could be best described as a lump of coal (definitely not a diamond in the rough *yet*) and polished him with her unfailing love and wisdom into the man he never imagined he could be. Many times during our life together she urged, "Honey, (or "Steven," if she *really* wanted to get my attention) DECIDE." Only to be followed by: "And then don't un-decide." I am forever grateful for her and I suspect that you (our readers) will be, too.

Barbara (Babs) Rossberg: My business partner and much-more-than-best friend for nearly 30 years. Babs labored untold hours transcribing, discussing, counseling, and compiling hundreds of my "great ah-has," revelations, and plain ordinarily "brain droppings" into a foot-high stack of pages that was the original manuscript for this book.

Robert Joseph Ahola: I greatly admire and appreciate Robert's abilities in structuring, organizing, and editing the content of this book. His gifts as an accomplished author/coauthor, playwright and director were extremely valuable as were his contributions of literary quotations and word-track clarity.

Kim Power Stilson: Kim is the "rising star" of public relations. Her expertise and counsel in the way these ideas are presented will help everyone become aware of the mission of this important and empowering project. She is our "recruitment poster girl," because she is already enthusiastically practicing what we are preaching.

Sylvia Shenk: My wife and sweetheart. I am forever grateful for her love and support of me, the thoughts I have, what I do, and who I am. They say that common sense isn't very common. This lovely lady not only has the sensibility about her, but also has the rare capability to express "unconditional love." They say that behind every "would-be" great man there is a woman rolling her eyes. Unfortunately I give Sylvia that opportunity much more often than even Babs, Kim, and Mona. I love you, sweetheart. (And so does The Guardian.)

Marina Peterson: Marina is an extraordinarily gifted organizer, editor, visionary thinker, versatile Renaissance woman and the best personal assistant a man could ever wish for—not to mention someone of phenomenal creative talent, critical judgment and consummate integrity. More than merely my "Director of Corporate Protection," she is my strong right arm. No man could ask for a better a friend or more loyal advocate.

William Shenk and Mini Gladys Shenk: I acknowledge, with love and admiration, my brilliant "animal husbander" (whisperer) and "curbstone philosopher" father, William H. Shenk, the source of much wisdom, and my lovely mother, Mini Gladys (Glady), the first woman (of many) in my life who stood behind me and rolled her eyes at my foolishness.

Index

'Act of God', 157
'Bad Stuff', 15, 59
'Cowboy Cadillac', 119
'Push Away', 124, 125, 127-129
A Bug's Life, 209
Abandoned Child, 239, 240
Abe Lincoln, 186, 210
Abraham Lincoln, 55, 78, 198, 209
Abuse, 29, 30, 49, 50, 82-84, 121, 127, 128, 227
Abused, 29, 31, 76, 127, 215
Abuser, 29, 83
Addiction, xv, 7, 29, 105, 215, 250-257
Addiction, xv, 7, 29, 105, 215, 250-257
Addictions, 227, 251-257
Afghanistan, 32
African, 34
Aldous Huxley, 186
Ancient Egyptians, 4
Ancient Toltec Wisdom Book, 197
Applications of Justice, 83
At-one-ment, 24
Atonement, 24, 54
Babe Ruth, 204
Barbra Streisand, 72
Beach Boys, 2
Benjamin Disraeli, 4
Benjamin Franklin, 165
Beverly Hillbillies, 222

Bible Revelations, 181
BIC, 170
Big Eraser, 15
Bind of Enablement, 45
BINMF (But It's Not My Fault), 37, 40
Book of Life, iv, xvi, 28, 187, 219, 257-261, 266
Book of Psalms, 107
British Empire, 205
Buddha, xi
Buddhist, 74
By-Products of Guilt, 29
C. S. Lewis, 208
Calvin Coolidge, 214
Carson City, 53
Carson City Memorial Hospital, 53
Carson-Tahoe Regional Medical Center, 53
Casanova, 129, 130, 133
Chosen One, 4
Christ, 17, 54, 84, 92, 105, 149, 166, 167, 190
Christ-like, 90, 106
Christian, 74, 85
Christianity, 26
Christians, 17, 54
CIA, 83
Cleve Backster, 83
Clint Eastwood Western, 218

Closure, 101
Codependency, 41, 43, 44
Cogito Ergo Sum, 160
Common Law, 81, 82
Conditional Love, 69, 86-88, 90, 91, 93, 94
Conditional Love That Destroys, 87
Creation Journal, 259
Critical Mass, 164, 165, 255
De-perfection, 164
Denis Waitley, 214
Dependency, 41, 42, 75, 183, 186
Depression, xvi, 7, 37, 38, 182, 194, 195, 226, 227
Descartes, 160
Disaster of Distance, 121
Distance Is Disaster, 117-119, 146, 219
Distraction of Action, 203
Don Juan, 129, 130, 133
Don Miguel Ruiz, 197
Done-untos, 37, 38
Dr. Bannister, 205
Egyptian Book of the Dead, 28
Emotional Blackmail, 44, 49
Emotional Terrorism, 44
Enablee, 44-48, 68
Enablees, 45
Enabler, 44-48, 68, 103, 256
Enablers, 45, 47, 48, 68
End of Time Events, 181
English Common Law, 81
English Olympic Team, 205
ETE, 181
Everything Is Fixed, 19
Examples of Faith, 200, 207
Explaining How Things Work, 5
Fault-finders, 28
Fault-finding, 27-29, 64, 87, 88, 98, 143
Finding Fault, xvi, 15, 20, 21, 33, 64, 126, 143, 168, 242
First Confusion, 142

Forbidden Zone, 215, 238, 251
Forbidden Zones, 215
Four Agreements, 197
Four Confusions, 139, 140, 142
Four Universal Laws, 61, 148, 150, 152-154, 197, 199, 208, 215, 250
Fourth Confusion, 151, 152
Fourth Universal Law, 140, 160, 188
Futurist, 267
Genuine Sympathy, 102
Gerald Lambeau, 128
GMO, 181
Goals and Objectives, 152, 169, 197-199, 225
Golden Rule, 188
Good Will Hunting, 128
Gratitude, 55, 83, 152, 198, 216, 217, 221, 222, 224-227, 258, 259, 261-263, 266
Gratitude Journal, 259, 261
Great American Prescription Drug Culture, 253
Great Facilitator, 106
Great Game of Chance, 9
Great Mirror, 70
Greek Oracle of Delphi, 75
Grief, 100-103
Grieving, 100, 101
Groucho Marx, 77
Guardian Code Formula, 260
Guardian Trash Removal Team, 14
Guardians, xi, xii, 5, 114, 219, 225, 261
Guilt Busters, 14
Guilt Creates Victims, 31, 35, 80, 149
Guilt Trash Removal System, 33
Guilt Trips, 27, 32, 129
Guilt-Assessment, 100
Guilt-cycle, 129
Guilt-defense, 121
Guilt-Free Zone, 33
Guilt-givers, 28

Guilty, xvi, 12, 13, 17, 27-33, 54, 62, 81, 82, 89, 99, 126, 127, 139, 149, 167, 177, 198, 222, 232, 241, 246, 248
Guru, 3, 219
Guru Line, 219
Haiti, 103
Hamlet, 75
Harry Potter, 209
Henry Wadsworth Longfellow, 138
Hidden Contract, 114
Hidden/Forbidden Zone, 215
Higher Source, 24, 213
Hilo, 186
Hollywood, 53
Holy Land, 32
Holy Spirit, 198
Horse Manure Principal, 25
How It Works, xvi, 85, 115, 136, 141, 159, 259
How People Think Things Work, 15, 20, 118, 130, 131, 149
How Things Really Work, xvi, 20, 21, 27, 30, 69, 85, 119, 120, 123, 130, 131, 139, 196, 259
How Things Work, xvi, 5, 7, 8, 13, 15, 18, 26, 29, 30, 32, 45, 54, 64, 66-68, 88, 89, 98, 109, 114, 116, 120, 123, 136-138, 140, 143, 149, 195, 196, 217-219, 227, 242
Hug, 9, 33, 63, 68, 69, 96, 102, 121-123, 125, 127, 128, 146, 147, 241
Hurricane Katrina, 103, 184
I Like Me Best, 61, 63, 74, 78, 131, 133-138, 145, 166, 168, 219, 249, 257
Independence, 42, 183
Indulgences, 26
Innocent, 14-17, 23, 26, 81, 82, 84, 147, 167, 168, 222
Institute of Transpersonal Psychology, 83
Internal Revenue Service, 28

INYF (It's Not Your Fault), 247
Iraq, 32
IRS, 33, 110
Israel, 167
Israeli, 47, 48
Israelis, 47
It's Not Your Fault Formula, 21, 22
J.D. Salinger, 258
J.K. Rowling, 209
Jehovah, 148
Jesus, 17, 54, 59, 67, 84, 92, 105, 149-151, 160, 166, 167, 190
Jesus Christ, 54, 84, 92, 149, 166, 167, 190
Jesus of Nazareth, 149, 166
Joe Gillis, 44
John Landy, 205
John Wilkes Booth, 210
Journal Of Knowledge And Reports, 260
Journals of Creation, 259
Judgment, 25, 26, 29-33, 39, 52, 75, 79-88, 90, 100, 149-151, 167, 168, 170, 171, 177, 180, 189, 241, 252, 264
Judgment Day, 25
Judgmentalism, 24, 27, 99, 151, 167, 226, 234
Julius Caesar, 10
Just Say No, 49
Kahlil Gibran, 101
Key Prevention Points, 237
Kim Power Stilson, 264
King of the Gods, 6
Kingdom of Heaven, 160, 166
Knight Commander, 205
LA Country Club, 77
La-Z-Boy, 261
Lack of Understanding, 130
Lack Thinking, 222-225
Lambeau, 128
Language of Understanding, 103

Lao Tzu, 68, 260
Las Vegas, 254
Law of Agency, 45, 247
Law of Creation, 72, 140, 160, 161, 164, 169, 177, 187-193, 195, 197, 198
Law of Familiarity, 145
Law of Justice, 140, 158-160, 179, 186
Law of Me, 60-62, 64, 66-71, 78, 92, 95, 108, 124, 125, 132, 142-144, 147, 149, 151, 154-156, 164, 166, 180, 189, 222, 234, 242
Law of Perfect Proximity, xii
Law of the Ten-Fold Return, 106
Law of Wrong, 148
Law, xii, 1, 33, 42, 45, 60-62, 64, 66-73, 78, 81-83, 85, 92, 95, 106, 108, 114, 115, 124, 125, 132, 133, 140-145, 147-151, 154-156, 158-161, 164, 166, 169, 177, 179-181, 184, 186-193, 195, 197, 198, 210, 214, 222, 225, 227, 234, 242, 247, 250
Laws of Health, 85
Laws of Justice, 250
Laws of Nature, 141
Laws of Physics, 141
Laws of Sickness, 85
Learn More About What Really Matters, 229
Legislation, 250
Letter of the Law, 148, 149, 151
Life Lessons That Cut Across All Species, 243
Life Zone, 229
Life-energy, 185
Little League, 10, 66
Los Angeles, 36, 77
Los Angeles Country Club, 77
Luke Skywalker, 207
Mahatma Gandhi, 109
Major League Baseball, 205
Man's Best Friend, 86

Mark Anthony, 10
Marriages, 7, 113, 114, 131, 146, 227
Marvelous Marmalade, 117
Matt Damon, 128
Mayan Calendars, 181
MBA, 111
McGuire, 128
Melba's Marvelous Marmalade, 117
Messenger of Light, 3, 4
Microsoft, 209
Middle Ages, 26, 84
Milton Hershey, 209
Mini Gladys Shenk, 264
Monsters, Inc., 209
Motivational Speaker, 267
Mr. Clean, 3
Mulberry Pie Café, 117
Murphy's Law, 1, 42, 73, 227
Muslim, 74
My Book of Life, iv, xvi, 187, 257-261, 266
My Book of Life Journal, 260, 261
My Creation Journal, 259
My Gratitude Journal, 259
My Journal Of Knowledge And Reports, 260
Nancy Reagan, 49
Napoleon, xiii, 58
Native American, 4
Native American Shaman, 4
Native Americans, 97
Negative Aspects, 85
Nelson Mandela, 109
Nevada, 53
New Orleans, 184, 186
New Testament, 149
New York, 16
NFL, 235
Nirvana, 240
Norma Desmond, 44
Nostradamus, 181

Obedience, 141, 246
Obsessions, 255
Oliver Cromwell, 200
Olympus, 6
Organic Guilt, 27
Original Sin, 26, 163, 166
Palo Alto, 83
Pandora's Box, 6
Past, xv, 21, 23, 25, 38-40, 50-60, 72, 75, 76, 78, 96, 98-100, 119, 126, 128, 129, 139, 144, 145, 158, 165, 169-171, 173-178, 180, 190, 191, 193, 194, 203, 242, 258
Patrick Henry, 185
Peace of Mind Through Ice Water Enemas, 4
Pearl Harbor, 64
Pearly Gates, 202
Perfect Building, 11, 12, 23, 68, 108, 125, 160, 215
Perfect Muscle, 17
Perfect Proximity, xii
Perfection, 11, 13-17, 23, 79, 105, 106, 163-168, 196, 197, 213, 215, 219
Philosopher Lao Tzu, 68, 260
PMA, 59
Political Correctness, 8
Pontius Pilate, 84, 167
Positive Mental Attitude (PMA), 59
Post-Traumatic Stress Disorder, 32
Power of Faith, 199
Power of Faith Visualization, 199
Power Struggle, 144-146
Powerball, 254
Powerstroke, 119
Prime Directive, xi
Principle of Distraction, 94, 95
Principles of The Guardian Code, iv, v, xi
Proverbs, 65, 160
Prozac, 253

PTSD, 32
Queen Elizabeth II, 205
Racism, 25
Rage, 24, 94, 95, 98, 101, 234
Ralph Waldo Emerson, 213
Reagan Presidency, 49
Red Cross, 202
Redskins, 235
Reinhold Niebuhr, 179
Rejection, 30, 31, 120, 198, 209, 254
Renaissance, 264, 267
Repentance, 32, 54, 247
Rescue Team, 121
Responsibility, xv, xvi, 21, 22, 26, 27, 37-39, 41, 42, 46, 54, 64, 75, 78, 80, 81, 94, 95, 109, 110, 115, 126, 129, 154-157, 167, 174, 177, 179, 186, 187, 192, 196, 200, 212, 215, 220, 222, 233, 234, 244, 247, 252-254, 256, 257, 266
Retirement, 37, 183, 187
Revolutionary War, 57
Ricky Henderson, 204
Roadrunner, 1
Robert Joseph Ahola, 263
Robin Williams, 128
Rodney Dangerfield, 70
Roger Bannister, 205
Role of the Teacher, 64
Roll of the Dice, 8, 9
Romans, 167
Rule of the Power Struggle, 146
Sadducees, 167
SBS (Shaken Baby Syndrome), 236. 237
Sean McGuire, 128
Second Confusion, 144
Second Universal Law, 45
Self Images, 29
Self-actualized, 44, 267
Self-Approval, 74, 89, 92, 93
Self-Aware, 143

Self-Discipline, 214
Self-esteem, xv, 31, 38, 41, 73-77, 87
Self-gratification, 74
Self-Image, 29, 30, 39, 62, 67, 69, 70, 74-79, 82, 87, 88, 93, 95, 98, 131, 164, 165, 227, 248, 254
Self-Image Guilt, 98, 164
Self-Images, 39, 73, 75, 82, 177, 227
Selfishly Unselfish, 64
Sensei, 27
Shaken Baby Syndrome (SBS), 236, 237
Shakespeare, 10, 75
Shangri-La, 240
Sherry Jane Shenk, 263
Sir Roger Bannister, 205
Six-Step Method, 33
Six-Step Process, 33, 173, 174
Social Security, 37
Socrates, 4, 152
South Africa, 109
South Boston, 128
Special Keys to the Guardian Code, 227, 229
Spirit of the Law, 148, 150
Spiritual Creation, 199
St. Peter, 202
Star Wars, 207
Start Out Perfect, 13, 18, 166
State of Perfection, 17, 23
Stay Perfect, 13
Steering Wheel Concept of Management, 206
Stellan Skarsgård, 128
Steven Jobs, 209
Sunset Boulevard, 44
Super-Guardian Six-Step Process, 173
Superman, 110
Sylvia Shenk, 264
Synthetic Guilt, 27, 28, 32
Talmud, 148
Tarzan, 222

Ten Commandments, 148, 154
Ten-Fold Return, 106, 107
Terrorist, 45, 47, 48, 83
The Atonement, 54
The Beatles, 144
The Better Angels, 198
The Big Push, 124, 127, 128
The Big Push-Away, 123, 124
The Chosen, 4, 5
The Creator, 106, 163, 191, 196, 209
The Dingo Concept, 84
The Dog, 68, 76, 85, 86, 246
The First Universal Law, 108
The Gospel of Love, 34, 85, 150
The Gospel of Love, 34, 85, 150, 151
THE GUARDIAN CODE Essentials, 266
The Guardian Council, 217, 224
The Jedi, 207
The Law of Displacement, 141
The Law of Perfect Proximity, xii
The Law of the Tenfold Return, 184
The Laws of Me, 187
The Lord, 107, 202
The Magic of Faultlessness, 18, 19, 21, 23, 180
The Man, xiii, 2-4, 10, 11, 39, 40, 68, 75, 84-86, 97, 105, 128, 137, 147, 149, 150, 157, 160, 166, 167, 180, 182, 183, 186, 191, 197, 200-202, 209, 210, 219, 220, 261, 263, 264, 267
The Mentality of Lack, 103
The New Yorker, 34
The Now, 59
The Past Does Not Exist, 21, 50, 58, 76, 78, 98, 99, 169, 171, 174, 190
The Past No Longer Exists, 23, 175, 176
The Pen Mightier Than the Sword, 168, 169
The Prophet, 101
The Right Law, 85

The Rockies, 117
The Steering Wheel Concept of Management, 206
The Trash Removal System, 12
The Wonder Hugger, 116, 117, 120-123, 196
Third Confusion, 148
Third Universal Law, 140
Thomas Edison, 58, 59
Tibetan Book of Life, 28
Toby Keith, 61
Tough Love, 49
Toy Story, 209
Trash Removal, 12, 14, 15, 21-23, 33
Trash Removal System, 12, 21, 33
Triumph, 60
Ultimate Validation, 134
Un-Original Sin, 24
Uncle Harry, 57
Uncle Rich, 56
Unconditional Love, 38, 89-91, 93-95, 97, 98, 100, 103, 105-107, 147, 150, 151, 235, 264
Unconditional Loving, 147
Understanding How Things Work, 7
Universal Law, 33, 45, 108, 114, 115, 133, 140, 142, 158, 160, 179, 184, 188, 214, 225
University of Michigan, 49
Upside of Guilt, 33
Valhalla, 240
Vicodin, 253
Victim Mentality, 38, 41, 75, 105, 252, 254

Victimization, xv, 26, 31, 40, 43, 44, 68, 101, 103, 105, 129, 202, 220, 222, 234, 251, 256
Victims, 27, 29-31, 34-38, 41-47, 54, 73, 75, 76, 80, 82, 84, 85, 100, 103, 125-127, 149, 167, 184, 202, 222, 237, 251, 253, 256
Vince Lombardi, 197, 214
Visualization, xvi, 199, 214
Visualize, 107, 161, 192, 195, 213, 214
Vivian Laramore, 50
Volcano, 186
Vulcans, xiv
Wall Street, 182
Welfare, 10, 75, 256
Wile E. Coyote, 1
Will Hunting, 128
William Blake, 216
William H. Shenk, 264
William Shenk, 264
Willpower, 214
Winston Churchill, 4, 163, 208
Wonder Hug, 33, 122, 123, 125, 127, 128, 146, 147
Wonder Hugger, 116, 117, 120-123, 196
Wonder Huggers, 123
Wonder Hugs, 147
World War II, 245
You Are What You Appear, 71
Your Fault Search and Rescue Team, 121
Zeus, 6
Zoloft, 253
Zorro, 110

THE GUARDIAN CODE
ESSENTIALS
(ORDER TODAY!)

The secrets of *The Guardian Code* are hiding in plain sight. Recognizing them and putting them into practice comes with daily application. Understanding that you have the ability to become everything you desire to be comes with assuming your responsibility to take the next steps. And the next steps are here...

MY BOOK OF LIFE
Begin with Gratitude, and take the Guardian Code's step-by-step program toward leading "the charmed life."

THE WISDOM OF
THE GUARDIAN
Pithy, poignant and to the point, *The Wisdom of the Guardian* is carefully crafted out of direct quotes from The Guardian presented to you in simple, direct, and memorable ways that anyone can grasp, share... and expand upon.

Available in print from:
www.Amazon.com • www.BarnesAndNoble.com • www.BooksAmillion.com
& other online retailers

Available in electronic format from:
• Amazon Kindle • Barnes & Noble • iBooks • Smashwords.com

About Steve Shenk

Author/Talk Show Host/Motivational Speaker/Entrepreneur/Futurist

A 30-year entrepreneur, Steve Shenk is a self-actualized Renaissance man who clearly walks his talk. Steve's book, *THE GUARDIAN CODE: It's Not Your Fault* is a life experience he felt impelled to share when he realized that, like every great truth, this Code contains secrets that have been used in every achievement by anyone who has ever made a difference in the history of the world—or anyone in their own chronicles of accomplishment and success.

THE GUARDIAN CODE was written to share the secrets to finding the magnificence hidden in each of us. And the Code and secrets from it are covered on Steve's weekly radio/internet/TV talk show of the same name… including his upcoming radio/audio broadcast series, "The Guardian Code [Chronicles]."

A frequent guest on talk shows, webinars and speaking engagements, Steve feels that every individual desperately needs to know how to take control of their lives, not only to survive, but to prosper and enjoy fulfilling relationships. In a time when it seems all life is crashing down around each of us, Steve shares his insights with the goal of helping each and every one of us to realize the magnificence and grandeur of who we are.

Raised by a father who was virtually an "animal whisperer," horses have been a part of his life since he started riding at age three. Steve has a sense and a love for animals that verges on extraordinary. In fact, his dog, Lexi, joins him at the office every day.

www.SteveShenk.com

www.ingramcontent.com/pod-product-compliance
Lightning Source LLC
Chambersburg PA
CBHW052014070526
44584CB00016B/1754